REMBRANDT
in the Mauritshuis

This book is published under the auspices of the
STICHTING JOHAN MAURITS VAN NASSAU, The Hague

REMBRANDT

in the Mauritshuis

AN INTERDISCIPLINARY STUDY BY

A.B. DE VRIES

MAGDI TÓTH-UBBENS

W. FROENTJES

WITH A FOREWORD BY

H.R. HOETINK

MCMLXXVIII

SIJTHOFF & NOORDHOFF INTERNATIONAL PUBLISHERS B.V., Alphen aan de Rijn

This publication was subsidized by
THE MINISTRY OF CULTURE, RECREATION AND SOCIAL WELFARE, The Hague
THE PRINS BERNHARD FUND, Amsterdam
THE M.A.O.C. GRAVIN VAN BYLANDT FOUNDATION, The Hague
THE DR. HENDRICK MULLER'S VADERLANDSCH FUND, The Hague

Translated from Dutch by James BROCKWAY

Published under the direction of Ernest GOLDSCHMIDT

Editorial assistant: Debora B. HENSBROEK-VAN DER POEL

ISBN 90 286 00280
Printed in Belgium

REMBRANDT IN THE MAURITSHUIS

ERRATA

p. 58: include number 21 next to lower right reproduction
p. 79: left column, lines 1 and 2 should read: "(Simeon in the Temple) . . ."
p. 100: left column, line 18: read "*orbitur*" as "*orditur*"
p. 105: left column, line 11: read "*mediating*" as "*meditating*"
p. 144: left column, line 5 should read: "bone black, Cologne earth . . ."
p. 147: left column, line 6: read "oeuvres" as "oeuvre"
p. 155: right column, line 18: read "married in 1835" as "married after 1835"
p. 159: left column, lines 1 and 2 should read: "posture – ignoring his facial expression – it is under . . ."
p. 187: left column, lines 5 and 6 should read: "since a photograph taken at that time shows the work . . ."
p. 187: right column, line 15 should read: "as the limit for his composition (Fig. 156). Since the . . ."
p. 206: left column, line 13: read "366 mm" as "366 nm"

Table of contents

Foreword

The publication of the present work fulfils a long-cherished wish. For it is the first time the thirteen paintings attributed to Rembrandt in the Mauritshuis collection, together with three other works associated with the artist and his circle, have become the subject of a comprehensive study. The initiative came from Dr. A.B. de Vries, director of the Mauritshuis at the time. A publication of this kind, however, required far-reaching technical, historical, iconographic and stylistic research before publication could be envisaged. To facilitate this work, the three authors worked in close co-operation with one another and each has accounted for his or her share in the *Introduction*.

The technical examination was performed by Dr. W. Froentjes, professor of Forensic Science at the University of Leiden. He was assisted by Mr. L. Kuiper, former restorer at the Mauritshuis, and since, chief restorer of the Department of Paintings at the Rijksmuseum in Amsterdam, and also by Mr. W. Verschuren, chief assistant at the Forensic Science Laboratory of the Ministry of Justice in Rijswijk.

Mrs. Magdi Tóth-Ubbens, former research assistant at the Mauritshuis, has subjected the available historical data to careful scrutiny and also undertaken her own research, which brought some new information to light. In addition, she paid special attention to some of the iconographic problems, working in co-operation with Dr. A.B. de Vries, who also assumed the responsibility for the criticism of style in respect of all sixteen paintings discussed.

The work was taken in hand in 1968. Most of the technical examination had been completed by 1970, but the editorial work proved time-consuming. During the last two years of his directorship, Dr. de Vries was kept fully occupied with other duties, while for some years after his retirement in 1970, commitments abroad prevented him from completing the work.

When I was appointed director of the Mauritshuis in January 1972, the material for the book was practically complete, but owing to Dr. de Vries's precarious health, it could not be cast in its final form until 1976. I have no hesitation in expressing my admiration and thanks for the perseverance and the energy Dr. de Vries has shown, despite all adversities, in bringing the work to its fruition. Not only had he familiarized himself with the scholarly aspects of Rembrandt's work during the almost twenty-five years that he was the Mauritshuis's director, but more importantly still, he had lived intimately with the paintings of the master in his care at the gallery. The fruits of his knowledge and insight will be found reflected in this book.

This book could never have come into being had not Mrs. Magdi Tóth-Ubbens and Dr. W. Froentjes made their individual contributions. Furthermore, the three authors were assisted by Mrs. Debora Hensbroek-van der Poel who devoted herself to the editing during the final year's work.

Although it has been the authors' endeavour to present as objective and unprejudiced an analysis as possible of the paintings they have studied, differences in appreciation, interpretation and approach—even where authenticity is concerned —are bound to remain in some instances. This is natural to all historical research, since the view we take of the past and of art can never be an exclusively rational one. We might make Malraux's question our own: "What does it matter if you do not approve of my answers, provided you cannot ignore my questions?". After all: "Non ad probandum, sed ad narrandum historia scribitur".

We are indebted to all those who have contributed in one way or another to making this publication possible. Here I am thinking of the highly experienced translator, Mr. James Brockway, of the members of the staff of the Forensic Science Laboratory in Rijswijk, who assisted Dr. Froentjes, Dr. A.H. Witte, the present Director, Dr. E.R. Groeneveld, Ir. R. Breek, H. van den Heuvel, the chief photographer, and Miss F.G. Patterson and Mrs. A.C. Meertens-van Wendel de Joode, both secretaries, the latter in Leiden.

In preparing the work for publication, much resort has been had to the many facilities offered by the Netherlands Institute for Art History in The Hague and the authors are most grateful to its Director Mr. J. Nieuwstraten and his staff. Their thanks are also due to the Municipal Archives Department of Amsterdam and particularly to the Deputy City Archivist, Dr. Isa H. van Eeghen, and various members of her staff, and likewise to Mr. W. Downer, Keeper of the City Archives in Leiden.

The publication of this work would not have been possible without generous contributions from the Ministry of Culture, Recreation and Social Work and from the *Prins Bernhard Fonds*. The *M.A.O.C. Gravin van Bylandt Stichting* has kindly met a considerable part of the cost of translation and the *Stichting Dr. Hendrik Muller's Vaderlandsch Fonds* kindly offered to finance the black and white illustrations. Our most sincere thanks go out to his Excellency, the Minister of Culture, Recreation and Social Work, and to the Board Members of the Foundations and Funds which have given their support.

We wish to express our gratitude to the publishers Sijthoff & Noordhoff International and in particular to Mr. Pieter Dijkstra and Mr. Arne Visser for the untiring attention they have devoted to the production of the book and to Dr. E. Goldschmidt, their adviser for the lay-out and for guiding the work through the final stages of editing and production.

Finally, it should be said that this work was commissioned by the *Stichting Johan Maurits van Nassau* which has fostered the interests of the Mauritshuis since 1956 and which has spared no effort in sponsoring the present publication dedicated to the most treasured paintings of the Mauritshuis collection.

H.R. Hoetink
Director of the Mauritshuis

Plate I. Selfportrait as a Young Man (No. 1)

Introduction

This publication appears much later than was originally planned and the reasons for the delay have accordingly been explained in the *Foreword.*

The authors are deeply indebted to the Members of the Board of the *Johan Maurits van Nassau Foundation* for their willingness to sponsor the work and for having made it possible, by means of a special contribution to include the seventeen colour plates. They are also grateful to Mr. H.R. Hoetink, the Director of the Mauritshuis, and his assistants for all the help they have given, despite the fact that they were not personally involved in the necessary research and the actual writing of the book. That is to say, by January 1972, when Mr. Hoetink took up his appointment as Director of the Mauritshuis, the research was already nearing completion and the main body of the text had been written. Thus, with his consent, no call was made upon Mr. Hoetink's collaboration, which in view of the advanced state of the work could have yielded him but scant satisfaction.

The work now published is modest in intention. It is confined to the fifteen paintings which W. Martin, Director of the Mauritshuis between 1909 and 1947, included in his *Catalogue raisonné* of 1935 under Rembrandt's name, plus one Rembrandt painting acquired subsequently. Even though Martin had his doubts about the correctness of attributing Nos. 2 and 3 to Rembrandt—paintings rejected (with No. 1) as genuine Rembrandts by the authors of the present work—he could not allow himself to express his opinion on the matter too categorically. Works which Bredius had loaned, then bequeathed (see Nos. III, IV, X, XI, XII, 1 and 2) stood quite literally at risk. We cannot be grateful enough to Martin for the tact and the self-abnegation he showed, to ensure that the works Bredius had loaned to the Mauritshuis and which he bequeathed to it after his death, in 1946, were preserved for the gallery and the nation.

The authors of this book enjoyed far greater latitude and complete independence, too, in their approach to their task. Obviously, one can question whether those who are, or were, closely associated with the gallery are able, or willing, to adopt an objective attitude towards works of art entrusted for so many years to their care. The authors, A.B. de Vries particularly, hope that they have shown sufficient critical acumen to enable them to state that in thirteen cases they consider the attribution to Rembrandt justified. Only in two cases (Nos III and IX) have they expressed certain reservations.

It has not been part of the author's purpose to supply a complete bibliography for each painting, nor could they see the usefulness of doing so. However, they believe they have read the most relevant literature and have consequently referred to it in the *Notes*.

In this Introduction, the authors have, in the main, confined themselves to facts and observations related to the paintings discussed in the book, but in view of the role the scientist has played in the project, he has gone into a few matters of a more general nature. He enjoyed an advantage over the other members of the team in that in many instances his findings meant new contributions to our knowledge of the paintings. The art historians taking part in our project were, however, sometimes disappointed by the uncertainty—the caution—which frequently accompanied the conclusion drawn from the technical examination. This caution, especially when it comes to interpreting one's findings, is enjoined by the complicated physical and chemical nature of the object examined. It is also due to the absence of knowledge concerning chemical and physical processes, i.e. the changes which have taken place in old paintings as the centuries have passed, and of influences brought to bear on them by their surroundings and by human intervention. If one also bears in mind the really very limited possibilities of research and checking arising from the valuable nature of the object examined, it goes practically without saying that the scientist often feels the need to make certain, sometimes far-reaching reservations, when stating his conclusions. This is particularly true with regard to a painting's original state.

The fact that the technical findings are often open to more than one interpretation may lead to the adoption of that interpretation which supports the art historian's hypothesis best but which is not necessarily the correct one. The chance that the investigations will ever be repeated is so slight that a mistake, once made, may persist for a very long time to come.

The same method has been adopted for each of the sixteen paintings, when describing the technical data. In *Appendix I,* the technical procedure has been briefly discussed, while a few words have also been devoted to expectations which determined the methods applied. It seemed to us superfluous to go into these techniques in greater detail. For the layman it would prove too difficult to follow and for the expert unnecessary.

The choice of method was determined by the task the technical and scientific investigation was called upon to perform, to support the art historian's work. This certainly meant that limits had to be imposed on the design and scope of the technical examination. Mention is made in *Appendix I,* note 2, of the reasons why no use was made of further and more sophisticated techniques. Briefly stated, it was because experience had shown that these other methods could not be expected to yield any information more relevant than that supplied by those actually used.

It was practically a matter of course that the results of the "surface examination" should be mentioned first of all. These investigations include photography in normal light, under ultra-violet and infra-red rays, and also examination by X-rays. The most important of all, however, is the careful examination of the surface using the binocular stereo-microscope, with a magnifying range between 10 and 40 times (the operation microscope). This method takes time—a rather large painting may easily require several days work—yet it gives information about the surface texture, and hints as to the authenticity of the paint layer, which can sometimes be very surprising. The examination most art historians carry out on a (hanging) painting with the naked eye, or using a simple magnifying glass, cannot be a proper substitute for the operation microscope to obtain comparable information.

Nowadays, the X-ray photograph falls more often than not within the domain of the art historian and many think they are able to read such a photograph without consulting an expert. In fact, however, an X-radiograph can only be properly judged—and here we are not thinking of *pentimenti* only—if one has the painting beside it and, above all, if one possesses the necessary knowledge of the structure of the various layers, with their relative thickness, the composition of their pigments, and is also aware of their significance as regards the X-ray image. In looking for *pentimenti,* it is sometimes forgotten that the radiograph only registers *pentimenti* painted with such pigments as white lead, lead-tin yellow or vermilion. Other, possibly more important ones, painted for example in yellow, red or brown ochres, in blue pigments or in organic dye-stuffs, are almost permeable by X-radiation and accordingly remain undetected.

In *Appendix II,* a brief and comparative account has been given of the technical data concerning the paint-layer structure and the palette, which account may be regarded as a new contribution to our knowledge of the technique Rembrandt employed. In those cases in which the attribution is open to question, it has not—except for No. II—brought us much closer to finding an answer to the most important question of all: Is the painting by Rembrandt or not? We have still too little knowledge of the methods and materials the painter employed throughout his career to evaluate and interpret such data when it comes to attribution. It is true that more technical information has been published about Rembrandt, particularly in recent years, than about other old masters. But it is only fragmentary and forms a whole of little consistency.

The almost exclusive interest so far taken in Rembrandt's technique calls for caution as long as research of the same kind into the work of his pupils, contemporaries and imitators continues to be neglected. Investigating the aspects in which he differs from them, after all, forms part of every attempt to recognize or characterize Rembrandt by his technique and the use he made of materials. In addition, it is often open to question whether, after three centuries of destructive influences on the paintings, one is still justified in interpreting certain features as characteristic of the artist.

Among the least satisfactory items of the technical research undertaken was the investigation of the signatures and dates. A number of factors which hamper the examination itself, and consequently the interpretation of one's findings, are mentioned in note 7a to *Appendix I.* Moreover, it has not proved possible to ascertain or even to argue the authenticity of a signature or date along other lines. The reason lies in the curious fact that, as far as we know, the existence of basic criteria has never been investigated. Therefore, where in this work, cautious statements have been made regarding the authenticity of signatures and dates, they have been based principally on the absence of evident anomalies or anachronistic features in the paint structure. As for the graphic forms, such statements depend more on intuition, supported by experience, than on a careful analysis of handwriting characteristics.

It is, for that matter, questionable whether one should expect to find signatures and dates in the original condition on the paintings, and one may ask whether they have not, in by far the majority of cases, been repainted or gone over to a greater or lesser extent. These considerations—and especially the lack of adequate methods of examination and incontestable criteria—make it hard to understand how some authors can have expressed their belief in the authenticity of Rembrandt's signatures—or their doubts on the score—with such aplomb. It is not clear on what criteria scholars who employ such terms as "a perfect signature", "einwandfrei signiert" and "unimpeachable signatures", base their statements. Being unsupported by arguments, these are actually nothing more than *ad hoc* assertions.

An interdisciplinary study would be highly desirable to help us emerge from what many consider a serious *impasse*. The handwriting expert would play a significant part in this research. He would have to be accustomed to work with the modern, i.e. statistical, methods of comparative investigation into handwriting and signatures and also equipped with a knowledge of the characteristics of 17th century handwriting (see also *Appendix I*, note 7b). The greatest difficulty such research would have to overcome, however, would be the problem of selecting a number of signatures and dates to serve as the starting point for the handwriting research—signatures and dates which could be taken with a reasonable degree of certainty to be authentic (or still authentic). It is difficult to forecast the extent to which a research project of this nature and scope would yield positive results, so that practical criteria deduced from them would make verdicts on the authenticity of signatures and dates at least acceptable. Negative results, too, can have their usefulness and may even have important consequences. It is conceivable that even exhaustive research might fail to produce clear-cut criteria for establishing authenticity—for example, on account of too great a degree of variability in the signatures examined. If, moreover, the "writing" were to prove so simple in its structure that signatures and dates could easily be imitated, thus rendering them indistinguishable from genuine signatures and dates, one would have disposed once and for all of the fairytale about the perfect signature.

The history and provenance of the thirteen paintings given to Rembrandt show that there is only one work which leads us with reasonable certainty to the collector who received it straight from the artist. This is No. XII, the *Homer*, which, if not commissioned, was certainly accepted by Antonio Ruffo, the Sicilian collector. In *Appendix IV* something is told of the people in Sicily and elsewhere involved in this transaction, which was conducted over what was then so great a distance. The text of the letter which Ruffo addressed to Rembrandt has also been given in full. Despite the enquiries made, it has still not been established when the *Homer* disappeared from the Ruffo collection, nor do we know the whereabouts of the painting between its being disposed of (by sale?) and its re-appearance in England during the last quarter of the 19th century. Although it is not possible to trace the entire history of the work, there can be scant reason for doubting that the *Homer* owned by Ruffo and the fragmentary painting in the Mauritshuis are one and the same work.

The *Simeon's Song of Praise* (No. V), one of the young artist's major works, painted when he was still in Leiden, can be identified with a certain degree of probability with the *Simeon in the Temple* "done by Rembrandt or Jan Lievensz" which is listed in the inventory of Frederick Henry's collection in the Noordeinde Palace (1632). Whether the commission was given via Huygens or came directly from the Stadhouder's residence is of minor importance.

Rembrandt moved from Leiden to Amsterdam in the latter part of 1631, taking up residence in the house of Hendrick van Uylenburch. It is possible that Hendrick van Uylenburch and he had already become acquainted in Leiden, since Van Uylenburch was acting as guardian to the children of his deceased brother,

Rombout van Uylenburch (1628) (see also *Dr. Nicolaas Tulp's Anatomy Lesson,* No. VI, and *Appendix IIIb*).

Rembrandt painted *Dr. Nicolaas Tulp's Anatomy Lesson* in Amsterdam in 1632. The work was most probably commissioned by the Surgeons' Guild, Tulp himself having a considerable say in the matter. It is almost certain that this large canvas was intended for the surgeons' Guild Room in the *Waag*. It is certainly surprising that this anatomy piece should not have been mentioned until 1693, and then only by Caspar Commelin. This is all the more so because this work is exceptional in its composition and a major work by a young artist who was making a name for himself at the time.

Prior to the reconstruction in 1690-91, the surgeons' Guild Room in the *Waag* had not been open to the public, yet it still seems strange that we have no evidence that this painting had any immediate influence, not even on Rembrandt's own pupils and other Amsterdam artists.

The basis of the Mauritshuis's collection of paintings was laid down by the Stadhouders William IV and V. When William IV acquired the *Simeon* (No. V) in 1733, he did not have any paintings by Rembrandt in his possession. Since the Stadhouder was interested in acquiring paintings of historical interest and especially those which had previously belonged to the House of Orange, it seems likely, if not proved, that he chose to buy precisely this *Simeon* from Rembrandt, since he would have known that it had formerly belonged to the dynasty.

Once William V had acquired the Van Slingelandt collection in 1768, the Stadhouder's collection contained four pictures by Rembrandt, *viz.,* Nos. I, V, VII and VIII. These, together with the greater part of William V's collection, were transported to Paris in 1795. In 1815, after the fall of Napoleon, the majority of these paintings returned to the Hague and were made accessible to the public in the Mauritshuis in 1822.

Rembrandt's *Dr. Nicolaas Tulp's Anatomy Lesson* was bought by King William I on behalf of the Government and hung in the Mauritshuis. William may not have had any special interest in, or knowledge of, painting, but he did understand that works of art of historical and aesthetic significance such as the *Anatomy Lesson* ought, if at all possible, to be preserved for the nation. After the political difficulties with Belgium (1831-1839), however, the means were lacking to make further acquisitions.

No more additions were made to the Rembrandts in the Mauritshuis between 1828 and 1890. In 1891, A. Bredius, who was the museum's director from 1889 to 1909, purchased the *Man with Grey Curly Hair* (No. IX) for the gallery at a price that was considerable at the time. This was followed by his acquisition of *Travellers Resting* (No. 3) and in 1895, of *Study of a Man Laughing* (No. II). Between 1890 and 1907, Bredius acquired Nos. III, IV, X, XI, XII, 1 and 2 for his private collection, loaning them to the Mauritshuis. It was a period when connoisseurship was highly esteemed and Bredius, together with Hofstede de Groot and Bode, ranked as a leading connoisseur of 17th century Dutch painting, and of Rembrandt in particular. There can be a very close association between connoisseurship and "discoveries". It is noticeable, for instance, that with the exception of the *Saul and David,* Bredius never paid high prices for the pictures destined for his private collection and this is characteristic of the connoisseur who relies wholly on his own eye.

In 1947, the *Self-Portrait in Later Life* (No. XIII) was purchased for the Mauritshuis, a work which was regarded for years as Rembrandt's last self-portrait.

One is struck by the preference the Stadhouders William IV and V and Govert van Slingelandt, too, showed for the work of Rembrandt's early period. In doing so, however, they were not deviating from the taste of the day in the Northern Netherlands. Of the four Rembrandt paintings in the Stadhouders' collection the *Self-Portrait in a Plumed Hat* (No. VII), c. 1637, is probably the latest.

The *Dr. Nicolaas Tulp's Anatomy Lesson* was an excellent and lucky purchase, made on historical rather than aesthetic grounds. It is true that Jonkheer J. Steengracht van Oost-Capelle, who was director of the Mauritshuis at the time, devoted a panegyric to the work in 1830 (*De Voornaamste schilderijen van het Koninklijk Kabinet tot 's Gravenhage,* The Hague, 1826-1830, No. 100), but this creates the impression of being obligatory praise rather than true personal appreciation, although the director was fully aware that the gallery had been enriched with a unique work by the master.

Of the Rembrandt paintings which Bredius acquired, either for the Mauritshuis or for his private collection, only two belong to the Leiden period (Nos. III and IV); one is of c. 1650 (No. IX) and the other three are of still later date (Nos. X, XI and XII). These paintings have greatly enriched the artist's image in the Mauritshuis. This is not the place to explain why the later Rembrandts were so much more highly prized in the last decades of the 19th century than they had been before. We will content ourselves with stating that Bredius followed this change in taste and tried to stop the incredible exodus of Rembrandt's paintings from the Netherlands, which had been going on since the end of the 17th century. This exodus continued until the 70s and 80s of the 19th century, when Victor de Stuers and Abraham Bredius—who held each other in a certain esteem but were far from being friends—began to bring their salutary influence to bear to rescue the nation's art treasures.

Finally, in 1947, it proved possible to purchase the *Self-Portrait in Later Life* (No. XIII). This work had hung in the Rijksmuseum in Amsterdam since 1925, on loan from a Berlin collector. In June 1940, it was confiscated by the occupying forces and destined for the Führer-Museum in Linz, Austria, which fortunately never materialized. After Germany's capitulation, it was among the first twenty-six pictures to be returned to the Dutch Government on the personal orders of General Eisenhower. The legal owners of this painting proved ready to sell and it should also be mentioned in this place that the Minister of Education, Arts and Sciences and the Minister of Finance, together with the President of the Bank of the Netherlands gave their personal consent to purchase it with pounds sterling (no problem) and American dollars (a big problem), at a time when funds were scarce, foreign exchange scarcer, and dollars almost unobtainable.

The two authors who have concerned themselves with the iconography of Rembrandt's work in the Mauritshuis are neither of them trained iconographers. This is particularly true of the former director of the gallery. They have nevertheless endeavoured to pay due attention to this aspect, although they make no claim to have conducted an exhaustive examination.

The contribution made by iconology, particularly to postwar research into Rembrandt's œuvre, has enriched our knowledge in many respects and, furthermore, deepened our insight into the master's work. The concept of "iconographic tradition" with respect to Rembrandt's creativity exerts a powerful influence on contemporary ideas about the artist. Whereas he was formerly described, perhaps to a somewhat exaggerated degree, as an artist who stood outside and above his time (as a genius ought to), the dominant tendency today seems to be to see him as in step with his time, as regards aesthetic theory as well as iconography and style.

It was not the purpose of the authors of this work to adopt any particular attitude as regards the significance and function of iconographical research into Rembrandt's work. Instead it has been their endeavour to apply the present method of research, especially where mythological (Nos. IV and 2), biblical (Nos. V, VIII and XI) and historical (No. XII) subjects are concerned. They have also made critical use of the material other scholars have brought to light concerning the sixteen pictures discussed.

Studies of heads and models which eluded identification (Nos. II, III, IX and X) and also portraits (No. 1; self-portraits, Nos. I, VII and XIII) and the group portrait (No. VI) account for more than half of the works examined.

As far as the identification of self-portraits, models or the artist's patrons is concerned, in many cases a tradition existed which at times proved to be correct, at times uncertain, and in some cases simply wrong. This check also forms part and parcel of the authors' iconographical investigation. During Rembrandt's Leiden period, there are many instances in which it is difficult to draw a strict dividing line between portrait and character study. This applies to a number of paintings and especially to some of Rembrandt's early etchings.

No. II in this work, now named *Study of a Man Laughing* is, in our opinion, first and foremost a study of physiognomy, the sitter being an unidentified person, formerly taken to be Rembrandt's elder brother. No. III, formerly referred to as Rembrandt's father, is both a portrait and a study of an elderly and possible ailing man at one and the same time. The sitter in No. IX, *Portrait of a Man with Grey Curly Hair,* is certainly an interesting model, yet he has so far remained unidentified. We can say with a reasonable degree of certainty that No. 1, on the other hand, does indeed represent the artist's mother, but the execution is not Rembrandt's work. The many copies and versions of the portrait probably indicate, too, that the work may also be looked upon as a character study of an old woman. During the 17th and 18th centuries there was an enormous interest in portraying facial expression.

The Mauritshuis's possession of three self-portraits is a remarkable and happy coincidence. They are of the years c. 1629, c. 1637 and c. 1666/69 (Nos. I, VII and XIII). We see Rembrandt before us as a young man of extremely well-groomed appearance; as a confident and successful artist, albeit in disguise; and, finally, as a man looking old for his years, whose expressive eyes have lost some of their intensity. These portraits represent three stages in a life which brought the artist fame and happiness but also sadness, disappointment, and eventually premature aging.

E. Panofsky was the first to refer to the absence of Perseus and the Dragon in the painting of Andromeda chained to the rock (No. IV) as a Rembrandtesque feature—a deliberate elimination he had noticed in some other works too. Chr. Tümpel drew attention to this once again, referring to this feature as "Herauslösung".

No. V was rightly re-named *The Song of Simeon* by a former assistant at the Mauritshuis, Dr. Lyckle de Vries. However, the title *Simeon's Song of Praise* has been adopted, since it conveys a more precise definition of the scene Rembrandt has painted here.

Both Heckscher and Van Eeghen are firm in their assumption that No. VI represents Dr. Tulp's second public anatomy lesson of 1632. Some authors emphasize the work's realism, while others justifiably point to the innovations the young artist has introduced. The authors of the present study believe that the artist's prime intention was to achieve a *group portrait* and at the same time to satisfy Tulp's desire to be shown as "*Vesalius redivivus*". As such, the painting can also be regarded as interpreting an event of the past. We accordingly see this work as a combination of realism and invention, a combination which was to reach its apotheosis in the *Night Watch*. Seen from this point of view, *Dr. Nicolaas Tulp's Anatomy Lesson* represents an important moment in Rembrandt's evolution.

a. Particles of paint with gold leaf *Study of a Man Laughing, Plate II.* (magnification x 75).

A curious story lies behind the iconographical explanation of the *Bathsheba* (No. VIII). Ten Dall's list, drawn up on the basis of the notes (unfortunately lost) made by T.P.C. Haag († 1812) who for years was the director of Stadhouder William V's collection of paintings (c. 1760-95), has shown that Haag rightly took the painting from Govert van Slingelandt's collection, which William V had acquired as a *Susanna Bathing,* to be a *Bathsheba.* Even before having come upon the article published in *Antiek* (1976, p. 171, No. 130), the authors of the present study had arrived at the same conclusion. In doing so, they had taken particular account of the fact that in this painting the traditional couple of elderly men in the Susanna story are missing, and had also borne in mind the influence exerted by certain of Buytewech's prints. If, therefore, Steengracht is found writing about *Bathsheba,* and then a few years later, in 1827, about *Susanna at the Bath,* the use of this latter title, which was kept from then on until a short time ago, was probably due to the importance the first director of the Mauritshuis attached to the authority Sir Joshua Reynolds enjoyed. This was his interpretation of the work, his writings having been republished in 1819.

b. Particles of paint with gold leaf. *Selfportrait,* Fig. 14 (magnification x 75).

Saul and David (No. XI) has been the object of varying interpretations, in which Rembrandt's early painting of the same subject was regarded as characteristic of the baroque and extrovert artist and the Hague canvas as an expression of the serene and introvert artist. It has now been established that the artist took the same biblical text as his starting point, but laid the stress rather differently. King Saul is both moved and disturbed by David's playing on the harp. He has half-hidden his face behind the curtain and is keeping a close watch on the young man, whom he will presently attempt—unsuccessfully—to slay with his javelin. In the view of the authors, Rembrandt certainly acquainted himself with the iconographic tradition of the Saul and David theme, but has assimilated it and deepened it in a highly individual way.

Finally, *Homer* (No. XII) must not be seen as the poet dictating his verses but as the poet instructing the young, he having, according to the pseudo-Herodotus, arrived on the island of Chios during his rovings.

We cannot avoid making a few remarks, in conclusion, concerning style and criticism of style. Here, the author concerned has observed a high degree of restraint. In the first place, it seemed superfluous to raise questions of style generally, since only a limited number of paintings by Rembrandt, spread over

Plate II. Study of a Man Laughing (No. II)

Plate III. Head of an Old Man (No. III)

Plate IV. Andromeda (No. IV)

Plate V. Simeon's Song of Praise (No. V)

Plate VI. Simeon's Song of Praise (No. V). Detail

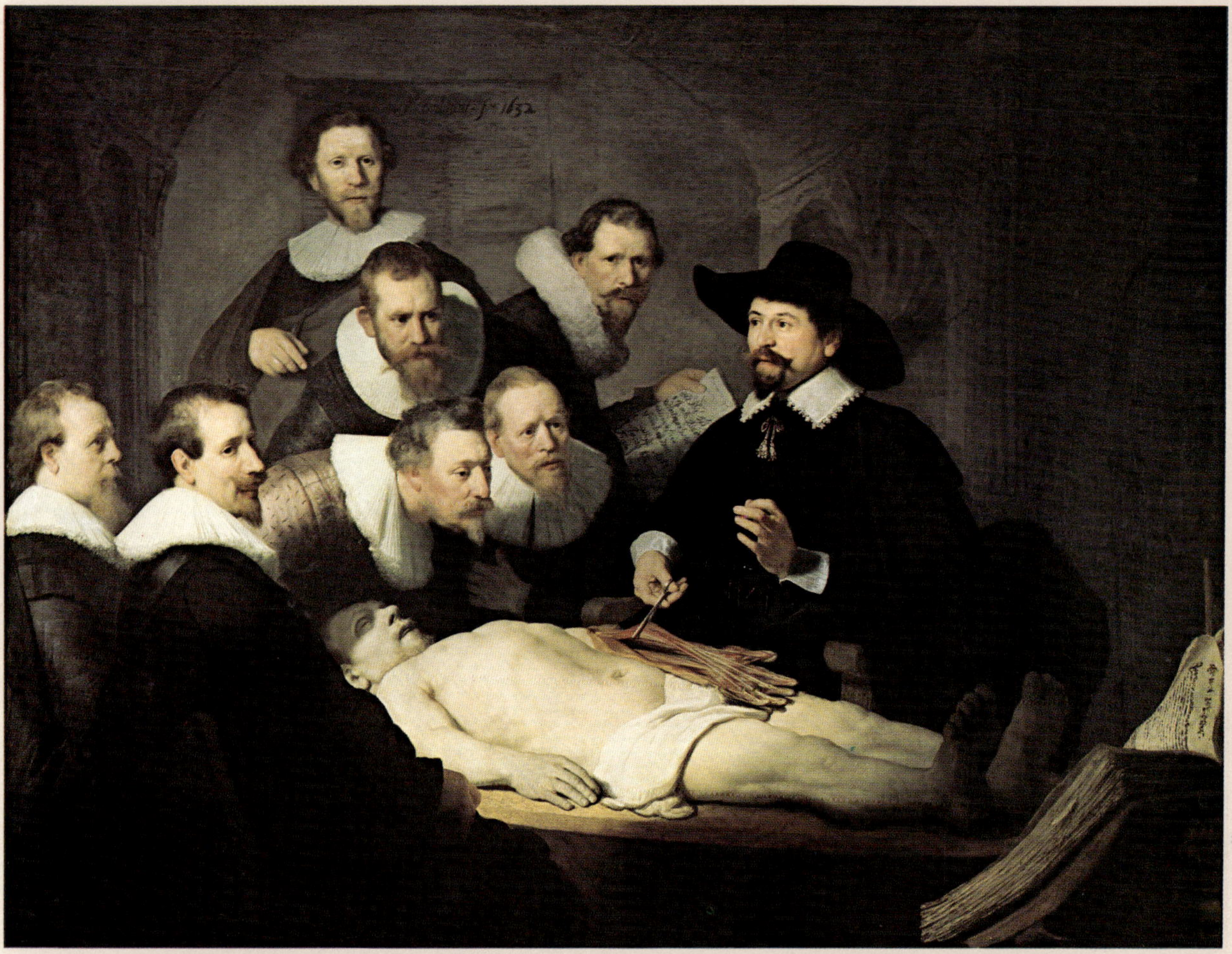

Plate VII. Dr Nicolaas Tulp's Anatomy Lesson (No. VI)

Plate VIII. Dr Nicolaas Tulp's Anatomy Lesson (No. VI). Detail

Plate IX. Self-portrait in a Plumed Hat (No. VII)

Plate X. Bathsheba (No. VIII)

Plate XI. Portrait of a Man with Grey Curly Hair (No. IX)

Plate XII. Two Negroes (No. X)

Plate XIII. Homer (No. XII)

Plate XIV. Saul and David (No. XI).

Plate XV. Saul and David (No. XI). Detail

Plate XVI. Saul and David (No. XI). Detail

Plate XVII. Self-portrait in Later Life (No. XIII)

various periods, are under discussion here. In the second place, he has observed restraint because the general characteristics of Rembrandt's style, varying during his lifetime, are familiar to us, even though our knowledge of them is far from complete and undoubtedly in need of some adjustment. This, however, was not our prime concern, although now and again we had to face problems of this nature. For example, the affirmation of the authenticity and dating of some pictures (Nos. III, IX, X, XI and XIII) naturally depended on the authors' evaluation of the artist's personal style and on the quality of the paintings.

Where, however, detailed investigation is involved, such as that in the present study, criticism of style and connoisseurship draw very close together. In many cases, their boundaries for that matter defy exact definition. Since our enquiry has been conducted along three lines—technical, historical and iconographic-stylistic—it was inevitable that the remarks about style should have been more concerned with the characteristics of the individual painting than with a general criticism of style.

The author responsible for this latter part of the study is fully aware that connoisseurship is not viewed very favourably by many younger art historians. It is true that the subjective nature of the connoisseur's verdicts does not make for credibility. They may be expressed in what are more often than not unsubstantiated and even unprovable opinions and, moreover, they may differ widely. Yet we are all too often indebted to connoisseurs of the first generation such as Bode, Bredius and Hofstede de Groot. Their successors, among them Martin, Valentiner, Benesch, Jacob Rosenberg, and today Gerson, have also achieved much and had they been less sanguine about the difficulties of Rembrandt research, younger scholars would not have much to go on. Greater appreciation of what are sometimes called superseded methods and insights would not be out of place, even granted that they have, indeed, often been replaced by more or less recent scientific methods and reniewed emphasis on historical and sociological investigation.

This is far from being an attempt to rehabilitate "connoisseurship". The author of these lines is nevertheless keenly aware that without this elusive concept, he would scarcely have been able to make his contributions to this study.

The paintings belonging to the Leiden period (Nos. I to V) have given no immediate rise to doubt as regards their authenticity. Confirmation came, as far as could be expected, from the findings of their technical examination. It is true that doubts have been uttered before this as to the attribution of the *Study of a Man Laughing* (No. II), and some still doubt it today. This certainly goes back to 1895 when Bredius purchased the work, advised by Hofstede de Groot. We believe that the technical examination has provided sufficient proof of Rembrandt's authorship. We have always clung to the attribution, since we see the young artist, especially in his Leiden period, as a highly impressionable youth—how could it have been otherwise?—who was fond of experimenting. We take the view that Rembrandt's œuvre should not be approached as though it followed a consistent line of development, lending itself to purely rational analysis.

No. I falls, in a certain sense, outside the series of familiar self-portraits (painted, drawn, etched) particularly because of the figure's well-groomed appearance. For this reason, we would suggest that the work might have been commissioned.

As regards No. III, we see no grounds for rejecting Rembrandt's authorship. It is nevertheless difficult to make a clear-cut distinction in all cases between

Rembrandt's, Lievens' and other artists' portraits and character studies done in the years 1626 to 1630.

Gerson has already dated the *Andromeda* (No. IV) on stylistic grounds as belonging to Rembrandt's Leiden period. We share his opinion. There is no certainty whether the panel was formerly of larger dimensions, although we do believe that this small painting was originally somewhat larger.

The rendering of space in *Simeon's Song of Praise* (No. V) and the "interplay" between space, light and darkness form the very remarkable main features of this masterpiece, painted during Rembrandt's last year in Leiden. As far as we know, little or no research has been done into Rembrandt's concept of space in his early work. It plays a striking role in this painting as does also the *chiaroscuro* he employed so effectively and with such refinement as a means of expression.

It goes without saying that *Dr. Nicolaas Tulp's Anatomy Lesson* has been the object of thorough investigation. It became clear that in this work—Rembrandt's first important commission—the composition presented the artist with problems. It is remarkable that no (drawn) sketches for the work have been preserved—and all the more so as it is hardly likely that he would have dispensed with them. This large canvas has suffered much damage, although the heads are fortunately well preserved. Their solid design and the very fluent brushwork would seem to suggest a certain rivalry with Rubens.

In discussing the *Bathsheba* (No. VIII) we have once again stressed the particularly strong resemblance between this nude and the *Susanna* in the Berlin painting. However much Rembrandt may usually have borne the iconographic tradition in mind and however much he may have gone to the Bible for his religious themes, this remarkable opportunity for making an interesting comparison demonstrates, in our view, that the artist's prime concern was to paint a youthful nude and that the story was only of secondary importance to him.

It is to be hoped that further research will one day produce evidence which will permit one to speak with more conviction about the painter of the impressive head of No. IX. Victor de Stuers attributed this painting to Carel Fabritius at an early date. The same opinion was expressed again much later on, but it carries no conviction for us.

The technical examination of *Two Negroes* (No. X) shows that this work has suffered severe damage in several places. There are, however, paintings which, despite all the defects of age, never lose their fascination. This, in our view, is the case with the picture showing two young negroes. The work is almost a monochrome, the gradations of colour ranging from a yellowish grey to yellowish brown and culminating in the deep brown of the heads. The light on these two heads is highly "Rembrandtesque". It has no immediately demonstrable source, yet it is in line with the artist's own individual treatment of lighting effects during his later period. One is struck by the way the tunic worn by the foremost figure has been painted and its all but abstract decoration. However subjective a view this may seem in the eyes of younger colleagues, we are of the opinion that the expressiveness of these two exotic figures knows no equal in 17th century Dutch painting and this latter remark may lend valid support to the attribution of the work to Rembrandt. It is not easy to find a place for the work in the artist's œuvre but we would suggest an earlier dating than that found on the painting.

It seems more appropriate to us to make no comment here on the *Saul and David* (No. XI). We will leave it to others to pronounce and explain their verdict on the work—a well-founded one, it is to be hoped. Let us wait and see.

From the point of view of style, the *Homer* (No. XII) comes close, in its finished but unfortunately mutilated state, to the painting in the Wallraf-Richartz Museum in Cologne. This is also a fragment, rightly interpreted, some years ago, as *Zeuxis Painting an Old Woman*. It seems to us that the broad strokes with which Rembrandt has painted the golden-yellow shawl over Homer's cloak, were added by him after he had received back the unfinished painting from his Italian Maecenas, Ruffo, for completion.

Then, finally, the *Self-Portrait in Later Life* (No. XIII) does not appear to fit in very easily among the late self-portraits Rembrandt painted from 1660 onwards. There can be no doubt, however, as to its authenticity. It is not inconceivable that a date between 1666 and 1669 will ultimately prove to be correct. As we have said, Rembrandt was a persistent experimenter, especially when painting portraits of himself.

In conclusion, we recall some words which are doubtlessly relevant to the present book and which were uttered by Jacob von Uxküll, in his day a widely known biologist, at the end of a lecture he delivered in Utrecht about fifty years ago. They were: "In the world of learning today's truth may be tomorrow's error".

This dictum reflects the general view of the three authors, who nevertheless believe that their joint efforts have resulted in some truthful information regarding Rembrandt's paintings in the Mauritshuis.

Key to bibliographical abbreviations

B.	A. Bartsch, *Catalogue raisonné de toutes les estampes qui forment l'œuvre de Rembrandt et de ses principaux imitateurs,* Vienna, 1797.
Bauch	K. Bauch, *Rembrandt Gemälde,* Berlin, 1966.
Benesch	O. Benesch, *The Drawings of Rembrandt,* 6 Vols., London, 1954-57.
Br.	A. Bredius, *The Paintings of Rembrandt,* Vienna, 1936.
Br.-G.	A. Bredius, *Rembrandt. The complete edition of the paintings,* Revised by H. Gerson, London, 1969.
Cat. Br. (1895)	*Catalogue raisonné du Musée Royal de la Haye,* The Hague, 1895 (Compiled by A. Bredius).
Cat. M. (1935)	*Catalogue Raisonné des Tableaux et Sculptures du Musée Royal de Tableaux à La Haye,* The Hague, 1935 (compiled by W. Martin).
Cat. H. (1977)	*Mauritshuis, The Royal Cabinet of Paintings, Illustrated General Catalogue,* The Hague, 1977 (compiled by H.R. Hoetink).
Drossaers-Scheurleer	S.W.A. Drossaers and Th.H. Lunsingh Scheurleer, *Inventarissen van de inboedels in de verblijven van de Oranjes, 1567-1795,* 3 Vols., The Hague, 1974-1976.
Dutuit	E. Dutuit, *Tableaux et dessins de Rembrandt,* Paris, 1885.
I. H. v. Eeghen, 1969	I.H. van Eeghen, "Rembrandt en de mensenvilders", *Amstelodamum,* 56, 1969, pp. 1-11.
von Einem	H. von Einem, "Rembrandt und Homer", *Wallraf-Richartz-Jahrbuch,* 14, 1952, pp. 182-205.
G.	Horst Gerson, *Rembrandt paintings,* Amsterdam, 1968.
van de Graaf	J.A. van de Graaf, *Het de Mayerne manuscript als bron voor de schildertechniek van de barok,* Mijdrecht, 1958, Dissertation (Utrecht).
Heckscher	W.S. Heckscher, *Rembrandt's Anatomy of Dr. Nicolaas Tulp,* New York, 1958.
Held, 1969	J.S. Held, *Rembrandt's Aristotle and other Rembrandt Studies,* Princeton, 1969.
Hoet	G. Hoet, *Catalogus of naamlyst van schilderyen, met derzelver pryzen,* 2 Vols. The Hague, 1752.
H.d.G. Urkunden	C. Hofstede de Groot, *Die Urkunden über Rembrandt,* The Hague, 1906.
H.d.G.	C. Hofstede de Groot, *A Catalogue Raisonné of the works of the Most Eminent Dutch Painters of the Seventeenth Century, 6, Rembrandt and Nicolaes Maes,* London, 1916.
Hollstein	F.W.H. Hollstein, *Dutch and Flemish etchings, engravings and woodcuts,* 19 Volumes published up to 1976 (Vols. 18 and 19: Rembrandt), Amsterdam (no year).
Hoogewerff, 1917	G.J. Hoogewerff, "Rembrandt en een Italiaansche Maecenas", *Oud Holland,* 35, 1917, pp. 129-148.
Houbraken	A. Houbraken, *De Groote Schouburgh der Nederlantsche Konstschilders - en schilderessen,* 3 Vols., Amsterdam, 1718-1721.
Judson	J.R. Judson, "Book review: William S. Heckscher-Rembrandt's Anatomy of Dr. Tulp", *The Art Bulletin,* 42, 1960, pp. 305-310.
Lugt	F. Lugt, *Répertoire des catalogues de ventes publiques intéressant l'art ou la curiosité,* 3 Vols., The Hague, 1938-1964.
Münz	L. Münz, *Rembrandt's etchings,* 2 Vols., London, 1952.
Münz, 1953	L. Münz, "Rembrandts Bild von Mutter und Vater", *Jahrbuch der Kunsthistorischen Sammlungen in Wien* 50, 1953, pp. 141-190.
Nuyens	B.W.Th. Nuyens, "Het Ontleedkundig Onderwijs en de geschilderde Anatomische Lessen van

het Chirurgijns Gilde te Amsterdam, in de Jaren 1550 tot 1798", *Jaarverslag Koninklijk Oudheidkundig Genootschap,* 1928, pp. 45-90.

Ricci — C. Ricci, *Rembrandt in Italia,* Milan, 1918.

Ruffo — V. Ruffo, "Galleria Ruffo nel secolo XVII in Messina", *Bolletino d'Arte* 10, 1916, pp. 21-64, 95-128, 165-192, 237-256, 264-320, 369-388.

Scheurleer — Th.H. Lunsingh Scheurleer, "De Stadhouderlijke verzamelingen", in: *150 jaar Koninklijk Kabinet van Schilderijen, Koninklijke Bibliotheek, Koninklijk Penningkabinet,* The Hague, 1967, pp. 9-50.

Terwesten — P. Terwesten, *Catalogus of naamlyst van schilderyen, met derzelver prysen,* The Hague, 1770.

Thijssen — E.H.M. Thijssen, *Nicolaas Tulp als geneeskundige geschetst. Eene bijdrage tot de geschiedenis der geneeskunde in de XVIIde eeuw,* Amsterdam, 1881, Dissertation (Amsterdam).

Valentiner — W.R. Valentiner, *Rembrandt - Des Meisters Gemälde*[3], Klassiker der Kunst, Stuttgart and Berlin, 1909.

PRELIMINARY NOTE

This *Introduction* was written before the dead-line, 30 January 1977, for completing the manuscript had expired. After this date an opportunity arose during the preparation of the English translation to make a few changes and additions on certain minor points, based on publications which appeared prior to 1 August 1977.

The dimensions of the paintings are given in centimetres, the height preceding the width.

Dimensions in the old Netherlandish texts quoted are generally given in "Rijnlandse voeten en duimen" and abbreviated as *V* or *v* and *D* or *d*. They correspond approximately to *foot* and *inch*, that is to say to respectively about 30 and 2.5 cm.

Netherlandish texts dating from before c. 1815, with the exception of those given in *Appendix IV*, as well as French and German texts in general have not been translated.

The English versions of the Italian texts quoted in *Appendix IV* are based on their translation from Italian into Dutch by Miss C. van Schendel, to whom the authors are much indebted.

The Paintings

I

Self-Portrait as a Young Man

TECHNICAL DATA

Pl. I; Fig. 1

Panel, 37.7 x 28.9 cm. Unsigned, undated; c. 1629.

Cat. Br. (1895), No. 148; Valentiner, p. 32; H.d.G., No. 544; Cat. M. (1935), No. 148; Br., No. 6; Bauch, No. 295; G., No. 39; Br.-G., No. 6; Cat. H. (1977), No. 148.

1. Self-Portrait as a Young Man.

The oak panel is bevelled on all four sides [1]. The flat middle section of the reverse has been covered with a layer of dark grey paint to which a thin layer of wax has been applied. This was presumably intended to protect the panel from atmospheric change and cracking [2].

Examination using ultra-violet and infra-red light did not reveal any special information.

The X-ray photograph does not show any *pentimenti* (Fig. 2). The layer of grey paint on the reverse of the panel is visible as a pale rectangle. The light areas of the head, painted in white lead, are clearly contrasted against the dark areas, which on the evidence of the radiograph were not underpainted in white lead. This was confirmed by further examination. The outline of the right shoulder and arm has been indicated with a stroke of white lead.

In the light areas of the face, the *craquelure* is very fine, forming a network of minute cracks. There are few traces of *craquelure* in the grey paint of the background, and this paint is so thin that in many places the grain of the wood is clearly visible through the thin top layer of paint. In the dark areas the *craquelure* is often a little coarser—in the shadow of the nose, for example. Yet it does not display the characteristic features of "premature" cracking which is experienced with poorly drying paint. Cracks are barely discernible in the blackish-brown paint of the eyes, which do not give the impression of having been retouched. There is a little retouching in the background and in the coat and hair.

Only chalk was detected in the ground. The flesh tones consist of white lead mixed with yellow and red ochre, thinly glazed with a red lake pigment. On the mouth, this red lake has been applied more thickly, on an underlayer of reddish-brown. Partial underpainting in dark brown or dark grey was not found in the light areas of the head as it was in most of the other paintings examined. The yellow of the hair is yellow ochre, the brown here consisting of brown ochre. The

2. X-ray photograph.

grey of the collar and the hauberk is composed of white lead and coarse grains of bone black. Traces of copper, silver and tin were shown to be present in the white lead, this being characteristic of old white lead. The paint of the coat is a dark, transparent brown with the properties of Cologne earth, mixed with carbon black and particles of a red lake pigment. The greygreen background is chiefly composed of yellow and brown ochres, a little white lead and a blue pigment, presumably azurite. Analysis of the coarse-grained grey paint on the back of the panel revealed the presence of white lead, chalk, umber, ochres and carbon black.

No signature is to be found on the painting and no remnants of one were found either.

HISTORICAL DATA

This portrait of Rembrandt as a young man has come, in common with Nos. VII and VIII, from the collection of Govert van Slingelandt, Seigneur of De Lindt and West-IJselmonde (1694-1767), Receiver-General of Holland and West Friesland. In 1752, he owned, according to Gerard Hoet, a gallery of 33 paintings [3]. One of the works listed in this collection was "Een Jongelings Hoofd, door denzelven [Rembrandt van Rijn], h. 1 v. 1 en een half d., br. 11 d.".

After this collector's death, eight paintings proved to have been added since 1752, for the sale catalogue dated 18 May 1768 shows 41 paintings in all [4]. Great interest was shown at home and also abroad in this auction, which had been announced months in advance. The collection was renowned and the paintings were "bien des originaux et parfaitement conservés". It was with these words that Desrivaux, the French chargé d'affaires in The Hague, sent the catalogue to the duc de Choiseul in Paris on 19 February 1768 [5]. Towards the end of 1767, the marquis de Vandières et de Marigny had already seen the collection, accompanied by the draughtsman and engraver Ch. N. Cochin [6].

Apart from the French, Stadhouder William V was interested too. A private bid was made on his behalf to acquire all the paintings *en bloc*. In the minutes of the "Confrérie Pictura" in The Hague, drawn up by Pieter Terwesten and dated 23 February 1768, we read: "De Prins heeft de schilderijen (41) van SLINGELANDT uit de hand gekocht voor f. 50.000" [7]. Thus an important collection was preserved for Holland and William V's collection enriched with 41 paintings, including three by Rembrandt. In the 1770 catalogue which Terwesten drew up of part of the Prince's collection, this portrait is described in the same terms as in Gerard Hoet's list [8].

Shortly after this, in 1774, or a little later, the Prince's paintings were transferred to a new gallery in a recently renovated house at No. 35, Buitenhof, in The Hague, where, during the brightest hours of the day, i.e. between 11 and 1 o'clock, the gallery ("sael") was open to visitors on request [9]. The painting we are concerned with here was described by F. ten Dall as follows: "Een Portrait, zijnde het Hoofd van een Jongeling, op Paneel, in een zwarte Lijst met Vergulde binnenkant door *Denzelven* [Rembrandt] 1 v. 1 1/2 - 11 d." [10].

More than 175 paintings from the Stadhouder's collection were transported to Paris in 1795. After the fall of Napoleon, 120 items, including this portrait of a young man, were returned to King William I in The Hague on 20 November 1815 [11]. From 1822 onwards the collection, which in 1816 had been put in the keeping of the State, was opened to the public in the former residence of Prince Johan Maurits von Nassau-Siegen (1604-1679), known as "The Mauritshuis" after him [12].

Collections

G. van Slingelandt, The Hague, 1752-1768
Stadhouder William V, The Hague, 1768-1795
The Louvre, Paris, 1795-1815
King William I, The Hague, 1815
The Royal Collection of Paintings, The Hague, 1816
"The Mauritshuis"—Royal Collection of Paintings, The Hague, 1822

Dimensions quoted

1752	1 ft. 1 ½ in 11 in = approx. 37.5 x 27.5 cm
1770	1 ft. 1 ½ in x 11 in = approx. 37.5 x 27.5cm
1874	37.5 x 29 cm
1977	37.7 x 28.9 cm

ICONOGRAPHY AND STYLE

The sitter, with his head turned almost to face the spectator, is portrayed in a half-lenght study, with no hands visible and turned slightly to the left. He is dressed in a dark coat over which he is wearing a hauberk. His shirt collar falls over the upright rim of the hauberk. The left side of the forehead is largely covered by the wavy hair, hanging down on either side as far as the neck, with a single lock reaching down to the left shoulder (Fig. 1).

3. Studio of Rembrandt. Portrait of Rembrandt as Young Man.
Nuremberg, Germanisches Nationalmuseum.

4. X-ray photograph of the portrait Fig. 3.

As far as we know it was Victor de Stuers who, in 1874, first recognized a "probable" self-portrait of Rembrandt at a youthful age in this portrait [13]. In 1875 and 1876, Wurzbach and Bode wrote articles in which the painting in The Hague and a portrait resembling it in many respects in the Germanisches Nationalmuseum at Nuremberg (Figs. 3, 4) were both reproduced as portraits of the artist. The latter work had already been taken to be a portrait of Rembrandt as early as 1832 [14]. It may be noted in passing that Wurzbach rejected the attribution of both portraits to Rembrandt, whereas Bode asserted it with conviction [15]. After Bode, both the identification of the Hague painting as Rembrandt and its attribution to the artist found general recognition.

It is not surprising that this identification should have come so late in the day, since in this work the young artist looks more refined and dignified than in most of the portraits he made of himself: studies in paint (Br.-G., Nos. 1, 2, 5 and 11) and completed

5. Rembrandt. Self-Portrait, 1629. Etching. B. 338.

self-portraits (Br.-G., Nos. 8, 9 and 12); etchings (B.4, 9, 10, 13, 27; B.338 (Fig. 5) was not yet considered a self-portrait at the time [16]); drawings (Benesch, I, Nos. 53 and 54) [17].

The hauberk may also help to explain why the work was not immediately recognized as a self-portrait. The hair-style is unusually fashionable, for Rembrandt has decked himself out with a lovelock.

6. Rembrandt. Self-Portrait. Drawing. *London, British Museum.*

This also occurs in the etching of 1629 (B.338) mentioned above [18]. Yet it is lacking in the drawing in London, also mentioned above (Benesch, I, No. 53), which in the composition and lighting bears a fairly close resemblance to the Hague self-portrait (Fig. 6).

The meticulous way of painting is very remarkable and also the rather haughty and reserved expression on the subject's face. How striking the contrast is between this and the two studies at Kassel and Munich (Br.-G., Nos. 1 and 2). Intensely fascinated as he was by facial expressions, Rembrandt portrayed himself in this Hague self-portrait as a proud young nobleman. May we perhaps conclude from this that the artist, who was acquainted with Huygens and probably, through him, with the Stadhouder's circle in The Hague, portrayed himself so elegantly here, because this self-portrait was possibly painted as a mark of homage to, or commissioned by, a prominent person [19]?

However this may be, the young painter's face seems narrower and longer than in the likenesses in Kassel and Munich. The nose is less knobbly and the mouth is closed. The treatment of the light is notable: the light and dark are divided vertically almost into halves, yet without interfering with the unity of

7. Valentine Green. "Prince Rupert", 1775. Mezzotint.

the face [20]. The strokes of the brush in this carefully finished portrait are distinguishable only in those places where the light is strongest: the nose, the right cheek and parts of the collar and hauberk.

Reference has already been made to the etching and this makes the dating of the painting as c. 1629 plausible.

The mezzotint by Valentine Green (1739-1813) (Fig. 7) deserves to be mentioned, even if it cannot have been made after the Hague painting [21].

Copies of later date are: a) J. Kronig collection, Monte Carlo, panel, 35 x 32 cm.; b) Statens Museum for Konst, Copenhagen, panel, 38.5 x 26.5 cm., Inv. No. 1634, listed as "after Rembrandt"; c) Rindermarkt, art dealers, Zurich (1962), provenance: Count Attems collection, Graz.

NOTES

1. J. Bauch has established that the last heartwood growth ring on this panel dates from 1595. (See also *Appendix I*, 2f).

2. Van de Graaf, p. 13, writes that this way of treating the reverse of a panel, employed by Van Eyck and other 15th century Flemish painters, may have contributed to the often fine state of preservation of paintings by the Flemish Primitives. According to Philip Hendy and A.S. Lucas ("The Ground in Pictures", *Museum,* 21, 1968, p. 272), numerous 14th, 15th and 16th century panels in Italy, Germany, the Netherlands and France received a layer of priming on the reverse, but such treatment of panels was extremely rare in the 17th century. It may be added that this early self-portrait of Rembrandt is in excellent condition. There are scarcely any cracks in the paint and almost no retouching.

3. Hoet, II, pp. 403-406.

4. Lugt, I, No. 1683. The only copy of this sale catalogue which Lugt mentioned (viz., that in the Bibliothèque Municipale at Orléans) was no longer to be found there after the Second World War.

5. Jonkheer B.W.F. van Riemsdijk, "Schilderijen-kabinetten in de 18de eeuw", *Oud Holland,* 10, 1892, p. 222; Scheurleer, p. 24 and note 41; Etienne-François, duc de Choiseul et d'Amboise (1719-1785), French statesman and minister under Louis XVI, was a great art collector.

6. Abel François Poisson, marquis de Vandières et de Marigny (1727-1781), brother of Madame de Pompadour (1721-1764), was Director and Administrator General of Royal Buildings, Gardens, Academies and Factories; C. Bille, *De Tempel der Kunst of het Kabinet van den Heer Braamcamp,* Amsterdam, 1961, pp. 107-108, p. 131, note 25.

7. A. Bredius, "Extract uit de notulen der Confrérie van Pictura te 's-Gravenhage, gehouden door Pieter Terwesten", *Oud Holland,* 19, 1901, p. 176; see also: C.W. Fock, "De Schilderijengalerij van Prins Willem V op het Buitenhof te Den Haag", *Antiek,* 11, 1976, p. 120.

8. Terwesten, p. 709: "Een dito Jongelings-Hoofdt, mede zeer exceellent en kunstig geschildert, door DENZELVEN op paneel 1 (V) 1 ½ (D) 0 (V) 11 (D)".

9. Scheurleer, p. 29; H. de Lussanet de la Sablonière, "De restauratie van Buitenhof 34 tot en met 38 te 's-Gravenhage...", *Bulletin van de Kon. Ned. Oudheidkundige Bond,* 74, 1975, pp. 97-126; Drossaers-Scheurleer, III, p. 202.

10. F. ten Dall (1758-1821) compiled a catalogue, using "Uit de Aantekeningen van den Overleden Heer Directeur *T.P.C. Haag*". Ten Dall's original manuscript is kept in the Royal Household Archives in The Hague (Inv. A 18, V, No. 41 A) and has been published in: Drossaers-Scheurleer, III, pp. 203-242. The Mauritshuis is in possession of two

transcriptions of this manuscript. One of these was left in 1882 by J.Z. Mazel, director of the Mauritshuis from 1841 to 1874. A note on this copy reads "bgl. 14 Octob. 1815 N. 61", which justifies the conclusion that the manuscript was used in 1815 in connection with the claim for the return of the Dutch works of arts transferred by the French to Paris in 1795 (see note 11). J.Z. Mazel was personally involved in this recovery, for, being a young lieutenant in the Engineers, he was attached to Colonel de Man, a member of the delegation whose task it was to arrange for the return of these works. (See A.B. de Vries, "Koninklijk Kabinet van Schilderijen" in *Koninklijk Kabinet van Schilderijen, Koninklijke Bibliotheek, Koninklijk Penningkabinet,* The Hague, 1967, p. 64.)
The original notes by T.P.C. Haag (1737-1812), curator of William V's collection of paintings from c. 1760 to 1795, have never been traced. Regarding T.P.C. Haag, see: A. Staring, in: U. Thieme and F. Becker, *Allgemeines Lexikon der bildenden Künstler...,* 15, Leipzig, 1922, pp. 384-385; Scheurleer, p. 22. Ten Dall was a friend of the director Haag, whose death was registered in The Hague by Ten Dall in 1812 (kindly communicated by the Municipal Archives, The Hague).

11. Scheurleer, pp. 30-32, pp. 38-39.

12. King William I's collection of paintings has never been officially transferred to the State. See A.B. de Vries, "Koninklijk Kabinet van Schilderijen" in *150 Jaar Koninklijk Kabinet van Schilderijen, Koninklijke Bibliotheek, Koninklijk Penningkabinet,* The Hague, 1967, pp. 61-62.

13. Victor de Stuers, *Notice historique et descriptive des tableaux et des sculptures exposés dans le Musée Royal de La Haye,* The Hague, 1874, pp. 123-124, No. 117, "Portrait d'un adolescent" and Note 2: "Le peintre lui-même a probablement servi de modèle pour cette étude".

14. According to information from the Germanisches Nationalmuseum in Nuremberg, Cat. 1909, 1919, No. 391, as "by Rembrandt"; was formerly said to be marked with an *R,* below, right. We share the opinion of Hofstede de Groot that this painting is a copy made when Rembrandt was a young man (*Verslagen omtrent 's Rijks verzamelingen van Geschiedenis en Kunst,* 16 (covering 1893), The Hague, 1895, p. 53). It should be pointed out that it is not a wholly exact copy. The face appears to be rather fuller, there are differences in the treatment of the hair and the expression in the eyes. Neither is the relation between the sitter and the total surface quite the same. The great resemblance between this painting and that in the Mauritshuis—as regards both structure and way of painting—is also revealed by the two X-ray photographs (cf. Figs. 2 and 4). For that matter, this technique is to be found in the work of other painters of the period besides Rembrandt. When the two X-ray photographs are compared, account should be taken of the slighter degree of contrast in that of the painting in the Mauritshuis as a result of the white lead preparation on the reverse.

15. A. von Wurzbach, "Zur Kenntnis Govaert Flinck's, resp. Rembrandt's", *Zeitschrift für Bildende Kunst,* 10, 1875, pp. 381-383; W. Bode, "Die ersten Selbstporträts des Rembrandt van Rijn", *Zeitschrift für Bildende Kunst,* 11, 1876, pp. 125-126; A. von Wurzbach, "Die 'grünen' Rembrandt's des Herrn W. Bode", *Zeitschrift für Bildende Kunst,* 11, 1876, pp. 222-224; W. Bode, *Studien zur Geschichte der holländischen Malerei,* Brunswick, 1883, p. 378, p. 558, No. 13.

16.

Bartsch No.	= Münz No.	= Hollstein vol. 18, p.	vol. 19, p.
4 (c. 1628)	1	2	1
9 (c. 1628)	2	4	5
10 (d. 1630)	6	4-5	5
13 (d. 1630)	7	6	6
27 (c. 1628)	5	13	16
338 (d. 1629)	3	151	257

17. Not all the works mentioned here could have been known to Bode before 1883.

18. M.M. Tóth-Ubbens, "Kaalkop of ruighoofd, historisch verzet tegen het lange haar", *Antiek,* 6, Jan. 1972, pp. 371-385, ill. 10. This fashionable hair-style is a sign that the young artist was not insensitive to features of high society life he had noticed in The Hague.

19. Some authors have already commented that the self-portrait in Boston (Br.-G., No. 8) may have been commissioned. See S. Slive, "The Young Rembrandt", *Allen Memorial Art Museum Bulletin,* 20, 1963, p. 148; Gerson in Br.-G., No. 8.

20. W. Pinder, *Rembrandts Selbstbildnisse,* Leipzig, 1943, p. 20, ill. on p. 10. See also H. van de Waal, "Rembrandt and Chiaroscuro" in *Steps towards Rembrandt,* Amsterdam, 1974, p. 15.

21. The mezzotint, published in London in June 1775, was based on a painting in the collection of a Mr. Edward Orme. Since the Hague portrait had been in the William V collection since 1768, it cannot be identical with the painting in the Orme Collection. Drawings, prints and books of Edward Orme's were auctioned in London on 12 January 1824 (Lugt, I, No. 10569). The mezzotint bears the title "Prince Rupert". It is not likely that this caption means that this print represents Prince Rupert of the Palatinate (1619-1682), third son of the Winter King, Frederick V, Elector of the Palatinate and former King of Bohemia. Rupert's features in this period are sufficiently familiar (see, *inter alia,* the portrait of him ascribed to G. Honthorst in the National Portrait Gallery, London, Cat. No. 4519). It is probable that Green, who travelled to the Netherlands and the Palatinate in 1775 and who was thereafter appointed court engraver to the Elector Carl Theodore, was seeking to pay homage to his employer as a descendant of Prince Rupert's. This Prince Rupert was, moreover, celebrated as the inventor of the mezzotint (see Orovida C. Pissaro, "Prince Rupert and the Invention of the Mezzotint", *The Walpole Society,* 36, 1956-1958 (issued 1960), pp. 1-9). J. Ch. Smith, *British Mezzotint Portraits,* 2, London, 1883, p. 583, No. 114, already doubted whether Green's inscription on the mezzotint was correct.

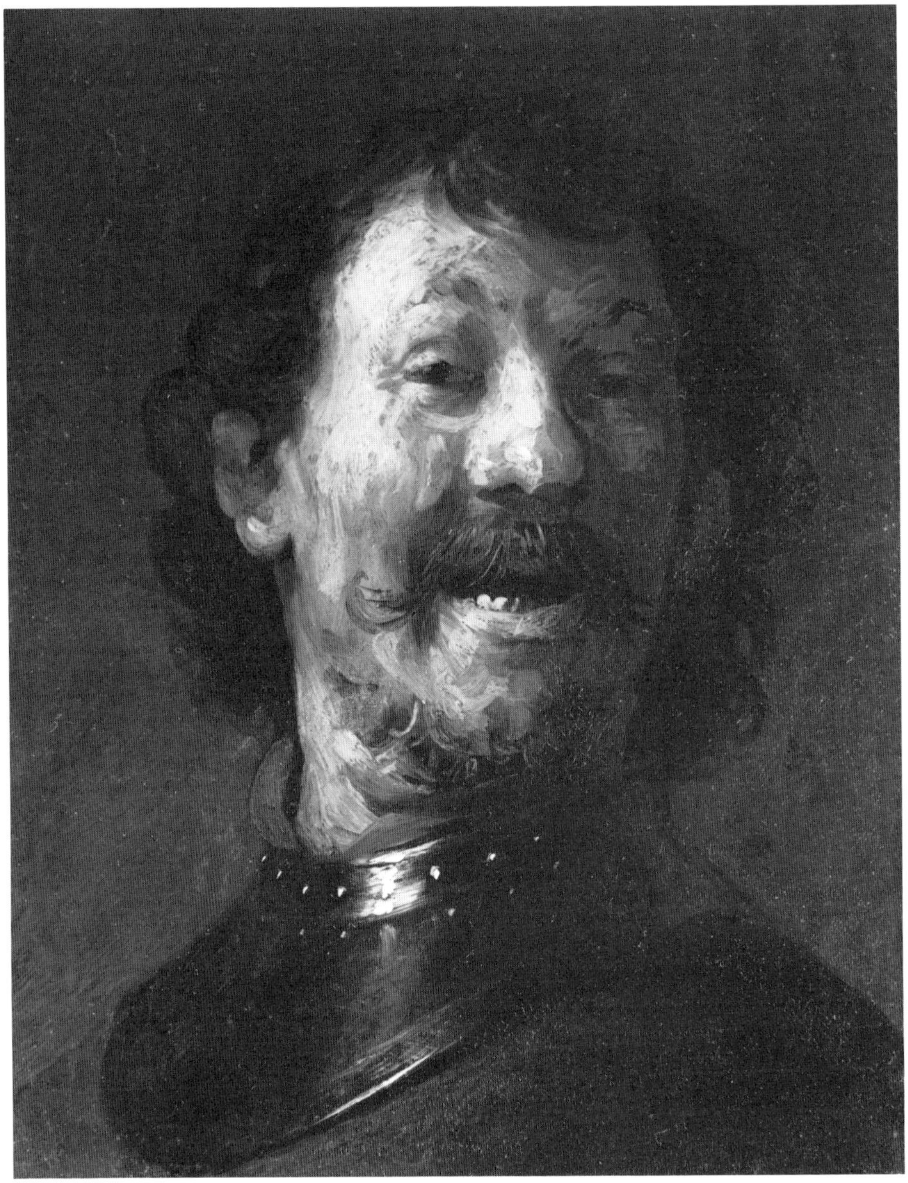

8. Study of a Man Laughing.

II

Study of a Man Laughing

Pl. II; Fig. 8

Copper, 15.3 x 12.2 cm. Unsigned, undated; c. 1629/30.

Cat. Br. (1895), No. 598; Valentiner, p. 29; H.d.G., No. 543; Cat. M. (1935), No. 598; Br., No. 134; Bauch, No. 113; Br.-G., No. 134 (not by Rembrandt); Cat. H. (1977), No. 598 ("the attribution to Rembrandt is not generally accepted").

TECHNICAL DATA

The work has been painted on a copper plate of approximately 1 mm thickness, mounted in a wooden frame with a cradle [1].

Apart from some retouching in the background and on the head, examination using ultra-violet and infra-red light did not reveal any special features; no remnants of a signature or date were found (see *Historical data* and note 6). Since the copper support does not allow X-rays to penetrate, electron emission radiography was employed for further investigation to trace *pentimenti* in the composition. The radiograph obtained did not deviate in any way, however, from the surface view of the painting (see also *Appendix I,* under 1a) (Fig. 9).

There are remarkably few cracks in the light areas of the head and the grey background, a very fine network of *craquelure* being visible only here and there. In the dark areas of the face, such as the red of the mouth, the black of the left eye and in the brownish-black shadows of the nose, neck and hair, wider cracks are, on the other hand, clearly visible in places.

The ground applied to the copper plate consists of a thin layer of greyish white, which has clearly turned green, owing to contamination by the copper. The ground consists of white lead mixed with a small quantity of chalk. Over the entire surface of this ground, an extremely thin layer of metallic gold, in the form of gold leaf, has been applied [2]. This gold leaf is particularly apparent on the edges of the painting (Pl. II) and also appears as glistening yellow dots in the very small areas where the surface of the paint has been damaged. These places include the hauberk and the forehead.

In places, too, where the paint has been applied very thinly, for example, above the right ear and near the right temple, or where a red or brown transparent paint has been used (ear and hair), it is possible, using a good magnifying glass and special lighting, to see the gold leaf showing clearly through the paint. The gold ground is also apparent in the yellow

9. Electron emission radiograph.

10. Macrophotograph. Detail of moustache. Scratching in wet paint (magnification x 7).

colour of a few strands of hair in the moustache and beard, where the painter has worked in the uppermost wet layer of paint with a point or the tip of the handle of his brush (Fig. 10). In these places, the greater part of the uppermost layer of paint has been removed in this way so that the yellow hairs are rendered by the underlying gold. This is, however, not visible to the naked eye.

For that matter, in other places, too, where the paint has been thinly applied to the gold, the purpose of this technique, which may perhaps have been to achieve more brilliant and durable colouring, is not evident [3].

The white in the painting is white lead, mixed in the flesh tones with yellow and red ochres and a little red lake pigment. Besides the red ochre and a red lake, a little vermilion has been used as a red paint, an example being the ear lobe, where it has been glazed over with a red lake pigment. A thin streak of blue pigment was detected in the outside edge of the right ear, consisting of small particles of a deep blue—probably azurite. The brownish-red colours, ranging to brownish-black, are composed of ochres, umber and (bone) black, while Cologne earth was found in the more transparent brown areas (edges).

In general, the pigments are of comparatively fine grain, although in various places coarser pigments have been used.

The painting bears no signature nor monogram and no remnants of either were found.

HISTORICAL DATA

This *Study of a Man Laughing* is probably identical with a small painting which was auctioned on 7-8 October 1783 at the "Kunst Confrérie-Kamer van Pictura" in The Hague, as item No. 72 [4]. It had come from the collection of Cornelia Steyn-Schellinger (1714-1783), widow of Mr. Pieter Steyn, Grand Pensionary of Holland and West Friesland [5]. One of the three small portraits by Rembrandt which were put up for sale at this auction was: "No. 72. Een fraay Krygsmans kopje, door *denzelven* [Rembrandt]; op *Koper*, hoog 6, breet 5 duim". In the 19th century this "small head" formed part of the collection of Dr. G. Munnicks van Cleeff of Utrecht, which was auctioned on 4-5 April 1864 at the Hôtel Drouot, Paris: "No. 79. Portrait d'homme (Rembrandt lui-même?). La tête de face est souriante, la bouche ouverte; le corps de trois quarts à gauche; hausse-col en acier, casaque brune. Fond neutre. A gauche, en haut, le monogramme *R^t^*. Sur cuivre parqueté. H. 0,22 - L. 0,19" [6]. According to a note in the copy of the sale catalogue kept in the Netherlands Institute for Art History in The Hague, this *Laughing Man* was sold for 2,000 francs. The small painting was auctioned once again in Paris on 19 February 1883, its provenance this time being the collection of Ch. de Boissière. It was announced in the catalogue as: "No. 40. Rembrandt van Ryn (Attribué à). Tête de soudard. C. H. 0^m^, 21. L. 0^m^, 17" and according to the note it was sold for 370 francs [7].

During the winter of 1894-95, C. Hofstede de Groot, at the time assistant director of the Mauritshuis, saw the painting at the F. Kleinberger Gallery, in Paris; according to the latter, it had come from the collection of a certain Langlois (perhaps a descendant of the engraver François Langlois, see below). After some hesitation, Bredius purchased it in March 1895 for the Mauritshuis, for the sum of 1,750 francs or 890 florins [8].

Collections

Cornelia Steyn-Schellinger, The Hague, 1783
Dr. G. Munnicks van Cleeff, Utrecht, 1864
Ch. de Boissière, Paris, 1883
Langlois, Paris
F. Kleinberger, art dealer, Paris, 1894-1895
"The Mauritshuis"—Royal Collection of Paintings, The Hague, 1895

Dimensions quoted

1783	6 in x 5 in = approx. 15 x 12.5 cm
1864	22 x 19 cm
1883	21 x 17 cm
1897	15.4 x 12.2 cm
1977	15.3 x 12.2 cm

Prices

1783	2 florins and 16 cents
1864	2,000 francs
1883	370 francs
1895	1,750 francs (890 florins)

ICONOGRAPHY AND STYLE

Bust of a man, laughing, with mouth open, chin-beard and moustache. He is wearing a hauberk (Fig. 8).

The records show that this painting was described in 1783 as the "Small head of a Warrior" and in

1864 was referred to, with some reservation, as a self-portrait. In the supplement to the Mauritshuis catalogue (1895, No. 598) Bredius observed that the sitter's features bear some resemblance to those of the artist but that in the year the work is said to have been painted (1629), the artist was younger than the *Laughing Man* seems to be. He considered the possibility that Rembrandt's eldest brother, Adriaen, had been portrayed here [9]. Since 1935 the painting has usually been called a *Study of a Man Laughing*.

11. Rembrandt. Portrait of the Artist with Cap, 1630, Etching, B. 316.

This study of an unidentified person does, in fact, bear a resemblance to a number of Rembrandt's self-portraits among his etchings [10] (Fig. 11).

The same "laughing head" was etched by J.G. van Vliet (active between c. 1600 and 1635); this undated etching is marked *J.G. van Vliet fec.* at the top, left, and at the top, right, bears the monogram and inscription *RHL inventor* (Fig. 12). It was used by the engraver Wenceslas Hollar (1607-1677) for a philosopher's portrait, showing Democritus laughing and Heraclitus weeping with a globe between them [11] (Fig. 13). Hollar also used another etching for this purpose, a head of Judas which Van Vliet etched in 1634 (after the Judas in Rembrandt's painting *Judas Returning the Thirty Pieces of Silver,* 1629; Br.-G., No. 539 A).

Finally, as Hofstede de Groot stated, the etching of the *Laughing Man* was copied by François Langlois, known as Ciartres (1589-1648), publisher, engraver and art dealer, and called by him *Democritus* [12], as Hollar's etching had been before it.

It appears from this that by virtue of their expression, figures by Rembrandt proved highly suitable models for depicting certain types [13]. He was intensely interested in the expression of human emotions,

12. J.G. van Vliet. Etching after Rembrandt's Study Fig. 8.

13. Wenceslas Hollar. Democritus and Heraclitus. Etching.

a theme upon which attention was also focused in 17th century philosophical treatises [14].

Van Vliet's etching causes one to wonder whether Rembrandt's *Laughing Man* was not perhaps intended as a preparatory study for a figure in some larger composition. For, just as Van Vliet took the head of Judas in Rembrandt's painting as his model, on account of its accurate rendering of a certain character, Rembrandt might have intended to employ this type, a laughing man, in a larger painting.

14. Rembrandt. Self-Portrait, c. 1629.
Stockholm, Nationalmuseum.

15. Rembrandt. The Mother of the Artist, c. 1629.
Salzburg, Residenzmuseum (Czernin Collection).

As a result of technical examination, it has been established that three small paintings, all of which are, or were, attributed to Rembrandt and date from the Leiden years, viz., *Study of a Man Laughing, Self-portrait* (Br.-G., No. 11) and *Rembrandt's Mother* (Br.-G., No. 63), were painted on copper plates of approx. 15 x 12.5 cm (old dimensions 6 x 5 in = duim), covered with gold leaf (see note 1) Figs. 14, 15).

Painting on copper became quite frequent in the Northern Netherlands as a result of the influence exerted by numerous Flemish painters who had immigrated during the last quarter of the 16th century [15]. Painting on gold leaf, however, seems so far to have been highly exceptional and has only been found in the small paintings mentioned above.

Whereas the dimensions and preparation correspond in the three works mentioned, there are striking differences in the execution. The painting in the *Study of a Man Laughing* is remarkable by reason of the strokes and touches of the brush, which seem to have been applied rapidly and with great assurance. As for the small portrait representing *Rembrandt's Mother,* it has been executed in far greater detail, while the brushwork in the *Self-portrait* is much more delicate. Sheer portraiture dominates in the last two works, although the old woman may also represent the prophetess Anna. In the *Study of a Man Laughing* the expression seems all the more emphatic since we are unable to identify the sitter.

In our view, it is plausible that all three small paintings are by Rembrandt, despite the differences referred to. Such differences may very well be explained by the young artist's urge to experiment. This apparently exceptional use of gold leaf also suggests that all three works were painted by one and the same artist. Finally, it should be pointed out that in various of his early etchings—studies of the face, wearing all manner of expressions, often studies of himself and of small dimensions—Rembrandt obtains effects similar to those evoked by the *Laughing Man.* It is as if with his brush, and by his colour, he was seeking to achieve various effects just as he had done when using the burin. Consequently, it is with conviction that we uphold the attribution of this *Study of a Man Laughing* to the artist [16].

There can be no doubt that Rembrandt familiarized himself with the work of Frans Hals and Adriaen Brouwer during his youth. In the handling of the paint and the characterization of the model we accordingly notice a certain likeness to Brouwer's *Bitter Medicine* (Frankfurt, Städelsches Kunstinstitut,

16. Adriaen Brouwer, Bitter Medicine. *Frankfurt, Staedelsches Kunstinstitut.*

17. Old Copy. *Present location unknown.*

No. 1076) [17] (Fig. 16). We know that Rembrandt owned six paintings (among them a *tronie* (face, mug) and two half figures) [18] and a volume with drawings by Adriaen Brouwer.

The etched self-portrait of 1630 (B.316) has an "impressionist" flavour, corresponding whit this study. In view of these correspondences, the *Study of a Man Laughing* is to be dated about 1629-30.

In the inventory of the estate of the painter Lambert Jacobsz. († 1636), drawn up on 3 October 1637, we find an item listed which may be an early copy of this *Study of a Laughing Man.* We read: "No. 15. Een soldaet met swart haer een Iseren halskraegh sluyer om den hals *na Remb.*" [19].

A copy (panel, 18.75 x 16.1 cm), formerly in the Baron M. Herzog collection, Budapest, and in 1966 at the art dealer's, J.K. Tannhäuser of New York, probably dates from the 18th century (Fig. 17).

NOTES

1. See W. Froentjes, "Schilderde Rembrandt op goud", *Oud Holland,* 84, 1969, pp. 233-237.

2. H. Kühn, "Untersuchungen zu den Malgründen Rembrandts", *Jahrbuch der Staatlichen Kunstsammlungen in Baden-Württemberg,* 2, 1965, pp. 189-210. In his research into the composition of the ground on 37 of Rembrandt's paintings, small ones included, Kühn did not find gold leaf on any. Kühn also examined *Tobias Healing his Father's Blindness* (now in Stuttgart, Staatsgalerie, formerly in the Arenberg Collection in Brussels; Br.-G., No. 502), which work according to W. Thoré-Bürger may have been painted on gold leaf (p. 200). For the remark concerning the gold ground, see W. Froentjes, "Schilderde Rembrandt op goud", *Oud Holland,* 84, 1969, p. 237, note 3.

3. A fair amount of painting on copper was done from the second half of the 16th century onwards, yet one will search in vain in the old and in more recent literature for a technique in which gold leaf was applied to the copper plate after priming, as the layer on which to paint. This technique proved to be unknown to the staffs of various museum laboratories, while an investigation into a number of old paintings done on copper, including some in the Mauritshuis, also failed to reveal any indication of a gold ground having been used. No response was received to a request made to readers by W. Froentjes in the article already mentioned to inform him of any paintings on copper known to them which may have a gold ground.

4. Lugt, I, No. 3615.

5. J.E. Elias, *De Vroedschap van Amsterdam, 1578-1795,* 1, Amsterdam, 1963 (unrevised reprint of the Haarlem, 1903 edition), No. 95a.

6. Lugt, III, No. 27807. The rather surprising *R^t* monogram is not otherwise mentioned. Technical research also failed to reveal any remnants of a signature. This monogram may possibly have disappeared when the work was cleaned by A. Hauser (see note 8).

7. Lugt, III, No. 42648.

8. See C. Hofstede de Groot, *Echt of onecht? Oog of chemie?* The Hague, 1925, p. 67: "During the winter of 1894-5, at Kleinberger's, the art dealer's, I saw a Small Head of a grinning-laughing man, attributed to Rembrandt and according to a print, which J.G. van Vliet made of it as early as 1634, either by or after Rembrandt. The small work had been enlarged and partially re-painted, but in the undamaged parts I was still able to recognize Rembrandt's touch. Bredius and Bode were originally disinclined to believe in its authenticity and A. Hauser, the celebrated restorer, to whom I had entrusted it for the removal of the over-painting, wrote me that he had begun to clean it but had stopped, since the entire picture struck him as being of recent date. On receipt of this letter I immediately telegraphed Hauser, saying: "Nur ruhig weiter putzen, Bild sicher echt" and the very next day I received a message from him, which read: "Was den kleinen Rembrandt betrifft, so musz ich gestehen, dass ich mich gründlich getäuscht habe".

9. K. Bauch, *Der frühe Rembrandt und seine Zeit,* Berlin, 1960, p. 168, also identifies the subject as Adriaen.

10.

Bartsch No.	=	Münz No.	=	Hollstein vol. 18, p.	Hollstein vol. 19, p.
13		7		6	6
316		12		146	254
6		301 (as by Van Vliet)		170 (under "Prints by Rembrandt only known in later states reworked by a pupil"; probably reworked by Van Vliet)	284

11. A. Bartsch, *Catalogue raisonné de toutes les estampes qui forment l'Œuvre de Rembrandt et ceux de ses principaux imitateurs,* Vienna 1797, Nos. 21 and 22; regarding the etching of the two philosophers, see A. Blankert, "Heraclitus en Democritus", *Kunsthistorisch Jaarboek,* 18, 1967, p. 117, No. 90, Ill. 44. The legend under Hollar's print reads: "I laugh at this Madd World: But I do Weepe That Bramsick Mortalls Such a Coyle Shuld Keepe". The print was published by John Overton (1640 - after 1708) "at the white horse neere the fountaine tavern without Newgate".

Hollar probably bought Van Vliet's prints while staying in Amsterdam in 1634 and took them back to England with him. In 1636 he entered the service of Thomas Howard, second Earl of Arundel (1586-1646), with whom the engraver crossed to England at the end of 1636. For this see exh. cat. *Wenceslas Hollar 1607-1677. Drawings, Paintings and Etchings,* Manchester (Art Gallery), 1963, p. 9.

12. H.d.G., *Urkunden,* No. 28; François Langlois, the French publisher, was employed by the Earl of Arundel as his agent. In 1637 Langlois travelled to London via the Netherlands. We know of this journey from two letters, viz., from the letter Nicolas Lanier addressed to Mariette (October 1637) and from one by the French painter Claude Vignon (1593-1670), addressed to his friend, Langlois. This letter is undated, but was probably sent from Paris in 1637. In it Vignon requests Langlois to visit various painters, among them Rembrandt (M.G. Bottari and S. Ticozzi, *Raccolta di lettere,* 4, Milan, 1822, No. CLXXXIX, pp. 445-447 and E. Guhl-A.Rosenberg, *Künstlerbriefe,* Berlin, 1880, p. 214, No. 83).

13. Publishers made a profitable use of these, issuing series of philosophers, princes or warriors and, employing these types or "characters" in arbitrary fashion.

14. *Renati Des-Cartes principia philosophiae,* Amsterdam, 1644; Johan van Beverwijck, *Heel-Konste, ofte Derde Deel van de Genees-Konste,* Amsterdam, 1652, p. 26; see also C.L. Thijssen-Schoute, *Uit de Republiek der Letteren,* The Hague, 1967, pp. 76, 79 and 240.

15. L. de Pauw-de Veen, *De begrippen "schilder", "schilderij" en "schilderen" in de 17de eeuw,* Brussels, 1969, p. 126, note 31. According to this authoress, engraved copper plates, apparently worn down by the printing process, were sometimes used as the support. This may possibly explain the correspondence in the size of these three paintings by Rembrandt.

16. The comment made by W. Sumowski in "Kritische Bemerkungen zur neusten Gemäldekritik", *Neue Beiträge zur Rembrandt-Forschung,* Berlin, 1973, pp. 94-95, to the effect that the fact that J.G. van Vliet signed his etching based on the *Laughing Man* with "J.G. van Vliet fec." and "RHL inventor" is a further argument supporting the attribution of the work to Rembrandt, appears to us to be correct, as does also his remark in this respect about the gold ground.

17. Both Frans Hals and Adriaen Brouwer painted on copper plates. See S. Slive, *Frans Hals,* 3, London, 1974, No. 8. It appears that the innkeeper-painter Barent van Someren (c. 1572-73 - 1632) advised Brouwer to paint on a copper plate. See Houbraken I, p. 323. As regards the painting *Bitter Medicine,* see G. Knuttel, *Adriaen Brouwer. The master and his works,* The Hague 1962, p. 150, No. 101.

18. Transcription of the inventory dated 25 and 26 July 1656 of Rembrandt's goods and chattels. H.d.G., *Urkunden,* pp. 193, 195. See also A. Heppner, "Brouwer's Influence Upon Rembrandt", *The Art Quarterly,* 4, 1941, pp. 40-54.

19. H.L. Straat, "Lambert Jacobsz., schilder", *De Vrije Fries,* 28, 1925, p. 72, No. 15.

18. Head of an Old Man.

III

Head of an Old Man

Pl. III; Fig. 18

Panel, 46.8 x 38.4 cm. Unsigned, undated; c. 1630.

Cat. Br. (1895), No. 265; Valentiner, p. 41; H.d.G., No. 676; Cat. M. (1935), No. 565; Br., No. 77; Bauch, No. 116; G., No. 36; Br.-G., No. 77; Cat. H. (1977), No. 565.

TECHNICAL DATA

The oak panel has been bevelled on all four sides but on the right-hand side the bevelled surface is narrower than on the other three. As a result, the panel is considerably thicker on this side, while the edge is clearly rougher than the others and bears no remains of ground and paint. A strip, approximately 3 ½ cm in breadth, has apparently been sawn off and this was presumably done after the painting had been finished [1].

Examination under ultra-violet radiation did not reveal any special features except for a little minor retouching here and there. The X-ray photograph shows that a few alterations were made to the painting (Fig. 19). The most striking of these is that originally an apparently small, dark cap had been painted on the head instead of the black soft cap seen in the finished work [2]. Direct observation, too, besides the X-radiograph, reveals that in those places where the black of the cap has worn off, not only does white lead become visible but this white is also mixed with yellow and here and there with red as well. The flesh tones of the originally uncovered portion of the forehead and head become visible in this red.

The infra-red photograph (Fig. 20) reveals a dark rim of shadow above the cap and from this we may deduce that the cap once reached up a little higher. The X-radiograph also shows that small alterations were made to the coat and the white collar. Finally, in the X-ray photograph, dark patches are seen to have been left in the background, to the left of the head, although no definite forms are distinguishable in them [3].

The texture of the panel is visible through the thin layer of paint almost everywhere, with the exception of the lights parts of the head and of the cap. There is little *craquelure* in the background. The light areas of the face display the network of fine cracks often found in old paintings on panels. In a few places the *craquelure* varies—for instance, in and near the right eye, where, in the shadowed areas, wide, star-shaped cracks occur. Wide cracks with

19. X-ray photograph.

20. Infra-red photograph.

21. Macrophotograph. Detail of the Cap. Abrasion of black paint (magnification x 3).

19

20

projecting edges are also present in the black of the cap. At the front, the black cap bears numbers of whitish-yellow spots, of varying size and shape, which produce a special effect. As already said, this phenomenon is, however, the result of the wearing off of the upper layer of paint. The black has worn away in this process, both in the upper regions of the original underlying layer of paint, which was applied fairly thickly, and in the projecting edges of the *craquelure* (Fig. 21).

The ground applied to the panel is of chalk. In the background, upper edge and near the cap, a thin brown intermediate layer was found—probably the *imprimatura*—in which brown ochre, umber and a little white lead were shown to be present. It seems plausible that the thin, light strokes visible here and there in the X-ray photograph—for example, under the coat—originate from this intermediate layer. Under the yellowish-white paint of the face, glazed here and there with a red lake pigment, lies a dark, brownish-grey underpainting. This is made up of a mixture of bone black, white lead and umber. In those places where the uppermost layer has been very thinly applied, for example in the right cheek, this dark underpainting is visible through the upper layer and results in a darker, bluish-grey colouring. This dark-grey layer also becomes visible in the collar, in those places where the white has worn away. The yellowish-white of the forehead consists of a mixture of white lead and yellow ochre, with very thin red lake glazing here and there. The yellow of the collar is also of yellow ochre mixed with white lead. The red of the ear proves to consist of a red ochre with vermilion, while some vermilion also seems to be present in the red of the right eye, in addition to red ochre and a red lake pigment. In the background, ranging from grey to olive green, ochres (yellow and red), grains of blue pigment (azurite) and carbon black have been used, mixed with varying amounts of white lead. Here and there in the face and moustache a light touch of white lead mixed with blue grains of azurite is to be found. The white lead, in the collar for example, contains impurities (silver and copper) characteristic of old white lead.

The painting is neither signed nor dated.

HISTORICAL DATA

This painting was purchased by Bredius in Paris, in 1892, for the sum of 6,000 francs and attributed to Rembrandt. The intermediary involved in this purchase was the Swedish painter Anders Leonard Zorn (1860-1920). The work had come from the collection of Lady Harrison of Sutton Place, near Seaford. Bredius loaned it to the Mauritshuis in 1892, bequeathing it in 1946.

Collections

Lady Harrison, Sutton Place, near Seaford, England, 1892

Dr. A. Bredius, The Hague, on loan to the Mauritshuis, 1892-1946

Bredius bequest, 1946

Dimensions quoted

1895 47 x 39 cm

1977 46.8 x 38.4 cm

Price

1892 6,000 francs

ICONOGRAPHY AND STYLE

A head and shoulders portrait of an old man with a moustache, goatee and chin-beard, turned to the left, with the head facing the spectator. He is attired in a fur-collared coat worn over an undergarment with a rucked collar. On his head he is wearing a cap (Fig. 18).

In the Mauritshuis catalogues compiled by Bredius (1895) and Martin (1935) this work is listed as "Tête d'étude, probablement d'après Harmen Gerritsz. van Rijn, père de l'artiste". There was apparently no certainty as to the sitter's identity, even though E. Michel had referred to this work in his monograph on Rembrandt (1893) as one of the best portraits of the painter's father [4]. Since then many paintings and etchings, studies of old men showing some likeness to the Hague panel, have been taken to be portraits of Rembrandt's father [5].

The drawing of an old blind man in the Ashmolean Museum in Oxford, bearing the inscription *HARMAN GERRITS. van den Rhijn* (Fig. 22) differs considerably from this series of portraits [6]. In 1906, Hind expressed the opinion that the Oxford drawing represented Rembrandt's father (1565-1630) and that the other portraits could not accordingly be likenesses of the Leiden miller [7]. Münz's detailed 1953 study concerning *Rembrandts Bild von Mutter und Vater* put a definite end to the assumption that the *Old Man* in the Mauritshuis represents the painter's father [8]. This same old man was portrayed repeatedly by Rembrandt, his contemporaries and his pupils [9].

Identification as Rembrandt's father is hampered by the fact that the 17th century tradition was lost

22. Rembrandt. The Father of the Artist. Drawing. *Oxford, Ashmolean Museum.*

23. Rembrandt. Man Wearing a Close Cap, 1630. Etching, B. 304.

as early as the 18th century: the 1679 inventory of Rembrandt's etching plates in the possession of the art dealer and publisher Clement de Jonghe includes under item No. 53 a portrait of "Rembrandt's father". In the inventories of later owners of these plates, however, Rembrandt's father is no longer mentioned [10].

It has become apparent from the X-ray photograph (Fig. 19) that the black cap which covers a large part of the forehead is a later addition. The artist had originally painted only a small cap on the old man's head (see *Technical data*). Both Michel and Bredius had noted the later addition of the cap as early as 1892, since the "empâtements des dessous" had remained "très apparents" [11]. This, too, has been confirmed by the technical examination. Since X-ray photographs did not exist at the time, Michel and Bredius must have detected this overpainting with the naked eye. Or did they base themselves on information from Zorn? From their remarks it appears that they were of the opinion that Rembrandt had painted the cap himself. However, the possibility must not be discounted that the painter Zorn added the cap, taking Rembrandt's etching of 1630 (B.304) as his model (Fig. 23) [12]. Michel had seen the painting at Zorn's studio in Paris.

The hue of the old man's face is highly remarkable. The strikingly yellow tint is not due to old layers of varnish and, as far as we know, is not to be encountered in any other study of a face in so striking a manner as here. The attention is also drawn by a number of accentuations in red in the sitter's right eye, on the under-edge of the nose and on the lobe of the right ear. Might the unusual (unhealthy?) hue of the face and these red, reflection-like touches permit

24. Rembrandt. Portrait of Nicolaes Ruts, 1631. Detail of the head. *New York, The Frick Collection.*

us to suppose that the work was painted by candle-light?

The distribution of light and dark on the old man's face is the same as in many other studies of faces during this period, from 1629 to 1631 (cf. *inter alia,* Br.-G., Nos. 79 and 82). While this *Head of an Old Man* must have been painted before Rembrandt left Leiden, we nevertheless note a resemblance to the portrait of Nicolaes Ruts (Br.-G., No. 145, dated 1631 and presumably painted in Amsterdam) at least as regards the painting of the latter's head, even though this portrait is certainly more powerful (Fig. 24).

Great attention has been paid to the details of the old man's face and to the wrinkles on his forehead and round his eyes. Partly on the grounds of the Rembrandt etching of 1630, which has been mentioned above and is closely associated with this painting, the date of the work is rightly put at circa 1630.

The authors are aware that a few scholars have expressed some doubt about the attribution to Rembrandt and even about the age of the painting. However, they wish to stick to the traditional attribution admitting the existence of divergent opinions concerning Rembrandt's authorship. As for the dating see note 1.

NOTES

1. J. Bauch has established that the last heartwood growth ring on the panel dates from 1569 (see also *Appendix I,* 2f).

2. The existence of this over-painting has been noticed before (see under *Iconography and style* and notes 4 and 11).

3. The suggestion that a hand might have been painted near the right ear seems unfounded.

4. E. Michel, *Rembrandt. Sa vie, son œuvre et son temps,* Paris, 1893, pp. 44-45, p. 44: "Une autre répétition, et assurément l'un des meilleurs de ces portraits du père de Rembrandt, que j'ai pu voir récemment dans l'atelier de M. Zorn, le peintre suédois bien connu, est aussi la reproduction à peu près exacte, mais en sens inverse, d'une eau-forte du maître, signée de son monogramme et datée 1630, la *Tête d'homme vu de face* (B.304). Même coiffure, une calotte de velours noir; même costume,...".

5. Br.-G., Nos. 73, 74, 76, 77, 78, 79, 80, 81, 82. Etchings:

Bartsch No.	=	Münz No.	=	Hollstein vol. 18, p.	Hollstein vol. 19, p.
263		46		119	203
286		51		137	244
287		52		137	244
292		37		139	249
294		36		140	250
304		39		142	251
321		32		148	255

The question remains as to how far Rembrandt was specially interested in portrait painting, at least during his Leiden period. He was undoubtedly always concerned with human beings, but nothing is known of commissions for portraits prior to 1631. During his Leiden period the dividing line between "character study" and "portrait" is very vague. Compare, for instance, the self-portraits of this period.

In Joachim Sandrart's biography of Rembrandt (in *L'Academia Todesca della Architectura, Scultura et Pictura: Oder Teutsche Academie der Edlen Bau-, Bild- und Mahlerei-Künste...,* Nuremberg, 1675, p. 327) special mention is made of his industry, patience and experience in portraying old people. According to Sandrart, he was especially good at rendering their skin and hair faithfully.

6. Concerning the blindness of Rembrandt's father, see J. Held, "Rembrandt and the Book of Tobit", *Rembrandt's Aristotle and Other Rembrandt Studies,* Princeton, 1967, p. 127.

7. A M. Hind, "The Portraits of Rembrandt's Father", *Burlington Magazine,* 8, 1906, pp. 426-431, ill. 1; Benesch, I, No. 56, ill. 57; K.T. Parker, *Catalogue of Drawings in the Ashmolean Museum,* 1, 1938, No. 182; We do not support L. Münz's opinion (Münz, 1953, pp. 177-180) that this drawing was not Rembrandt's work and that the sitter was probably not Rembrandt's father.

8. Münz, 1953, p. 164 and pp. 166-167, ill. 186. Except for the drawing in the Ashmolean Museum at Oxford, all that has come down to us concerning portraits of Rembrandt's father is to be found in documents: two descriptions of good and chattels and one inventory (see H.d.G., *Urkunden,* Nos. 101 and 350, and D. de Hoop Scheffer and K.G. Boon, "De inventaris-lijst van Clement de Jonghe en Rembrandts etsplaten", *De Kroniek van het Rembrandthuis,* 25, 1971, p. 10, p. 16, No. 53).

9. Also illustrated in Münz, 1953, ills. 182, 187, 188, 198 and 199.

10. D. de Hoop Scheffer and K.G. Boon, "De inventaris-lijst van Clement de Jonghe en Rembrandts etsplaten", *De Kroniek van het Rembrandthuis,* 25, 1971, p. 10, p. 16, No. 53; D. de Hoop Scheffer, "Nogmaals de inventaris-lijst van Clement de Jonghe", *De Kroniek van het Rembrandthuis,* 26, 1972, pp. 128-130.

11. For this see note 2; the technical examination does not permit any pronouncement as to the date of the overpainting. E. Michel, *Rembrandt. Sa vie, son œuvre et son temps,* Paris, 1893, p. 45, note 1: "La calotte de velours noir a été ajoutée après coup, sans doute pour masquer la calvitie, et les empâtements des dessous sont restés très apparents". Bredius wrote (cat. 1895): "Le peintre a ajouté ultérieurement la calotte. On voit apparaître comme repentir la couleur du front, primitivement éclairé d'une lumière intense".,

12. B. 304 = Münz, 39 = Hollstein, Vol. 18, p. 142, Vol. 19, p. 251. See also the etching by Lievens, B. 21; Hollstein, Vol. 11, p. 35 with illustration.

IV

Andromeda

Pl. IV; Fig. 25

Panel, 34.0 x 24.5 cm. Unsigned, undated; c. 1630.

Valentiner, p. 104; H.d.G., No. 195; Cat. M. (1935), No. 707; Br., No. 462; Bauch, No. 254; G., No. 55; Br.-G., No. 462; Cat. H. (1977), No. 707.

25. Andromeda.

TECHNICAL DATA

The oak panel has been bevelled on the right-hand side and the top but not along the left-hand side and bottom edge. From this we may deduce that it has been presumably larger [1]. *R. Rembrand, no. 32,* has been painted at a later date on the reverse, in black lettering, probably by a former collector.

Examination and photography using ultra-violet light clearly revealed a fair amount of retouching (Fig. 27). The infra-red photograph did not yield any particular information, except that Andromeda's hair shows up more clearly on this photograph than in the painting itself (Fig. 28).

X-ray photography brought a number of very striking *pentimenti* to light (Fig. 26). Thus the X-radiograph shows that Andromeda was originally a full-length figure, with her feet rendered in detail. In the work as we now know it, the feet, ankles and lower part of the legs are hidden from view by the rock in the foreground. The X-radiograph also shows that the cloth draped round the hips and legs was originally of a different shape and concealed far less than it does now. For instance, the entire left leg, almost up to the hip, is clearly visible in the X-ray photograph (Fig. 29). It must accordingly have been overpainted at some later stage. There is, on the other hand, little of the right leg to be seen in the X-radiograph, so that this leg must have been largely covered by the loin cloth. It appears that a fold of this garment also originally hung down beside the uncovered left leg. The pattern of the fringe of this original portion of the loin cloth, which was painted over later on, is still clearly discernible in the form of white lead outlines at the same height as the knee (Figs. 29, 30). This pattern seems to be the same as that of the fringe visible in the painting where the loin cloth has not been altered and where it hangs down in front of the right leg.

There are also indications that about the hips the garment was originally much narrower and that the upper parts were added later. That is to say, both in the X-ray photograph and by examination with a

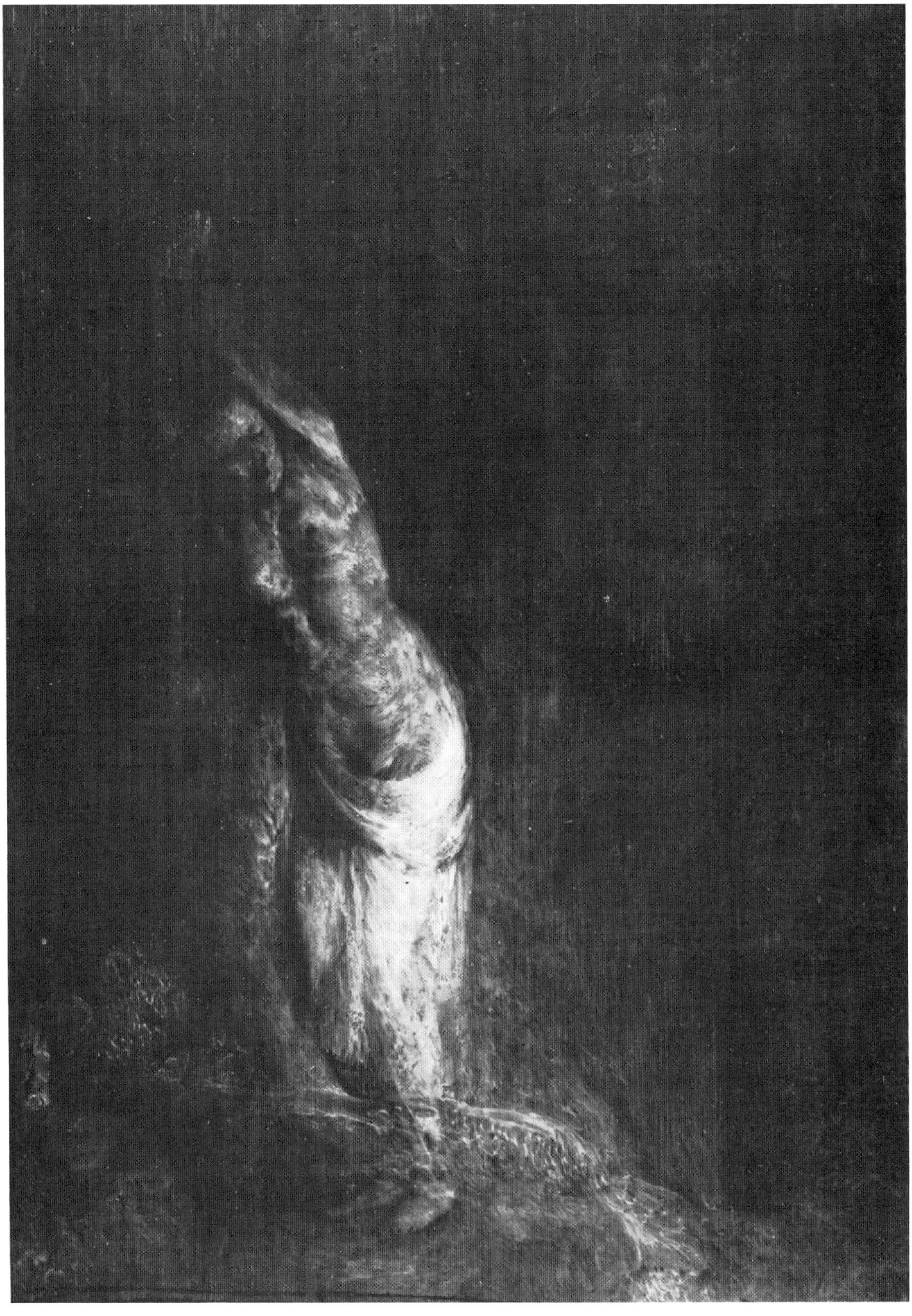

26. X-ray photograph.

27

28

29

30

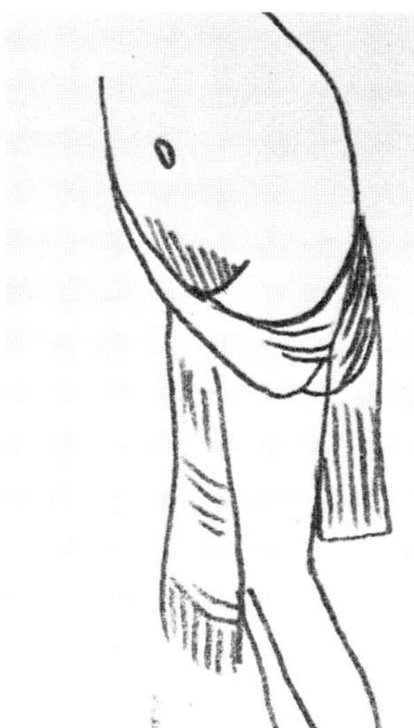

27. Ultra-violet fluorescence photograph.

28. Infra-red photograph.

29. X-ray photograph of the legs. Detail of Fig. 26.

30. The presumable original loin-cloth. Drawing by the restorer L. Kuiper.

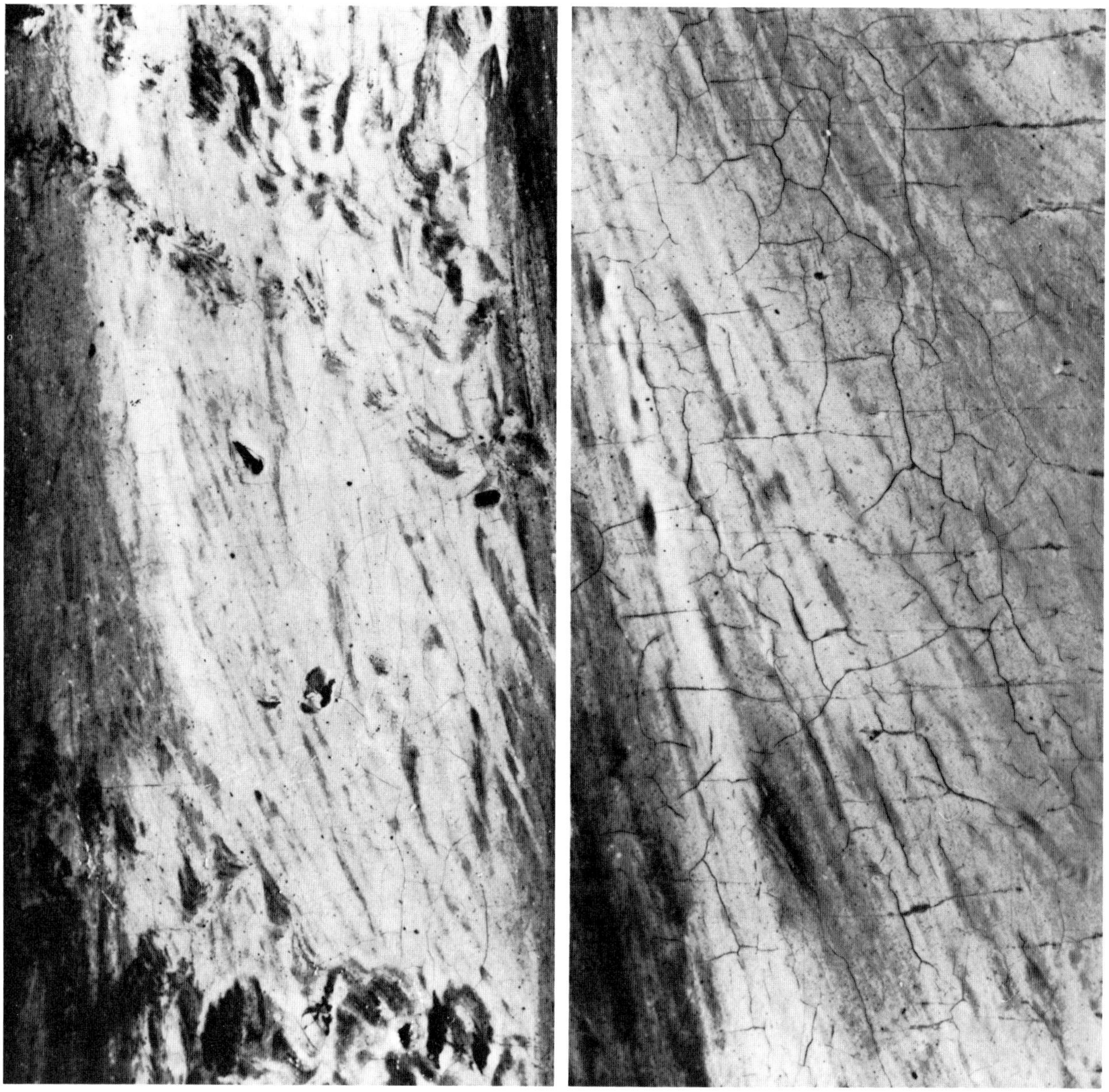

31. a) Detail of the original loin-cloth with fine cracks. b) Detail of the overpainted cloth over the left upper leg with coarser cracks (magnification x 8).

magnifying glass, one can still discern the vague contours of the upper part of the leg under the uppermost part of the loin cloth, in the groin.

The X-ray examination did not reveal any special features in other parts of the painting. No indication whatever was found of a figure of Perseus and a sea-monster having originally been included in the composition, nor did electron emission radiography and infra-red examination reveal any such evidence (see *Iconography and style*).

The surface of the paint is fairly smooth; only here and there, in the vegetation and rocks, has the paint been applied a little more thickly. There is very little *craquelure* in the background (sky and sea); here the paint film is so thin that the texture of the panel is visible in many places, while there is also a fair amount of retouching.

According to the radiograph, the figure has been painted rather thinly in white lead. Fine, scarcely discernible cracks are accordingly found here, which continue normally into the cloth round the hips. It is noticeable that the *craquelure* is of finer structure in the figure and in the loin cloth which originally hung down to the left of it than in those portions of the cloth which were added later, and where the cracks are clearly wider (Figs. 31a and b). A number of

32. Detail: The vegetation (above to the right). Outlines drawn in wet paint.

instances of retouching in the cloth (see Fig. 27) accompany this coarser network of cracks, which must have been caused by overpainting on paint which had already dried.

In this painting, too, the artist has drawn in the wet top layer of paint either with a point or with the wooden tip of his brush. This is the manner in which the vegetation to the right of the rock has been rendered. The outlines of leaves, stalks and grass, which to casual inspection seem to have been painted with a brownish-yellow ochre, appear on examination with a stereo-microscope or even with a good pocket lens to have been drawn in the wet paint, so that the colour of the vegetation is partly determined by the yellowish-brown of the panel (Fig. 32).

The thin ground on the panel was identified as chalk. On the upper edge and in the background, a very thin intermediate layer of white lead was found, while in other places (at the right side) a thin yellowish-brown intermediate layer—probably the *imprimatura*—was detected. Beneath the light parts of the figure, painted in white lead, there is a thin blackish-brown underpainting, which becomes visible in the areas of shadow.

The grey of the sky and the sea is composed of white lead mixed with a large quantity of coarse black pigment, consisting of either ivory black or bone black. A little azurite was also found in these places. The same blue pigment is present in the irises on the right, lower down, where malachite also occurs. This green malachite has been mixed with grains of yellow, brown and white pigment. The red in these plants consists of a red lake pigment. This is also encountered in the flesh tones and in the shadowed areas of the main figure. The yellow in the rock in the foreground is yellow ochre, mixed with black and blue. The whitish-yellow, rather transparent paint, in the flowers to the left of Andromeda consists of white lead with a fair quantity of chalk. It may be that this chalk has been derived from a bleached organic yellow pigment precipitated on chalk. The dark areas of the background consist of ochres and umber with a fair quantity of coarse grains of white and black pigments.

Comparative spectrographic analysis of the white lead from the cloth as originally painted, and that from the part added later on, revealed practically no differences in composition: both consist of white lead with trace elements of copper, silver, tin and manganese, characteristic of old white lead. Accordingly, this result does not permit any conclusion regarding the time which elapsed between the painting of the original composition and the later alterations. It may have lasted one or more years, since the difference in the *craquelure* and the X-ray photograph indicate that the overpainted parts must have been thoroughly dry before the concealing cloth and rock were painted in.

There is no signature on the painting, nor were any remnants of one detected.

HISTORICAL DATA

During the last quarter of the 18th century, this painting belonged to the collection of the banker, Charles - André - Melchior Count de Proli (1723-1786), whose family, originating from Friuli near Venice, had settled in Antwerp in 1684. When his bank failed, in 1785, De Proli was obliged to sell his collection of paintings and other works of art.

In the sale catalogue of 23 July 1785, this small panel is described as follows: "No. 17. Rembrandt. Andromède ayant les bras au-dessus de la tête liés à un rocher, elle est à deminue: à la droite sont quelques roseaux, une mer calme & un ciel sombre; tout y est d'une touche hardie, fière & pateuse: la figure y est d'un grand relief & d'un dessein correct, on y découvre une couleur argentine, & une magie du clair-obscur qui se manifeste dans tous ses ouvrages, & qui a comme scellée la réputation de ce Peintre. Haut 12 ¼ po. large 9 B[ois]". According to the note in the copy of the catalogue in the Netherlands Institute for Art History in The Hague, the painting was sold for 44 florins and 10 cents [2].

A. Bredius acquired the work in 1905 from the estate of Jonkheer R.L. van den Bosch (1815-1905) in Brussels. It was loaned by him to the Mauritshuis in 1907 and bequeathed in 1946.

Collections

Ch.-A.-M. Count de Proli, Antwerp, 1785

Jonkheer R.L. van den Bosch, Brussels, 1905

Dr. A. Bredius, The Hague, on loan to the Mauritshuis, 1907-1946

Bredius bequest, 1946

Dimensions quoted

1785 12.15 pouces x 9 pouces = approx. 33.07 x 24.3 cm

1910 34.5 x 25 cm

1977 34.0 x 24.5 cm

Price

1785 44 florins 10 cents

ICONOGRAPHY AND STYLE

A semi-nude young woman, with hair untied, is standing chained to a rock, with her arms raised above her head. Handcuffs have been attached to her wrists. Both legs are covered by a cloth. She is looking beyond her left arm towards the sea. Irises and bulrushes are growing at the water's edge. Plants and shrubs are seen here and there on the rock (Fig. 25).

The scene has been described in the fourth book of Ovid's *Metamorphoses* (verses 663-739), which recounts how the Ethiopian princess Andromeda, as a punishment ordained by her presumptuous mother, Queen Cassiopeia, was chained to a rock as prey for a dragon, but was rescued by Perseus, the son of Jupiter and Danaë.

The usual depiction of this story shows us Andromeda fastened to the rock as Perseus, descended from the skies, is fighting the dragon.

The technical examination of the *Andromeda* failed to reveal any traces of a Perseus figure and monster. Although it appears that the panel was perhaps larger on the lefthand side and below, it is hardly likely that Perseus and the monster were originally to be seen [3]. Rembrandt apparently concentrated on Andromeda's reaction at the moment she first caught sight of the monster approaching: her attitude is all tension, her gaze full of anxiety. C. Tümpel has remarked that on several occasions Rembrandt concentrated on fewer figures than are generally shown in illustrations of biblical or mythological scenes, thereby achieving greater thematic intensity. [4].

Andromeda is generally depicted completely or all but naked [5]. Only in a print by Jacob de Gheyn II (1565-1629) is the princess seen chained to the rock with a cloth draped down to her feet (Fig. 33). Another analogy between this print and Rembrandt's *Andromeda* is the absence of Perseus. De Gheyn made the print in question for a book on the heavenly constellations, meticulously copying the illustration of

33. Jacob de Gheyn II. Andromeda, 1609. Engraving.

34. Anthonis Blocklandt. Perseus and Andromeda. Drawing. *Brussels, Musées Royaux des Beaux-Arts de Belgique (Collection De Grez).*

the Andromeda constellation from a 9th century manuscript for this purpose [6].

As the X-ray photograph clearly shows (Fig. 26), Rembrandt, too, originally painted Andromeda full-length. At first, the cloth covered less of her legs than it does now. It is possible that the painter was influenced in this respect by De Gheyn's or some other earlier representation of the scene. It is, in any event, obvious that he has broken away from the mannerist ideal of beauty, even though he had occasionally been influenced by works of art of that

35. Hendrick Goltzius. Perseus and Andromeda, 1583. Engraving.

36. Joachim Wtewael. Perseus and Andromeda. *Present location unknown.*

period; see, for example, a drawing of the same subject by A. Blocklandt (Fig. 34), an engraving by H. Goltzius (Fig. 35) and a painting by J.A. Wtewael (Fig. 36) [7]. Rembrandt was not endeavouring to idealize the model but setting himself to paint a realistic version of a naked figure [8].

There can be no doubt that this painting belongs to Rembrandt's Leiden period and should be dated circa 1630 [9]. In the manner in which the foliage has been painted there is a clear correspondence between this work and Rembrandt's panel *The Prophet Jeremiah Lamenting in the Wilderness* (Amsterdam, Rijksmuseum, cat. 1976, No. A.3276; Br.-G., No. 604), dated 1630. In both panels the artist has drawn in the vegetation and foliage in the wet paint in practically the same manner. The strong contrast between the darker and lighter parts and the summary depiction of the landscape motif also point to Rembrandt's Leiden period. K. Bauch was mistaken in writing that the *Andromeda* is a grisaille [10].

Reference has already been made to the alterations in the original composition of the painting (see *Technical data*). As regards the loin cloth Andromeda is wearing, it is not improbable that considerations of modesty prompted the alterations and that they accordingly date from *after* Rembrandt's day. It is not possible to establish whether the rocky foreground which now hides Andromeda's naked legs and feet was added by overpainting at some later date, or whether this is an alteration made by Rembrandt himself. The technical investigation yielded no clue to this. It is, however, likely that in making this addition the artist was trying to add depth to his composition.

An old copy of this painting was in the Karl Rosner Collection in Berlin in 1938.

NOTES

1. J. Bauch has established that the last heartwood growth ring on the oak panel dates from 1603 (see *Appendix I,* 2f).

2. Lugt, I, No. 3926.

3. The panel was presumably larger on the left-hand side and lower edge, but this can have made little difference to the composition.

4. C. Tümpel, "Studien zur Ikonographie der Historien Rembrandts", *Nederlands Kunsthistorisch Jaarboek,* 20, 1969, pp. 160-161, ill. 42. For the iconography, see also E. Panovsky, "Der gefesselte Eros (Zur Genealogie von Rembrandts Danaë)", *Oud Holland* 50, 1933, p. 214, note 1; J. Bialostocki, *Stil und Ikonographie. Studien zur Kunstwissenschaft,* Dresden, 1966, p. 134.

5. Cf., for instance, H. Goltzius's prints illustrating the same theme: Hollstein, Vol. 8, p. 34 with ill. and the engraving by Goltzius after the drawing by A. Blocklandt (see note 7), J. Vuyk, "Blocklandt in Parijs", *Oud Holland,* 59, 1942, ill. 4. See also Ingrid Jost, *Studien zu Anthonis Blocklandt,* Cologne, 1960, p. 118, note 3.

6. De Gheyn made this print for an edition of *Syntagma Arateorum* by Hugo de Groot (1583-1645), published in 1600 by Chr. Raphalengius at Leiden. A miniature from the Carolingian manuscript of the *Syntagma Arateorum* was taken as the model for this illustration. See exh. cat. *Leidse Universiteit 400,* Amsterdam, Rijksmuseum, 1975, C 73 and C 74, with illustrations on p. 156 and p. 158. The four characters in the story of Andromeda, Andromeda herself, Perseus, Cassiopeia and Cepheus also hang next to each other as constellations.

7. See, *inter alia,* the drawing by Anthonis Blocklandt van Montfoort (1532? - 1583), Andromeda chained to the rock, with Perseus on the right, attacking the monster with

drawn sword (Brussels, Musées Royaux des Beaux-Arts, Collection De Grez), published by W. Sumowski, "Einige frühe Entlehnungen Rembrandts", *Oud Holland,* 71, 1956, p. 111, ills. 7 and 8. The closest parallel to Rembrandt's *Andromeda* is found in a painting on the same theme by J.A. Wtewael (1566-1638). Here, too, Andromeda is standing with arms raised above the head and chained to the rock. Perseus's struggle with the dragon is shown here merely as a reminder (see C. Tümpel, "Studien zur Ikonographie der Historien Rembrandts", *Nederlands Kunsthistorisch Jaarboek,* 20, 1969, note 106, ill. 43).

8. See, for example, regarding G.A. Bredero, Garmt Stuiveling, introduction to the exh. cat. *G.A. Bredero,* Historisch Museum, Amsterdam, 1968, no page numbering: "But the wonderful thing about Bredero is not merely this predilection for the people but the honest objectivity he showed in portraying them, the realism of which rivals that of the Dutch school of painting".

9. It appears that during these years Rembrandt interested himself in mythological subjects from Ovid's *Metamorphoses,* such as "The Rape of Proserpine" (*Metam.* V, verses 420 et seq.; Br.-G., No. 463), "The Rape of Europa" (*Metam.* II, verses 401 et seq.; Br.-G., No. 472).

10. K. Bauch, *Studien zur Kunstgeschichte,* Berlin, 1967, p. 133: "Es handelt sich bei dem kleinen Bild offenbar nicht um eine Teilstudie oder Skizze, sondern wohl um ein fertiges Bild, grau in grau gemalt, also vielleicht für eine Radierung geschaffen."

37. Simeon's Song of Praise.

V

Simeon's Song of Praise

Plates V, VI; Fig. 37

Panel, 61.0 x 48.0 cm. Monogrammed and dated *RHL 1631.*

Cat. Br. (1895), No. 145; Valentiner, p. 23; H.d.G., No. 80; Cat. M. (1935), No. 145; Br., No. 543; Bauch, No. 52; G., No. 17; Br.-G., No. 543; Cat. H. (1977), No. 145.

TECHNICAL DATA

The oak panel has been bevelled on either side and along the bottom edge. A piece of oakwood, rounded in the form of an arc and of a maximum height of 13 cm, has been added along the top edge of the original panel. This part is now almost completely covered by the frame, only the rounded-off corners of the original panel remaining visible [1]. The wood has been entirely pasted over with a thin piece of linen, presumably to reinforce the seams and an ancient crack, 17 cm from the right-hand edge. A mixture of wax and white lead was used for this purpose. This piece of linen was temporarily removed when the X-ray photographs were taken.

Examination under ultra-violet light and infra-red photography produced little information, partly because of the interference caused by the varnish (Fig. 39). The X-radiograph produced an image corresponding with the surface view of the painting (Fig. 38). Underpainting in white lead was revealed in the group of figures in the centre and in the foreground. Above the head of Infant Jesus a crescent halo appears to be omitted in the white lead underpainting. Remnants of white lead paste on the reverse of the panel make it difficult to arrive at a satisfactory interpretation of the radiograph.

The *craquelure* varies according to the composition and thickness of the paint layers and their structure. In large sections of the background and foreground, where the paint film is thin and the grain of the wood shows through, there is a network of very fine cracks. In the central group, too, where, generally speaking, more white lead has been used in the underpainting and in the top layer, the *craquelure* is hardly visible to the naked eye.

The cracks are wider and more irregular in Simeon's cloak, which has been underpainted in purplish-red and yellowish-brown. Wide cracking is evident in the paint, in those places where yellow ochre or umber has been added thinly to a fairly transparent intermediate layer of dark reddish-brown paint. In these places we see very wide, premature

38. X-ray photograph.

39. Ultra-violet fluorescence photograph.

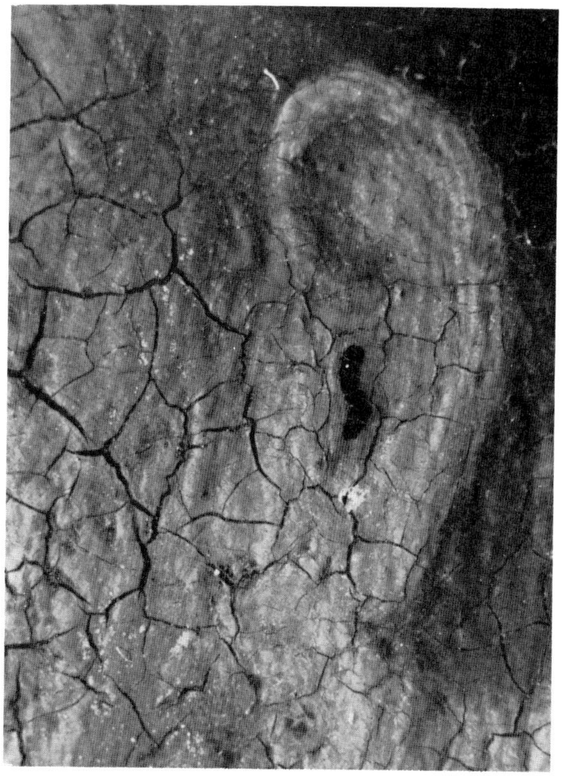

40. Macrophotograph. The ear of one of the scribes. Premature cracks in the paint layer (magnification x 6).

cracks, often proceeding from a triple fork and highly irregular in shape (crow's foot type). This is a characteristic result of the uneven drying process of the paint layers. The ear of one of the scribes—in the foreground, right—has been reproduced here (Fig. 40). Similar cracks in the paint which has been ap-

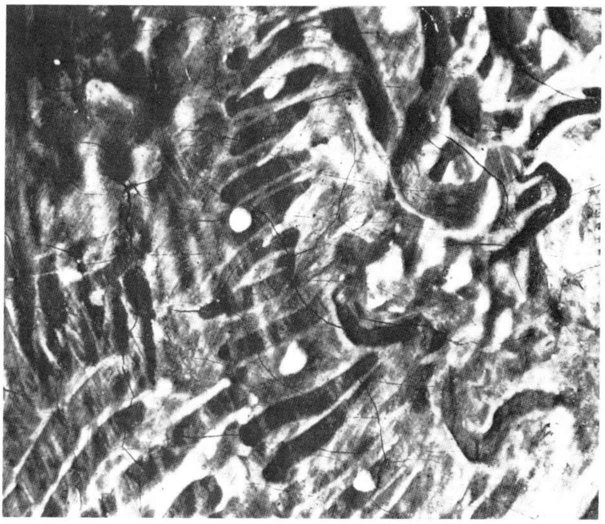

41. Macrophotograph. Detail of the cloak of Simeon. Scratching in wet paint (magnification x 6).

plied to dark-brown underpainting are also present —*inter alia,* in the darker parts of the cloak worn by the prophetess Anna, in the dark areas to the right of Simeon, and in the background figures. The edges of the cracks often project slightly upwards.

The design on the cloak Simeon is wearing has been scratched into the wet top layer of yellowish-white paint with a point or with the pointed tip of the brush (Fig. 41). In these places, the top paint layer has been partially removed, so that the purplish-red, yellow and greyish-brown underpainting and the raised edges of the furrows in the top layer combine to create this special effect.

Chalk only was detected in the ground. The white top paint layers consist of white lead. The blue in Maria's gown is azurite, which has been applied to the white lead in the form of "scattered blue", very finely distributed. Apart from red ochre, a red lake pigment has also been generously used as red colouring matter—*inter alia* in the areas of shadow, and for glazes in the background. Vermilion has been used very sparingly. It was found in Simeon's hand among other places. The yellow in this work consists principally of yellow ochres, sometims mixed with white grains of white lead. The bright, pale yellow in

Simeon's cloak proved, however, to consist of lead-tin yellow. The greenish-grey to olive brown colours in the background and in the flagstones in the foreground are composed of umber and white lead, ochre, smalt, bone black and a red lake pigment. The brown, which in the darker areas is present as a half-transparent layer, and which in various places—the foreground included—was also detected as underpainting, is Cologne earth mixed with bone black, red lake and ochres, in varying proportions. Green pigments were not detected on the painting; the green colouring in Anna's headdress appears to be an optical illusion, caused by unblended blue lying adjacent to areas of yellow.

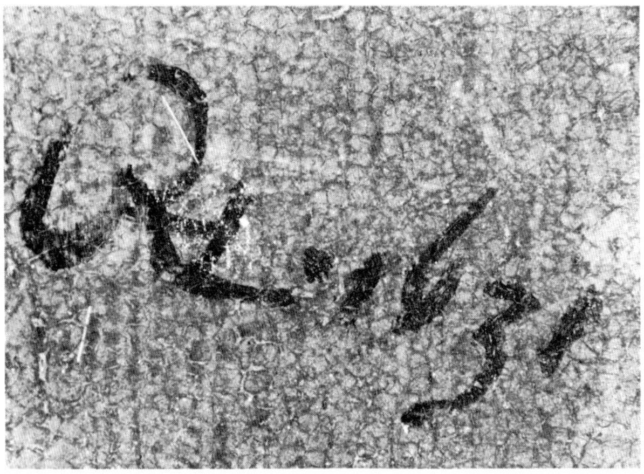

42. Monogram and date.

The monogram and date *RHL 1631* are painted in black on the olive green of the bench in the foreground, right (Fig. 42). The paint used for this signature bears cracks which are part and parcel of the *craquelure* of the surface layer to which it has been applied [2]. Apart from the probability that the monogram and date were slightly reinforced at some time in the past, there is no reason to doubt their authenticity.

HISTORICAL DATA

One of the first paintings purchased by Prince William IV of Orange (1711-1751) was the *Simeon in the Temple* (1733). A year beforehand, the Prince had completed protracted negotiations with the King of Prussia concerning matters of inheritance and, as a result, had acquired the palaces *Huis Ten Bosch,* near The Hague, and *Het Loo,* near Apeldoorn, among other property [3]. The painting had come from the collection of Adriaan Bout (1661-1733), councillor and agent in The Hague of the Elector of the Palatinate who had his residence in Düsseldorf [4].

Adriaan Bout was the son of a cloth merchant of Leiden and lived in The Hague. From 1691 on he is listed as "army solicitor"; in 1701 and 1703 he served as intermediary for the equipment of four infantry and cavalry regiments for John William Duke of Gulik, Kleef and Berg, the Elector Palatine (1658-1716). He was appointed his agent in 1714 and held this same office for the Elector's brother, Carl Philip (1716-1742), who succeeded John William. The office of solicitor was apparently a lucrative one, for we note that the art dealers and collectors Michiel van Hoeken and Willem Lormier, both in The Hague, exercised the same function [5].

The Bout auction, which included porcelain and paintings, was announced in a Hague paper, *De 's Gravenhaegse Vrijdaegse Courant,* of 7 August 1733, and was held on 11 August 1733 in that town [6]. Three other works by Rembrandt were auctioned in addition to this *Simeon in the Temple* [7]. The description in the sale catalogue reads as follows: "No. 82. Simeon in den Tempel curieus en uytvoerig geschildert, vol Beelden, van zijn alderbeste en uytvoerigste tyd, hoog 23 breet 18 en een half duym". According to the annotated copy kept at the Netherlands Institute for Art History in The Hague, the Simeon was acquired for the sum of 430 florins by Van Dijk, who was probably acting on the Prince's behalf [8].

The *Simeon in the Temple* came to hang in his private collection at *Het Loo.* From the inventory dated 7 June 1763, which at the request of William V's guardian, the Duke of Brunswick-Wolfenbüttel, had been drawn up "naer de forme en order van den ouden inventaris" of 1757, it appears that the *Simeon in the Temple* was of the same dimensions as Gerard Dou's *Young Mother* (Fig. 43) since these two works hung as a pair on either side of the *Gloria in excelsis Deo* of C. van Poelenburgh [9] (Fig. 44). According to the dimensions recorded, a rounded piece of wood must have been added at the top of the *Simeon* between 1733 and 1757 (see *Technical data*).

During the autumn of 1763, a large number of paintings were transferred from *Het Loo* to the Stadhouder's residence in The Hague. The inventory dated 8 October 1763, drawn up by the collection's director T.P.C. Haag (1737-1812), who was also court painter, indicates that Rembrandt's and Dou's paintings were again hung as a pair, but no longer with the Poelenburgh between them [10]. In 1774, or a little later, they were removed to the Stadhouder's new gallery next to the *Gevangenpoort* and during the French occupation suffered the same fate as many other paintings in William V's collection—they were

43. Gerrit Dou. The Young Mother. 1658. *The Hague, Mauritshuis.*

44. Cornelis van Poelenburgh. Gloria in Excelsis Deo. *Gray (France), Musée Baron Martin (on loan from the Museé du Louvre).*

carried off to Paris. The greater part of these paintings, the *Simeon in the Temple* among them, were brought back to The Hague in 1815.

In the 1632 inventory of the collection of the Stadhouder Frederick Henry, item 111 is described as follows: "Een schilderije daerinne Symeon, sijnde in den tempel, Christus in sijne armen heeft, door Rembrandts oft Jan Lievensz. gedaen." [11]. The uncertainty as to whether this is a painting by Rembrandt or Lievens hampers its identification. For that matter, Jan 's Herwouters, the "controller" who drew up this inventory, is often vague or mistaken when attributing paintings to Rembrandt and Lievens. For instance, he attributed Rembrandt's *The Rape of Proserpine* (Br.-G., No. 463) to Lievens [12]. We cannot be too sure of his ability to distinguish between a Rembrandt and a Lievens. It should, however, be said that in certain cases it is still difficult even today to distinguish between these two artists (see note 13).

The *Symeon* is no longer mentioned in later inventories of the Stadhouder's collection and we have no information regarding the date at which the work disappeared from it.

Although the *Symeon* in the above-mentioned 1632 inventory is sometimes identified with Rembrandt's painting *Simeon in the Temple* in Hamburg (Br.-G., No. 535) [13], we believe that it is more likely that the *Simeon's Song of Praise* in the Mauritshuis is identical with the *Symeon* in Frederick Henry's collection.

Just as the Elector of the Palatinate came to own the paintings of the Passion which Rembrandt made to the order of Frederick Henry [14], it is very likely that his agent, Adriaan Bout, acquired the *Symeon* from the same collection, possibly via the Elector. It may very well be that the paintings Rembrandt made of the Passion were given by Amalia von Solms during her lifetime to her daughter, Albertina Agnes, since the list of the sale of Albertina Agnes's estate (1696) includes paintings which could be identical with Rembrandt's Passion series [15]. It is probable that the *Simeon* left the Orange collection by the same route, since, under item No. 313 on the said sale list, we find a painting described as *Van Simeon in den tempel* [16]. Rembrandt's name is not mentioned, but this does not exclude his authorship as no names at all are given in this list.

It is likely that out of the four Rembrandt paintings at the Bout auction William IV chose precisely this *Simeon* on account of its probable provenance from an ancestral Orange collection. His interest in history and dynastic matters is quite evident from the purchases he made. We even know that William IV was an important buyer at an auction of the estate of one of Amalia von Solms's heirs [17].

The Hamburg *Simeon* was owned by the Hague collector Martinus de Jeude and was auctioned on 18 April 1735. Does the fact that William IV did not purchase this painting perhaps suggest that this Hamburg *Simeon* should not be identified with the Simeon in the 1632 inventory? [18]

Collections

Stadhouder Frederick Henry, The Hague, 1632?
Princess Albertina Agnes van Nassau-Dietz, 1696?
A. Bout, The Hague, 1733
Stadhouder William IV, "Het Loo" (Palace at Apeldoorn), 1733-1751
Stadhouder William V, "Het Loo", 1751-1763; The Hague, 1763-1795
The Louvre, Paris, 1795-1815
King William I, The Hague, 1815
Royal Collection of Paintings, The Hague, 1816
"The Mauritshuis"—Royal Collection of Paintings, The Hague, 1822

Dimensions quoted

1733 23 in x 18 1/2 in = approx. 57.5 x 46.25 cm
1763 2 ft. 6 in x 1 ft. 8 in = approx. 75 x 50 cm
1874 73 x 48 cm
1895 60 x 48 cm
1977 61.0 x 48.0 cm

Price

1733 430 florins

ICONOGRAPHY AND STYLE

Simeon is holding the Infant Jesus in his arms in the temple at Jerusalem. Arranged in an arc around him are Joseph and Mary, both kneeling, and three elderly men, standing; in front of them stands a full-length figure in a long robe, wearing a head-cloth. The gesture suggests that it is pronouncing a blessing. Two scribes are seen seated on a bench to the right. In the background, is a flight of steps on which many figures are seen under a baldachin, among them the high priest, distinguishable by his staff (Fig. 37).

45. Rembrandt. The Presentation of Jesus in the Temple. *Hamburg, Kunsthalle.*

46. Rembrandt. The Presentation of Jesus in the Temple with the Angel, 1630. Etching. B. 51.

The title in the sale catalogue of 1733 (*Simeon in he Temple*) is still used for this painting in the Mauritshuis today. However, a comparison with two other works by Rembrandt illustrating the story of Simeon and dating from his Leiden period has led to a more precise description of the work as *Simeon's Song of Praise* [19]. Both the panel in the Kunsthalle in Hamburg (Br.-G., No. 535) (Fig. 45) and the 1630 etching (B.51) (Fig. 46) represent the moment at which Simeon, with the Infant Jesus in his arms, addresses himself to Mary [20]. In the painting Anna is shown bestowing a blessing, in the etching she is shown being led to the Child by an angel (see St. Luke, 2, 33-39).

In the painting in the Mauritshuis the emphasis has been slightly shifted. Here, too, the words of the Gospel of St. Luke, Chapter 2, provide the theme, but this scene is based on verses 28-32, with its reference to the Song of Simeon, the *Nunc Dimittis:* "Lord, now lettest thou thy servant depart in peace". Simeon is seen singing his song of praise (Fig. 47): the salvation of the Lord had come, as Isaiah had prophesied (Isaiah, 49, 6). The story in the Bible has fired Rembrandt's imagination: he has concentrated the light on the group with Simeon and the radiant Infant Jesus. For Simeon sang of the light of salvation which the Lord had prepared for all peoples: "A light to lighten the Gentiles and the glory of thy

47. Macrophotograph: The head of Simeon.

people Israel!" (St. Luke, 2,32). The figures grouped around him share in the revelation. The two figures sitting on the bench are drawn into the scene by the ray of light, while the throng in the temple continues to move in darkness. The figure seen from the rear with hands raised can be none other than the prophetess Anna [21]. Since the two prophets, Anna and Simeon, both of them devout Jews with the Holy Ghost upon them, appear together in this scene from the Gospel according to St. Luke, 21, 25-39, Rembrandt has devoted equal attention to each, to the aged Simeon and to Anna, who was 84 years old. Both, at one and the same moment, recognize in the Infant Jesus the Saviour of Jerusalem and the Jewish people. The two men on the bench may be seen as scribes, who witness this event from a distance and discuss it between them.

This picture, painted in 1631, is rightly regarded as one of the masterpieces among the works of the artist's youth. Its composition is particularly well-balanced and daring though it is the treatment of the light and colour, concentrated on the main group, which has led to a harmonious result.

Rembrandt has situated the scene in a corner of a lofty, vaulted temple, the architecture of which owes much to the imagination. It is possible that one of the late Gothic church interiors in Leiden led him to such a conception, but we are unable to point to any definite model. A flight of steps leads up from the main scene to the throne of the high priest, beneath a lofty baldachin. The etching of 1630 (B.51), already mentioned, shows a similar flight of steps with many small figures on it, but seen from a different angle.

In none of his early biblical or historical pieces did Rembrandt succeed in solving the problems of space and light so splendidly as here. Spatially, the scene he has conceived is highly convincing and well-ordered, and this he has achieved partly by the linear perspective created by the flagstones of the temple floor, which accentuates the effect of depth, and by the small figures on the steps. Light is the determining factor in this evocation of space. Proceeding from the central group of figures on which the light is concentrated, the space expands via the outstretched hand of the prophetess Anna and the three main figures, Simeon, the Infant Jesus and Mary, reaching towards the flight of steps and, via a strip of light on the floor, towards the area in the background.

48. W. de Poorter. Copy after Rembrandt. *Dresden, Staatliche Kunstsammlungen, Gemäldegalerie.*

There is an old copy painted on wood by William de Poorter (1600 - after 1648) of roughly the same size as the original but not, of course, rounded off at the top. It is in the Dresden gallery (Inv. No. 391) (Fig. 48).

Many copies are known, some based on the original painting, some on a print or a reproduction: a.o. the Madame de Marolles collection, Fercé par Noyon sur Sarthe (1963); A. Soós collection, London (1965); Eliseo Vives collection, Barcelona (1965); D. Ghouy collection, Saint Symphorien, Belgium (1974); Von Wattenwyl collection, Berne (based on a print).

NOTES

1. J. Bauch has established that the last heartwood growth ring on the panel dates from 1589 (see also *Appendix I*, 2f).

2. According to Gerson (G., No. 17) the monogram and the date have been "redrawn".

3. Scheurleer, pp. 17-18.

4. Hoet, I, p. 391. Hoet calls Bout "Raad en Agent van zijn C:F:D: van Trier".

5. *Bericht van constitutie van alle de Illustre Vergaderingen*

en Collegien in 's-Gravenhage. Met de benamingen van alle de Leeden die daar inne sessie hebben: derselver Ministers Beampten en Suppoosten mitsgaders aanwijsinge van hunnen woonplaatsen. 's-Gravenhage, 1728 (o.a.). Bout lived in the Raamstraat at the time. A "solicitor" (solliciteur) is a person who advances sums at a certain rate of interest to meet soldiers' pay and certain other military expenditure.

6. "Dinsdag den 11 Augusty, zal men ten Sterfhuyze van wylen den Heer Agent Bout, verkoopen, deszelf Cabinet Porceleyn, en Schilderyen; als ook nog eenige Juweelen en Meubelaire goederen. Alles drie dagen voor de Verkooping te zien" (Gemeente-Archief, The Hague).

7. *Abraham and Hagar* (No. 80), bought by Michael van Hoeken; *Joseph, Mary and the Child* (No. 81), bought by Hans Berge; *A small piece* (No. 152). The prices were 105, 150 and 47 florins respectively.

8. Lugt, I, No. 427. Against Gerard Hoet, *op. cit.* (see note 4): 830—probably a misprint. Philips van Dijk (1680-1752) was a painter and art dealer. He also lent his services to William VIII, Landgrave of Hesse and lived in The Hague from 1719 onwards.

9. Louis Ernest (Ludwig Ernst), Duke of Brunswick-Wolfenbüttel (1718-1788) was William V's private guardian from 1759 onwards. The copy of the catalogue in the Mauritshuis archives shows: "No. 86 Een vrouwtje met het kintje in de wieg op hout door Gerhert Douw, verg. lyst 2-6 1-10 1/2" and "no. 88 Simeon in den Tempel met het kindeken, op hout door Rembrandt in dito lyst 2-6 1-8"; the painting by Dou mentioned here is now in the Mauritshuis (inv. No. 32). See also *Technical data.* The painting by Poelenburgh was one of the works removed to Paris in 1795 and not returned to The Hague in 1815. It is still in the possession of the Louvre in Paris and was on loan to the Baron Martin Museum, Gray, inv. No. 1694. See exh. cat. *Le siècle de Rembrandt,* Paris, Petit Palais, 1970-71, p. 160, No. 162, with illustration.

10. See Drossaers-Scheurleer, II, pp. 651-652. The inventory is kept in the Koninklijk Huisarchief, Inv. A. 18, No. 38e; published in Drossaers-Scheurleer, III, pp. 18-28. A copy made by Jonkheer M.J.V.J. de Jonge and dated 4 March 1875 is in the Mauritshuis archives; Nos. 1 and 2. The *Simeon* is also included in Terwesten's catalogue, pp. 708-709; "Een uitmuntend Stuk, verbeeldende: Simeon in den Tempel met het kind Jezus op zyn Armen, waar by Maria, Joseph en meer andere Figuuren, verwonderlijk schoon, zoo van Ordinantie als Dag, schaduw en uitvoerigheid door REMBRANT VAN RHYN; op paneel 2 (V) 6 (D) 1 (V) 8 (D)". The description in the catalogue compiled by F. ten Dall, based on T.P.C. Haag's notes, is practically identical; for Haag's list, see I, *Self-Portrait as a Young Man,* note 10. (See also Drossaers-Scheurleer, III, p. 227.)

11. Drossaers-Scheurleer, I, p. 186, No. 111.

12. Drossaers-Scheurleer, I, p. 184, No. 82.

13. S.W.A. Drossaers, "Inventory of the furnishings of the Stadhouders' Quarters, with the 'Speelhuis', and of the House in the Noordeinde at The Hague, with annotations by C. Hofstede de Groot and C.H. de Jonge", *Oud Holland,* 47, 1930, p. 205, No. 64; Drossaers-Scheurleer, I, p. 186, No. 111 and note. The reason for this identification is presumably that the Hamburg painting is more like Lievens than the Hague one although it bears a signature. This would make 's Herwouters' hesitation comprehensible. A recent view regarding the relationship between Rembrandt and Lievens can be found in the exh. cat. *Geschildert tot Leyden anno 1626,* Leiden, Museum De Lakenhal, 1976-1977, pp. 51-56. *Simeon's Song of Praise* was not included in the exhibition.

14. Drossaers-Scheurleer, I, p. 285, No. 1240 and note.

15. Drossaers-Scheurleer, I, p. 285, No. 1240 and note; II, p. 237, Nos. 312, 318, 319, 326, 328 and 329.

16. Drossaers-Scheurleer, II, p. 237, No. 313.

17. William IV was especially interested in subjects related to the history of his country and the Orange dynasty and tried to recover former possessions of the House of Orange (Scheurleer, pp. 17-18; Drossaers-Scheurleer, III, p. 158: William IV was an important buyer at auctions of former Orange collections).

18. Hoet, I, p. 437, no. 101. Lugt, No. 447. Catalogue, Kunsthalle, Hamburg, 1956, p. 124, No. 88. At this auction William IV did buy a painting by A. van der Venne, viz., the *Zielevisserij; allegorie op het twaalfjarig bestand* (1609-1621). Described in the De Jeude sale catalogue as "door den Fluweelen Breugel", cat. No. 91. Now in the Rijksmuseum, Amsterdam, Cat. 1976, No. A 447.

19. L. de Vries drew attention to the text in which Simeon sings the praises of the Lord. See also C. Tümpel, "Studien zur Ikonografie der Historien Rembrandts", *Nederlands Kunsthistorisch Jaarboek* 20, 1969, pp. 189-190.

20. B. 51 = Münz, 191 = Hollstein, Vol. 18, p. 26, Vol. 19, ill. p. 40.

21. W. Stechow, "Rembrandt's 'Presentation in the dark manner'", *The Print Collector's Quarterly,* 27, 1940, pp. 370-371, was the first to identify this figure as Anna; H. Schulte Nordholt in "Rembrandt van Rijn: Simeon in de tempel", *Openbaar Kunstbezit,* 4, 1960, No. 40 believes that this figure represents a priest.

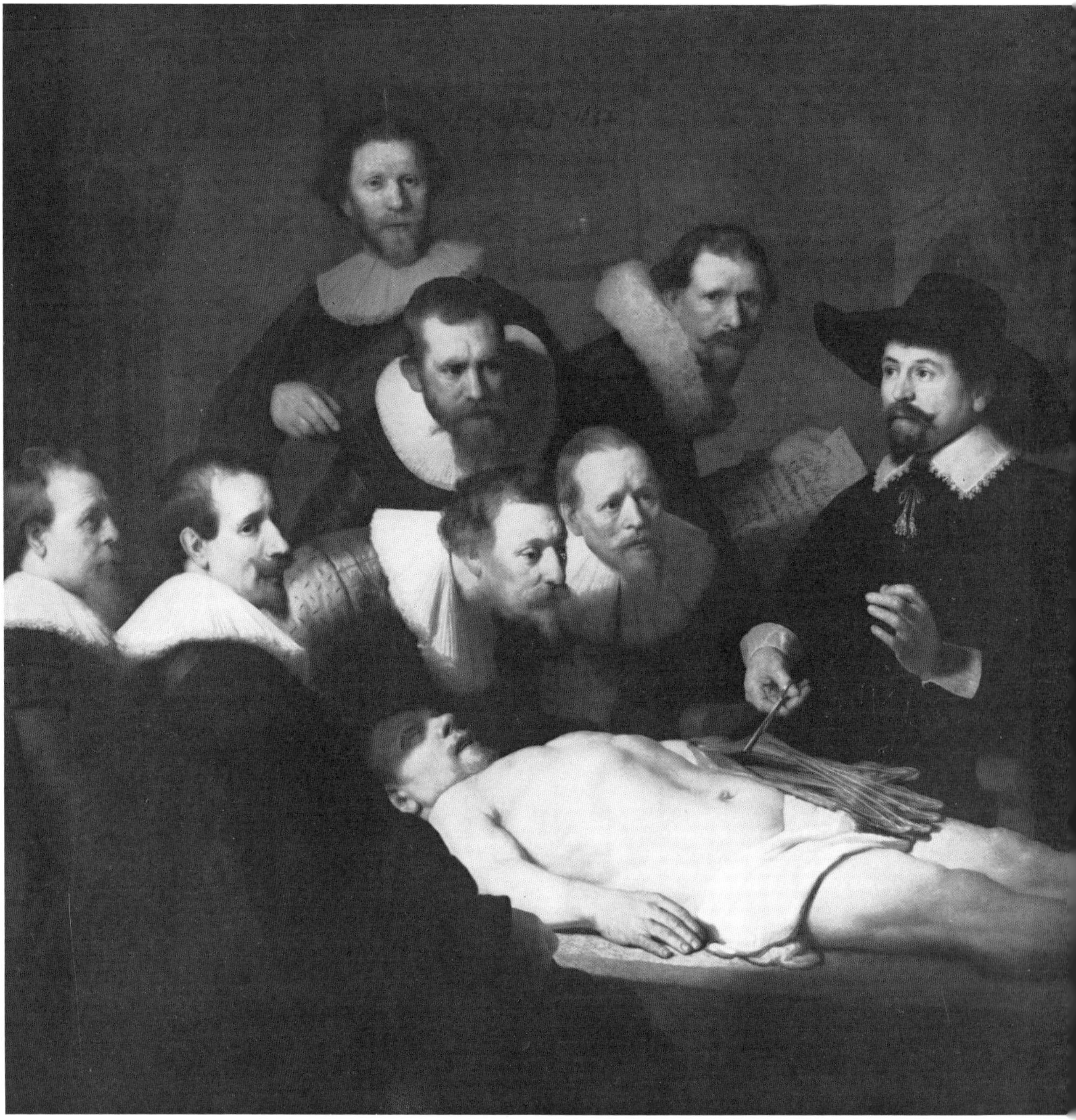

49. Dr. Nicolaas Tulp's Anatomy Lesson.

Frans Jacobsz. van Loenen (No. 8)

Hartman Hartmansz. (No. 3)

Jacob Dielofse Block (No. 2)

Dr. Nicolaas Tulp (No. 1)

Jacob Jansz. Colevelt (No. 7)

Mathys Evertsz. Calkoen (No. 6)

Adriaen Cornelisz. Slabberaen (No. 4)

Jacob Jansz. de Witt (No. 5)

VI

Dr. Nicolaas Tulp's Anatomy Lesson

Plates VII, VIII; Fig. 49

Canvas, 169,5 x 216,5 cm. Signed and dated *Rembrant. ft: 1632.*

Cat. Br. (1895), No. 146; Valentiner, p. 69; H.d.G., No. 932; Cat. M. (1935), No. 146; Br., No. 403; Bauch, No. 530; G., No. 100; Br.-G., No. 403; Cat. H. (1977), No. 146.

TECHNICAL DATA

The original canvas of the painting is made up of 15 warp and 18 weft threads per sq. cm. There are two re-lining canvases.

On the X-ray photograph, a vague dividing line, stretching across the entire width of the painting 12 cm above the middle, shows up. The obvious explanation of this is that it is the join in a canvas consisting of two pieces of linen (see also No. XI). Careful scrutiny of the X-ray photographs, however, failed to provide any convincing confirmation of this. An examination of the surface of the painting with the naked eye also brought no such confirmation. Yet it would be highly unusual for a seventeenth century painting of these dimensions to have been painted on a single piece of canvas. If it had, one would have to seek an explanation of this dividing line in a re-lining at a later date.

Examination using ultra-violet light produced no special information. The infra-red photograph taken in the Rijksmuseum in 1950 indicates a few *pentimenti* (Fig. 51). For instance, the shape of a black hat which the upright figure (No. 8) in the background was originally wearing can be identified and dark areas to the right of this figure, and above the hat Dr. Tulp is wearing, also point to changes in the composition.

In the X-ray photograph (Fig. 50 a and b) one is struck first by the fact that the heads of six of the figures stand out considerably more clearly than do those of the remaining two, i.e. those of figure No. 3

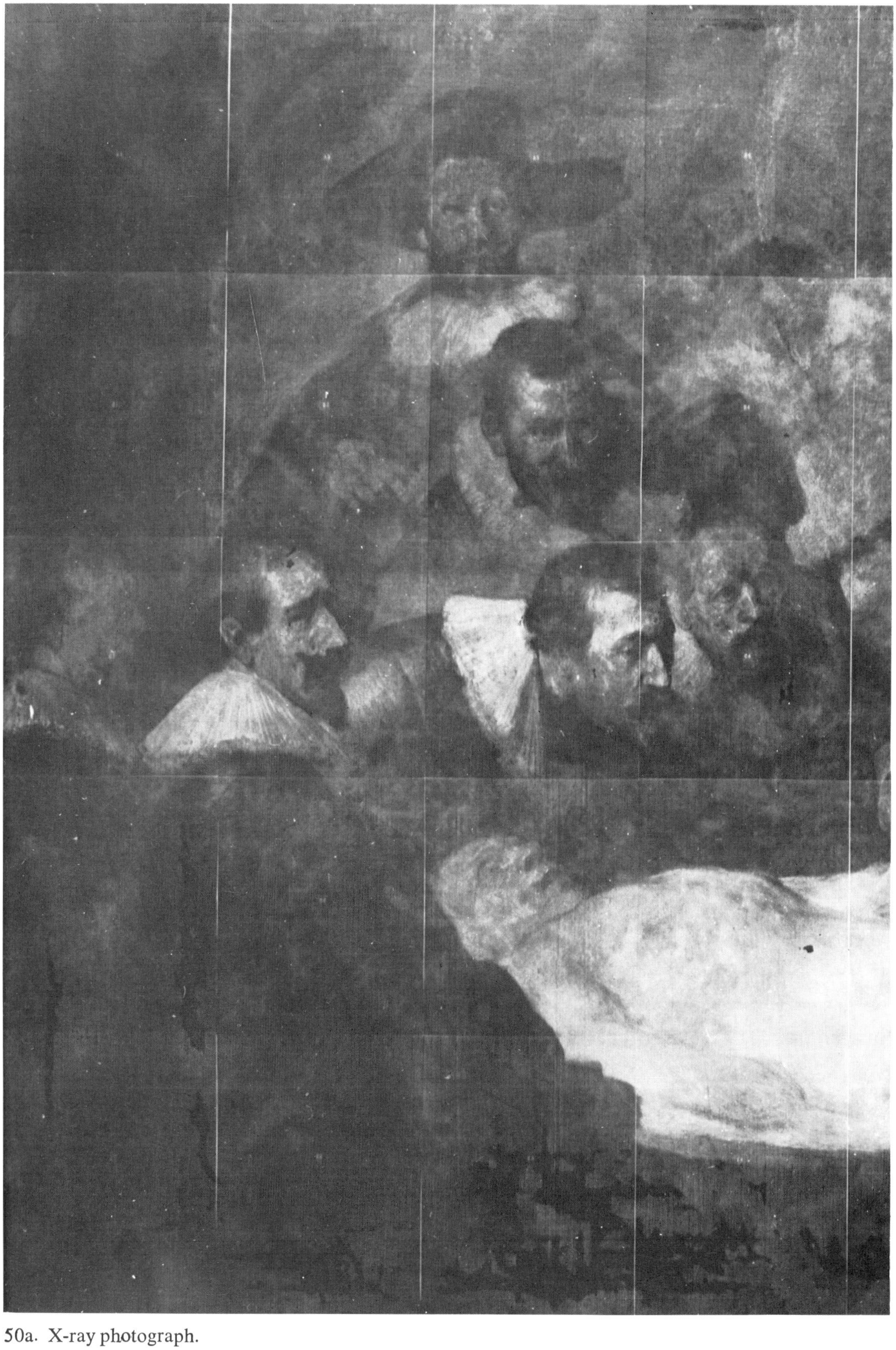

50a. X-ray photograph.

50b. X-ray photograph.

51. Infra-red photograph. Before the 1951 restoration.

and No. 7. As a result of the deliberate omission of the dark areas (eyes, hair) in the white lead underpainting and also as a result of the brushwork, there is a marked resemblance between the X-ray image of these six heads and their appearance in the painting. In contrast to this, the head of the seated figure on the far left (No. 7) and the collar, too, are much fainter in the X-radiograph. Here the painting in white lead is much thinner, the dark areas are far less clearly outlined and they were, apparently, painted on a layer containing white lead. To illustrate this difference, the head and ruff of this figure and of the figure sitting next to him (No. 4) have been reproduced (Figs. 52 and 53).

In the radiograph the head of the standing figure (No. 3) on Dr. Tulp's right also shows less contrast, and here, too, the cause must be sought in the white lead of the under-layer, especially in the dark areas (eyes, hair). Here, however, in the light areas of the head, it is clear that more white lead has been used than for figure No. 7, while in the immediate vicinity too, that is, to the left of the head, light and dark shapes can be discerned in the radiograph which are not traceable in the present state of the painting and are clear indications of alterations to the original composition. One can deduce from the outlines of these X-ray shadows, and from what can be seen in this area in the infra-red photograph, that in the original arrangement figure No. 3—head and ruff—was situated further to the left. This provides a sufficient explanation for the slightness of contrast obtained in the radiograph of the figure we now see because this figure had to be re-painted on a paint layer containing white lead.

Striking among the other *pentimenti* is the clear picture we get of the hat originally worn by the figure in the far background (No. 8). As the X-ray shows, not only was this hat left blank in the underpainting, which contains white lead, but it must almost certainly have been painted in and completed in the original composition, in view of the evidence supplied by the infra-red photograph. Dr. Tulp's hat appears

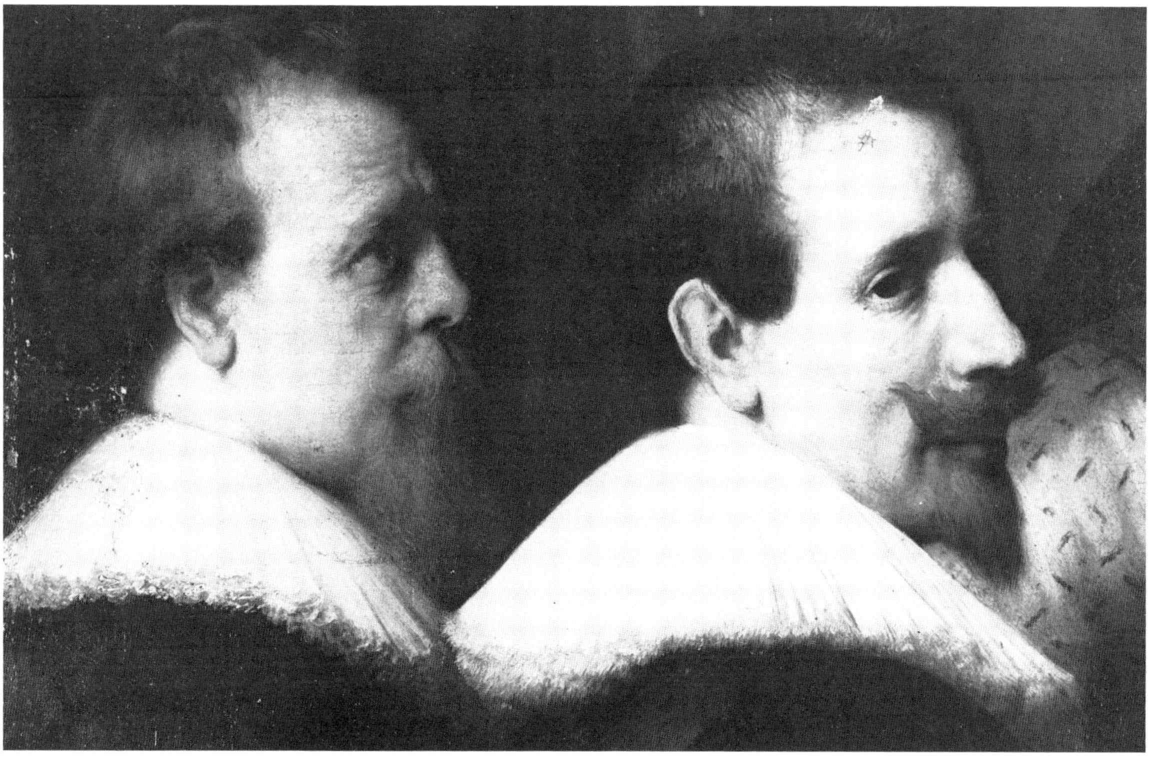

52. The heads of Colevelt (No. 7) and Slabberaen (No. 4).

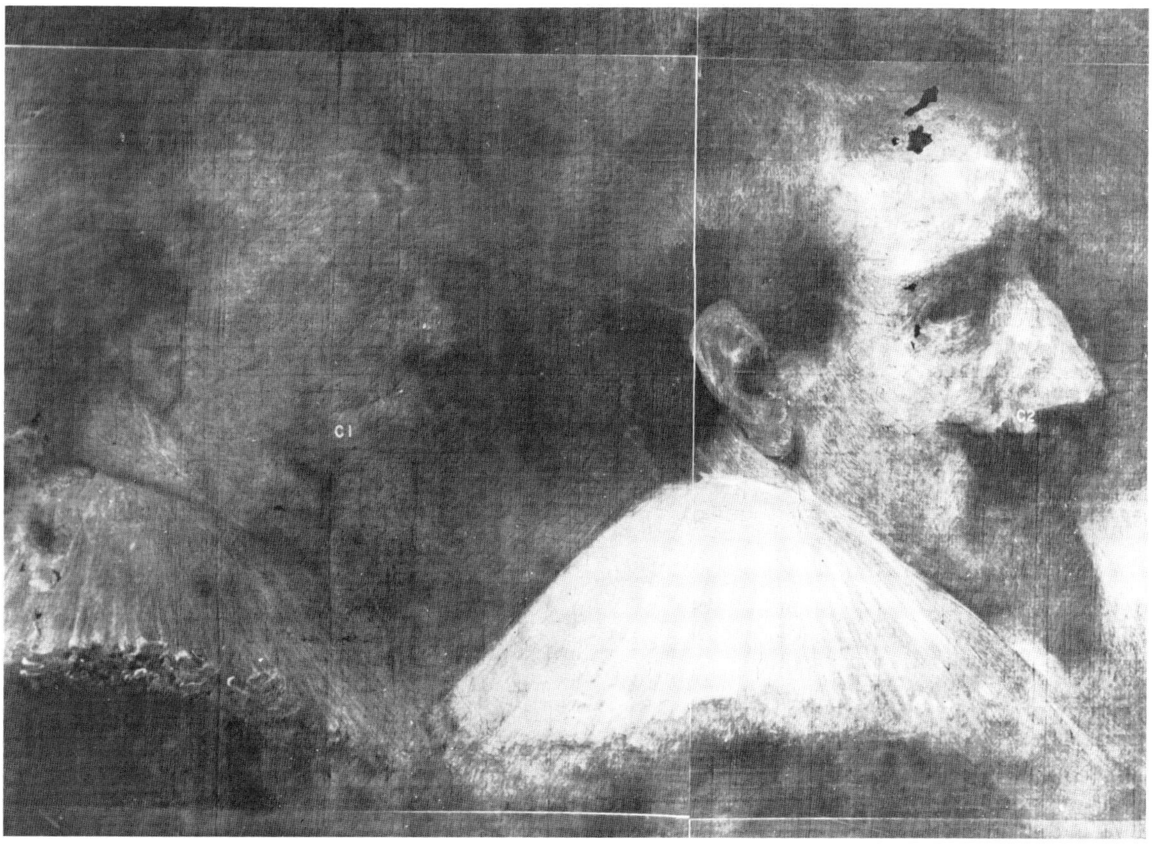

53. X-ray photograph. The heads of Colevelt (No. 7) and Slabberaen (No. 4).

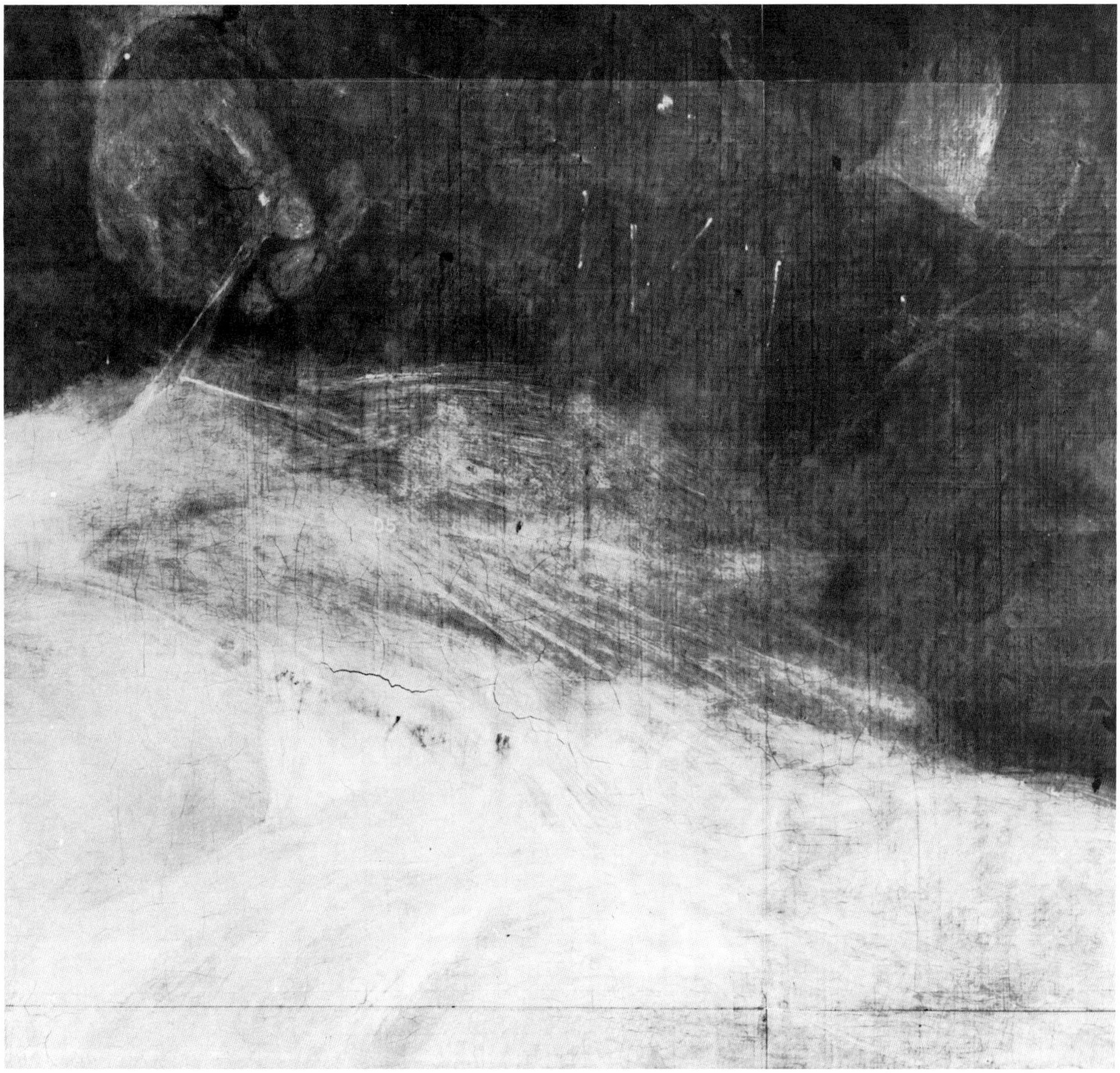

54. X-ray photograph. The dissected arm and *pentimento.*

to have had a higher crown too, originally, while changes have also been made in the brim. The shape of his white collar has likewise undergone evident alteration, but the damage sustained by the old paint of the collar and the hat, clearly visible in the radiograph, makes it plausible that these alterations were the work of a later restorer. We know, for instance, from the painting's history, that the coat Dr. Tulp is wearing had to be entirely repainted in 1732, as a result of the effect heat and smoke had had on the paint, and that later on as well, in 1780, fairly considerable repairs were carried out (see *Appendix IIIc).* It seems reasonable to assume that quite a few changes were made to the damaged collar during one of the restorations and that the hat was altered too. The lengthening of the cuff on the left sleeve and the alteration to Tulp's moustache must likewise be attributed to these restorations.

An interesting *pentimento* is to be found above the dissected lower left arm of the corpse (Fig. 54). In this place, the radiograph does reveal a light area partially painted in white lead, which links up directly with the X-ray image of the dissected lower arm now visible. Though one can distinguish the tendons and shape of the fingers fairly easily in the X-ray image of the dissected arm, no anatomical structure can be seen in the *pentimento.* What we are concerned with here, apparently, is a first design for the dissected arm. The white line which begins next to the tweezers, or forceps, and runs to the right in the streaky white of the *pentimento,* could possibly be a tendon. In the same *pentimento* one can also distinguish a forceps which was originally shorter (higher) and is lifting the tendon and, with it, the arm [1].

A faint *pentimento* can also be distinguished in the upper contour of the chest, which was originally painted a little higher. Finally, the X-ray photograph provides us with a good picture of the damage sustained in many places in times past, especially in the lower areas, where the paint had apparently suffered most.

The *craquelure* in the top layer of the paint largely resembles that usually found in old paintings. The white lead areas, including the collars and ruffs, the flesh tones and the corpse display a regular network of cracks and the same applies to the background as well. Wider cracks are present only in the dark paint of the eyes which has been applied to brownish-black underpainting. A sharp point, probably the wooden tip of the brush, has been used in some places to scratch into the wet top layer of paint —that is in the corpse's beard and on the book (Figs. 72 and 73).

A very remarkable feature is the presence, everywhere in the painting, of numerous small round holes in the paint film, 0,1 to 1 mm in diameter, often

55. Macrophotograph. Holes in the paint film (magnification x 3).

in the cracks, but next to them also (Fig. 55). Those holes penetrate to the underlaying layers, for they appear as black dots on the X-ray photograph. In the lighter areas of the painting they appear as dark dimples and in the darker as light ones; some of them have clearly discernible raised edges, resembling

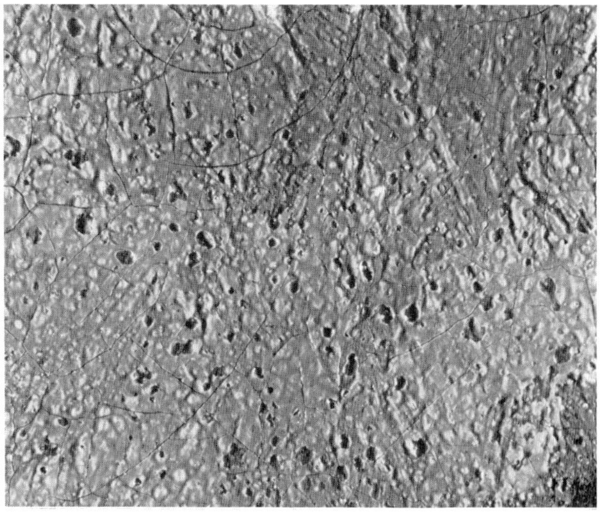

56. Macrophotograph. Holes in the paint film from Rembrandt's Self-Portrait. 1658. *New York, The Frick Collection* (magnification x 3). See note 2.

the rims of craters. Their presence is also connected with the thickness of the white lead painting and white lead underpainting. The thicker these layers are, the fewer, generally speaking, are the holes. They do not, for instance, occur at all in the corpse and are infrequent, too, in the background and the book.

A likely explanation for this phenomenon would appear to be the development of gas in the layers of paint. A proces of this kind can develop, if during the first fifty to a hundred years of its life, when the layers of paint have still not completely hardened, a painting is exposed to too high temperatures, for instance, from a fire; or when it is re-lined. It is conceivable that the gases which are then emitted by volatile oils, resins and moisture would, in certain circumstances, make small, crater-like holes, when escaping through the as yet unhardened paint of the top layers. The fact that many of these small holes correspond with the cracks in the paint-film indicates that they came about *before* these cracks were present, possibly during the first hundred years therefore. We know, for that matter, that the painting was indeed exposed to the heat of fire and precisely during this period [2].

The first ground layer in this work is of a brownish-red colour. Microscopic examination reveals a mixture of yellow and red ochres, fairly homogeneous in character, with comparatively small grains of pigment. This ground has been mixed with a little white lead and a trace of chalk and is covered everywhere with a grey second ground layer, composed of white lead, chalk, carbon black, yellow ochre and umber. This layer makes a bluish, rather transparent impression and appears to contain a comparatively large quantity of binding medium. The top layer has usually been painted on this grey layer, for instance, in the dark parts of the background, which contains Cologne earth, umber and bone black among other pigments. In the light areas of the heads a blackish-brown layer of underpainting was found, consisting of Cologne earth and bone black. No dark underpainting was found in the collars, although here the white lead has been mixed with carbon black. The ruff worn by figure No. 7 forms an exception. Here a blackish-brown layer did prove to lie under the white, while in places a grey layer was found, too, separated from the second and lower layer of grey by the blackish-brown layer.

The white consists of white lead, containing traces of copper and silver. The yellow in the painting is yellow ochre and the red pigments consist of red ochre with here and there a little vermilion. There is also very rich glazing with a red lake pigment, *inter alia* in the faces, in which yellow and red ochre have been mixed with the white lead to render the flesh tones. A red lake pigment has been applied very liberally in the dissected left arm of the corpse. The costumes consist to a large extent of dark-brown ochre mixed with a large quantity of black pigment.

a

b

c

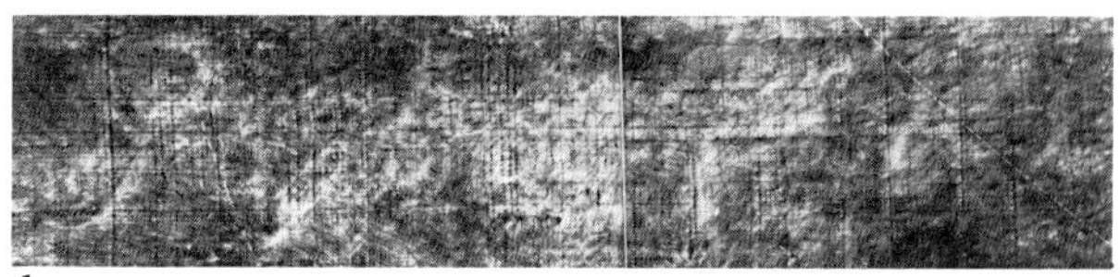
d

57. a. The present signature and date; b. The facsimile of the signature and date from the Cat. M. (1935, p. 277); c. Infra-red photograph. The signature and date before the 1951 restoration; d. X-ray photograph (1968). Signature and date.

To the right of the head of figure No. 8 at the back we find the signature and date: *Rembrant. ft: 1632* (Fig. 57a). This signature came to light when the work underwent thorough cleaning in 1951, on which occasion part of the signature then visible was removed, together with the old layers of varnish [3]. A facsimile of the old signature and date is to be found on p. 277 of the 1935 catalogue (Fig. 57b) [4]. The infra-red photograph taken in 1950 shows the signature and date in this former state (Fig. 57c). Here we must remember, however, that an infra-red photograph can show us more than scrutiny in visible light can, and that such a photograph may therefore reproduce more than the facsimile of the same signature mentioned above, because in the infra-red photograph black parts of a still older underlying signature, possibly covered and restored with a thin layer of paint, may become visible.

That this is indeed the case becomes apparent when one compares the facsimile and the infra-red photograph of the former signature with the photograph of the present signature (Fig. 57a). Such a comparison yields the following information: the present signature is shorter than that in the facsimile; the letter *m* is now closer to the *e*; the present letter *b* has also moved up one place to the left and now occupies the place where remnants of a vague letter *b* have been drawn in the facsimile. The second part of the letter *m* and the letter *b* in the former signature have disappeared entirely as a result of cleaning, their places having been taken by the now present letters *b* and *r* respectively. The remnants of a letter *a*, which, according to the facsimile, stood immediately before the *r,* appear to belong to the *a* of the present signature. The letters *r, a, n* and *t* of the former signature have also been completely obliterated in the cleaning process, the letters *n* and *t* taking their places, in addition to the letter *a* already mentioned. In the facsimile this *t* has, moreover, already been drawn in the form of a stroke, pointing upwards next to the letter *a.* In the space created by the removal of the *n* and the *t* of the former signature there is now merely a full-stop [5]. The letter *f* and the hint of a *t* (of *fecit*) deviate a little in their present state from the facsimile, but here, too, there is a question of the retouching of older lettering, which was restored to its original form during cleaning. Finally, the date *1632* now agrees, as regards its place and shape, with the facsimile version, except for the fact that the bottom stroke of the *3* is now shorter.

The infra-red photograph of 1950 provides complete confirmation that the signature and date we now see were already present before the cleaning. That is to say, the letters *m, b, r, a, n* and *t* of the present signature can be clearly distinguished in this photograph next to, and through, the characters of the signature which was then visible. Another interesting feature is that in its original form, the capital letter *R* has the stem joined to the cap as in the present version of the signature, and this is also clearly visible in the infra-red photograph. In the facsimile, however, the *R* then visible was quite different in shape and showed no such join. The same applies to the shape of the letters *f* and *t* of *fecit,* the colon and the brief lower stroke of the *3,* the present forms of which are also clearly discernible in the infra-red photograph.

There can accordingly be no doubt that the present signature and date go back a long way and are most likely original. The date has probably been done over, as it is blacker in tone than the signature. The cracks in the paint surface continue through the letters and figures. White lead is also present in the signature but this could just as likely have come from the old, original paint as from the paint used in the past for retouching. Regarding the X-ray photograph of this signature, as far as we are able to decipher this, we may say that the *R* differs from the present *R* and still more from the *R* of the facsimile (Fig. 57d).

HISTORICAL DATA

When the "Bataafse Republiek", following the example set in France, dissolved the guilds in the Netherlands by an order issued in 1798, all the paintings belonging to the Surgeons' Guild, among them *Dr. Nicolaas Tulp's Anatomy Lesson,* came into the possession of the Surgeons' Widows' Pension Fund [6]. In 1828, in view of the Fund's poor financial position, it was decided to put *Dr. Nicolaas Tulp's Anatomy Lesson* up for auction together with other works. The date of this auction was fixed for 4 August 1828. It was to be held in the auction room of Mrs. Roos, widow of the late C.S. Roos. The sale was advertised on the auction bill in bold capital letters as follows: "... Als mede HET WYD VERMAARDE EN ALOM BEROEMDE MEESTERSTUK VAN REMBRAND, Verbeeldende het Ontleedkundig Onderwys door den Hoogleeraar N. TULP, behorende aan het CHIRURGYNS WEDUWENFONDS, te Amsterdam" [7] (Fig. 58).

In AMSTERDAM, Anno 1828.

JERONIMO DE VRIES,
ALBERTUS BRONDGEEST,
ENG^T. MICH^L. ENGELBERTS,
EN
CORNELIS FRANÇOIS ROOS,
MAKELAARS,

Zullen op Maandag, den 4den Augustus 1828, en volgende Dag, des Voormiddags ten Tien Uren precies, ten Huize van de Wed. C. S. ROOS, in *Het Huis met de Hoofden*, op de Keizersgracht, tusschen de Leliegracht en Heerenstraat, door een daartoe bevoegd BEAMBTE,

VERKOOPEN:

EENE UITGEBREIDE EN VOORTREFFELYKE
VERZAMELING
VAN ZEER FRAAIJE
SCHILDERYEN

Waaronder veele door voorname Oude en Hedendaagsche Nederlandsche Meesters, en eenige mede van voorname Meesters uit de Fransche, Spaansche en Italiaansche Scholen.

Onder de Nederlandsche Meesters munten uit,
DIE VAN:

L. BACKHUIZEN,	J. VAN DER HEYDE,	J. RUISDAAL,
N. BERCHEM,	J. KOBELL,	D. TENIERS,
D. VAN BERGEN,	F. VAN MIERIS,	J. VAN DER ULFT,
G. BERKHEYDEN,	A. VAN OSTADE,	W. VAN DE VELDE,
G. DOU,	C. POELENBURG,	A. VAN DER WERFF,
A. VAN DYK,	P. POTTER,	PH. WOUWERMAN,
G. VAN DEN EEKHOUT,	P. P. RUBBENS,	

Als mede
HET WYD VERMAARDE EN ALOM BEROEMDE
MEESTERSTUK
VAN
REMBRAND,
Verbeeldende het Ontleedkundig Onderwys,
door den Hoogleeraar *N. TULP,*
behorende aan het
CHIRURGYNS WEDUWEN-FONDS,
te Amsterdam.

Al hetwelke Verkocht zal worden ten Dage, Ure en Plaatse bovengemeld.
De Katalogussen zyn by gemelde Makelaars, (à 25 Cents voor den Armen) te bekomen.
Alles twee Dagen voor de Verkoopdagen voor een ieder te zien.
Iemand nader onderrigting begeerende, spreke met de Makelaars:

58. Bill of the auction of paintings on 4 August 1828 in Amsterdam.

On 13 May 1828, the auctioneer C.Fr. Roos wrote to Jonkheer J. Steengracht van Oostcapelle, director of the Mauritshuis, as follows, with respect to a number of paintings due to be put up for sale: "By die veiling zal het fameuse Schildery van Rembrand van de Anatome kamer alhier gevoegd worden; daar mijns bedunken veel vreemdelingen om over zullen komen; dus eene geschikte gelegenheid om iets te verkoopen" [8].

King William I forbade the public sale of the painting, wishing to acquire it himself. Jonkheer J. Steengracht van Oostcapelle and C. Apostool, Director of the Mauritshuis and Director of the Rijksmuseum respectively, had been appointed by royal decree of 19 July 1828 as valuers and they entered into negotiations with J. de Vries and C.Fr. Roos, the valuers acting on behalf of the Surgeons' Widows' Pension Fund. The outcome was that the King purchased the painting for 32,000 florins and ordered it to be hung in the Mauritshuis. Should the Rijksmuseum in Amsterdam wish to acquire the painting for its own collection, the municipality of Amsterdam would have to pay the purchase price [9].

It is rather remarkable that so little should have been written prior to 1828 about this "widely renowned and universally praised masterpiece" belonging to the Surgeons' Guild. According to Heckscher, Barlaeus was the first to have made any reference to it. This was in 1639 when at the opening of the new *Theatrum Anatomicum,* in a street known as the *Nes,* he praised Dr. Nicolaas Tulp's great gifts. Heckscher also assumes that the painting was hanging there at the time [10]. This does not appear to have been the case. Barlaeus' epigram "*In locum Anatomicum recens Amstelodami exstructum*" was composed about the year 1639 in connection with the newly equipped anatomy theatre in the *Nes.* Two lines from this epigram

Hic loquitur nobis docti facundia Tulpi,
Dum secat artifici lurida membra manu,...

("Here the eloquent Tulp is addressing us, as he severs the lurid limbs with skilful hand") praise Tulp's eloquence and dexterity. With these words, Barlaeus who had also studied medicine, was paying homage to Dr. Tulp; it was, after all, the latter who had taken the initiative for the reconstruction of the premises and who was to continue to perform his public dissections and lessons there until his retirement on 27 January 1653 [11].

It is possible to deduce from the various 17th century descriptions from Amsterdam that from 1639 onwards the surgeons held their public lessons and dissections in the anatomical theatre above the *Kleine Vleeshal* in the *Nes.* Their Guild Room, however, where hung the portraits of the members or the officials of the guild and their prelectors, continued to be housed in the *St. Antonies Poort* or *Nieuwe Waag* where the surgeons had had their dissection theatre and Guild chamber since 1619 [12].

The paintings were praised by two of the city's historians, Melchior Fokkens in 1662, and Caspar Commelin in 1693. Moreover, the pictures by Rembrandt were the only two to have the artist's name mentioned by the latter author: "In dese kamer hangen groote kostelijkke Schilderyen alle die de Kunst der Heelmeesters aangaan" (Fokkens) and "Dese Kamer is niet alleen verçiert met eenige menschen en beesten Geraamtens, maar ook van verscheyde Schilderyen, gedaan door bysondere konstige Schilders, daar onder twee door den vermaarden Rembrandt gedaan, welke boven al uyt munten; deselve verbeelden in 't midden een subject van een Mensch dat ontleed word door de in der tijd zijnde *Professor Anatomiae,* daar by en om geplaatst staan, de in dienst zijn de Overluyden" (Commelin) [13]. Unfortunately Commelin's description has caused some confusion. The names of the sitters and their respective functions were apparently unknown to this author [14].

It was not until about 1750 that mention was made of the names of the surgeons portrayed in *Dr. Tulp's Anatomy Lesson.* It was the surgeon Johannes Monnikhoff who recorded them in the same order as adopted in the sketch-book one of their company is holding. In the *Na-reeden* (Epilogue) appended in manuscript to the book of *Privilegiën, Willekeuren en Ordonnantiën* of the Surgeons' Guild of Amsterdam (published in Amsterdam in 1736 and kept in the University Library of that city), Monnikhoff wrote as follows: "In het jaar 1632 wierd bij de voorgaande Schilderijen op de Gilde-kamer gevoegd dat fraaij en uijtmuntend stuk, waar in door den vermaarde *Rembrand* zeer konstrijk afgebeeld zijn Dr Nicolaas Tulp, Mr Jacob Block, Hartman Hartmansz., Adriaan Slabbraan, Jacob de Wit, Mr Matthijs Kalkoen, Jacob Koolveld en Frans van Loenen".

Monnikhoff also compiled a list of the wardens of the guild showing the year of their appointment. In this list, covering the administrative year September 1631-September 1632, we find the names of Jacob Jansz. de Witt and Adriaan Cornelisz. Slabberaen. In the following year, Jacob Jansz. de Witt is listed as "bosmeester" (treasurer) and Adriaan Cornelisz. Slabberaen as "overman" (warden) [15]. In 1632 the other surgeons Rembrandt portrayed did not yet hold office in the guild.

The well-known 18th century historian of Amsterdam, Jan Wagenaar, also described the interior of the surgeons' Guild Room (in 1765) at the same time, noting down the names of those portrayed: "De schoorsteen is, met de uitgehouwen wapens van eenige Overluiden versierd, en de wanden, rondsom, behangen met oude en nieuwe schilderstuk-

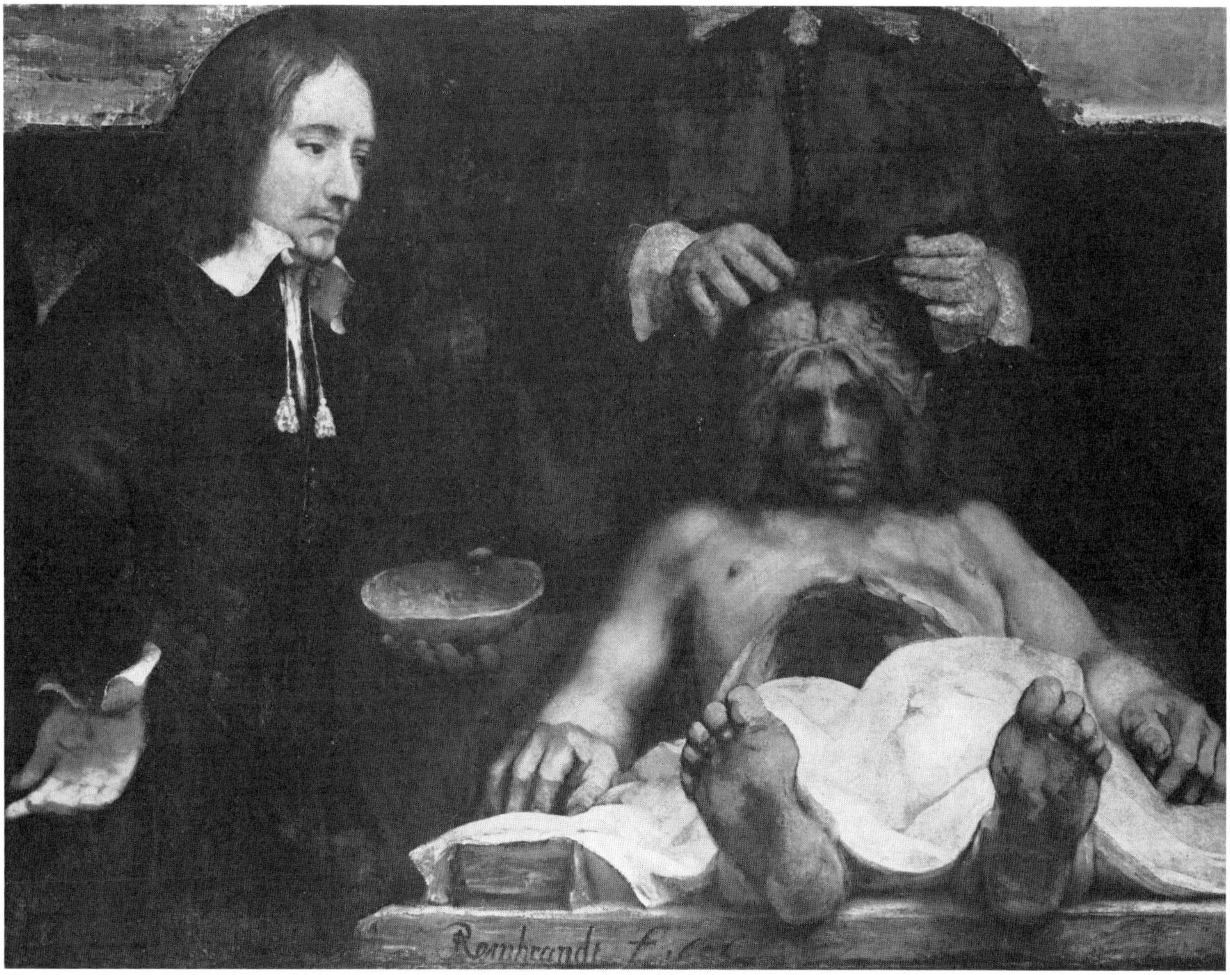

59. Rembrandt. Dr. Johan Deyman's Anatomy Lesson, 1656. *Amsterdam, Rijksmuseum.*

ken, tot twaalf of meer in getal, doorgaands, gezelschappen van Overluiden of Chirurgijns, en Voorlezers of Professoren in de Ontleedkunde verbeeldende... Doch de twee oudsten en fraaisten zyn beide van Rembrand: het schoonste van de twee is in 't jaar 1632 geschilderd, en vertoont Doctor Tulp en de Chirurgyns Jacob Blok, Hartman Hartmansz., Adriaan Slabberaan, Jacob de Witt, Matthys Kalkoen, Jacob Koolveld en Frans van Loenen, die allen, behalve den laatsten, ook Overluiden geweest zijn" [16].

In addition to the accounts left by the Amsterdam town historians and by the surgeon Monnikhoff, who was able to draw on the guild's archives, two further descriptions have been preserved, recorded by travellers who visited the *Nieuwe Waag* in Amsterdam, and saw Rembrandt's anatomy paintings. On 20 February 1711, the German traveller Zacharias Conrad von Uffenbach visited the anatomy theatre and Guild Room, his preference being for Dr. Tulp's Lesson: "Eines rechter Hand des Camins ist demselben weit vorzuziehen und war unvergleichlich. Auf diesem Stück verrichtet der berühmte Anatomicus Tulpius die Section" [17].

It appears from his travel diary of 1781 that the English painter Sir Joshua Reynolds, on the other hand, preferred the *Dr. Deyman's Anatomy Lesson* (Fig. 59). Of Rembrandt's painting of 1632 he writes: "The Professor Tulpius dissecting a corpse which lies on the table, by Rembrandt. To avoid making it an object disagreeable to look at, the figure is but just cut at the wrist. There are seven other portraits coloured like nature itself, fresh and highly finished. One of the figures behind has a paper in his hand, on which are written the names of the rest: Rembrandt has also added his own name, with the date 1672 [incorrectly read; authors' note]. The dead body is perfectly well drawn (a little foreshortened,) and seems to have been just washed. Nothing can be more truly the colour of dead flesh. The legs and feet which are nearest the eye, are in shadow: the principal light, which is on the body, is by that means preserved of a compact form. All these figures are dressed in black" [18].

It is strange, all the same, that so many questions regarding *Dr. Nicolaas Tulp's Anatomy Lesson* should have remained unanswered despite some investigations made during the latter half of the 19th century and more recent and systematic research in the Amsterdam archives, carried out particularly before and after the Second World War [19].

This seems the proper place to say something about the artist's removal to Amsterdam in 1631. As far as we know, this *Anatomy Lesson* was the young painter's first large commission—a group portrait with seven (eight?) figures—after his arrival in the city. Then we may ask who commissioned the work and what the requirements were.

Although Orlers, the historian of Leiden, wrote that Rembrandt left for Amsterdam "about the year 1630", various records show that he could only have done so after 19 November 1631 [20]. For some years the young Leiden artist had been in touch with Hendrick van Uylenburch, an art dealer in Amsterdam (see *Appendix IIIb*), in whose house, in the Jodenbreestraat, he was staying on 26 July 1632 [21].

Rembrandt had already done portraits of Amsterdam citizens in the period 1631-1632 (Br.-G., Nos. 145, 165 and 166). He must have come to the city from Leiden more than once during 1631, for stays of varying length. It does not seem unlikely that Uylenburch acted as an intermediary and perhaps introduced him to the wardens of the Surgeons' Guild and/or to Dr. Tulp.

Since, according to Monnikhoff, the finished painting had been added to the other anatomy pieces in the Guild Room in the *Nieuwe Waag* by 1632 (see note 11), we may certainly assume that the work had been commissioned, with the approval of the officials of the guild, by the surgeons portrayed and their prelector, Dr. Tulp. The *Anatomy Lesson* of 1632 and the painting by Aert Pietersz., of 1603, are the only anatomy pieces in which not only wardens of the guild appear with their prelector. This is also one of the reasons why it is so difficult to ascertain who actually commissioned Rembrandt's *Anatomy Lesson.* We may presume that the surgeons portrayed paid the artist's fee jointly. How much each of them had to pay, and what Dr. Tulp's contribution may have been, remains unknown [22].

The annual anatomical demonstrations and public lessons in Amsterdam harked back to a prerogative decreed by King Philip II in Brussels on 13 March 1555 [23]. These dissections were to take place under the supervision of a qualified physician.

Later, on 11 January 1606, a bye-law was issued entitled "*Ordonnantie voor den Chirurgijns op 't stuk van de Anatomie*" (see *Appendix IIIa*). It is evident from this bye-law that in addition to the dissection performed on this one occasion in the year upon an executed criminal, others were performed by the surgeons privately, also, without doubt, on animals and prepared specimens [24]. For that matter, it is known from Dr. Tulp's *Observationum...* that he performed more than one partial autopsy in the presence of colleagues (both doctors and surgeons), in his work as a pathologist [25].

The public demonstrations of anatomy, quite apart from being a "public entertainment", were also occasions of scientific significance and served, in Dr. Tulp's own words, to distil truth from the shadow [26]. According to Dr. V.F. Plemp, during the public dissection performed on 31 January 1632 and the days following, Dr. Tulp paid particular attention to the *valvula coli.* This author does not, however, make any mention of the dissection of the arm [27].

Finally it should be said that it is only by way of deduction that this painting can be connected with Dr. Tulp's public lesson and dissection which took place on 31 January 1632 and the following days. The historical data do not allow one to go any further than this.

ICONOGRAPHY AND STYLE

In a vaulted chamber, the prelector Dr. Nicolaas Tulp is seen demonstrating to seven master-surgeons the operation of the muscles in a dead man's dissected left arm and hand (Fig. 49). Tulp is seated in an armchair in front of a niche and is turned three-quarters to the left. He is attired in a black cloak with a flat white collar and white cuffs. The surgeons are all dressed in their best, with large flat ruffs, Hartman (No. 3) excepted. He is wearing a much thicker, old-fashioned ruff.

In his right hand Dr. Nicolaas Tulp is holding a forceps, with which he is raising a bunch of muscles above the dissected arm, while with his left hand he is making a rhetorical gesture. The corpse is lying on a wooden table, placed diagonally. At the corpse's feet stands a pile of books against which an open folio volume has been propped. Four surgeons, in various attitudes, are ranged on Tulp's right. One is situated at the head of the table—opposite the prelector—another is seated next to the latter's right and the seventh is sitting (as it would seem) between the

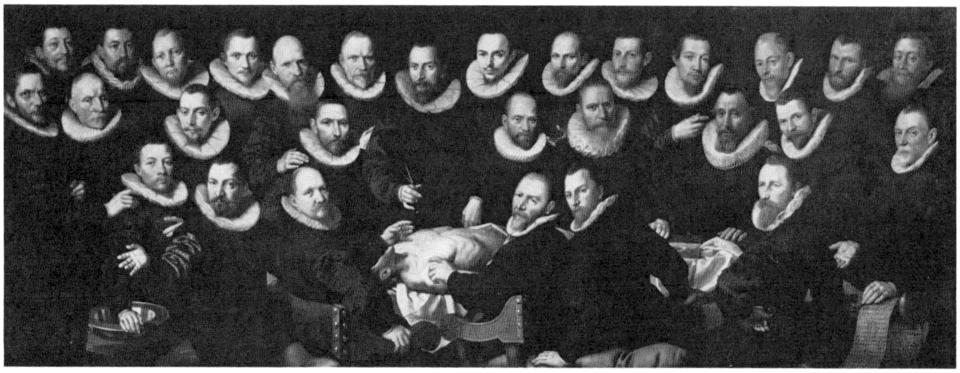

60. Aert Pietersz. Dr. Seb. Egbertsz.'s Anatomy Lesson, 1603. *Amsterdam, Rijksmuseum.*

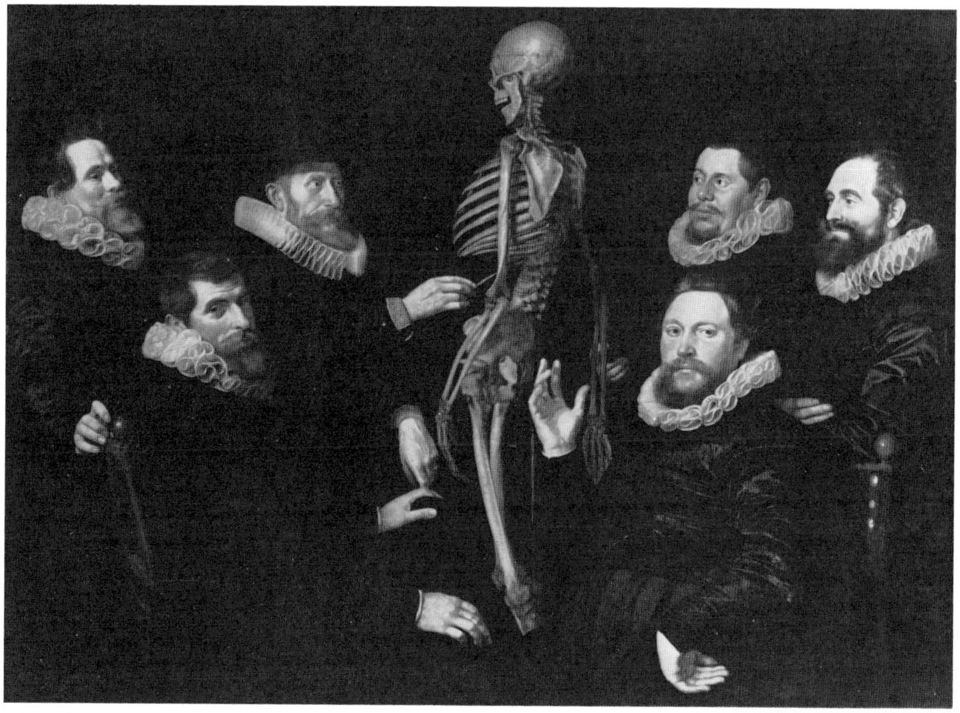

61. Thomas de Keyser. Dr. Seb. Egbertsz.'s Anatomy Lesson, 1619. *Amsterdam, Rijksmuseum.*

62. Nicolaes Eliasz. (called Pickenoy). Dr. Johan Fonteyn's Anatomy Lesson, 1625. Fragment. *Amsterdam. Amsterdams Historisch Museum.*

63. Dr. Nicolaas Tulp (No. 1).

64. Jacob Dielofse Block (No. 2).

65. Hartman Hartmansz. (No. 3).

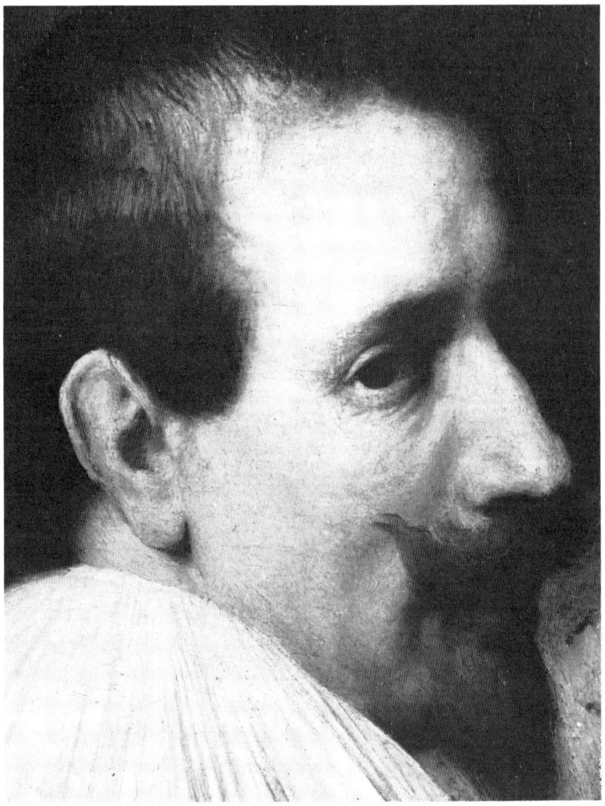

66. Adriaen Cornelisz. Slabberaen (No. 4).

67. Jacob Jansz. de Witt (No. 5).

68. Mathys Evertsz. Calkoen (No. 6).

69. Jacob Jansz. Colevelt (No. 7).

70. Frans Jacobsz. van Loenen (No. 8).

last two. On the wall at the back, a scroll is hanging from a rod.

From the information supplied by Johannes Monnikhoff (see *Historical data*) it appears that Rembrandt's *Dr. Nicolaas Tulp's Anatomy Lesson* joined the other, earlier paintings in the Guild Room in 1632. However, it is unfortunately not possible to be quite certain whether the work, dated 1632, refers to the first or to the second public lesson Dr. Tulp delivered.

It seems only natural that, in preparing himself for his task, Rembrandt would take account of the way his predecessors had set about similar commissions. The earliest anatomy piece known to us, completed in 1603 by Aert Pietersz., portrays Dr. Sebastiaan Egbertsz. de Vrij, prelector between 1595 and 1621, surrounded by all 28 members of the Surgeons' Guild (Fig. 60).

In 1619 this prelector had himself portrayed once more, this time with five wardens ranged about the skeleton of a young man (Fig. 61). In 1625 Dr. Johan Fonteyn, prelector from 1621 to 1628, had himself painted by Nicolaes Eliasz., called Pickenoy, in the company of ten master-surgeons. Only a fragment of this painting survived the fire in the Guild Room in 1723. It shows the prelector and five surgeons (Fig. 62).

These three works are primarily group portraits of the prelector and a number of master-surgeons. The secondary emphasis is laid on the prelector's anatomy "lesson", though we should add that it is not known what subjects were being treated. The first work shows us a corpse which is still intact; the second a skeleton, from which we can at least deduce that this was not one of the annual public demonstrations of anatomy but a lecture in osteology. In the third work, all we see is a cranium, which once again hardly suggests a public anatomy lesson.

It was thus that portraits of the prelectors and the surgeons decorated the walls of the Surgeons' Chamber in the *Nieuwe Waag,* that is to say as representatives of their profession and their guild and accordingly dressed, as was the custom, in their best attire. In some ways Rembrandt appears to have followed the tradition, breaking away from it in some very essential respects, however (see below, p. 103 ss.).

It is known that Dr. Tulp gave his first public lessons—including dissections—in January 1631 and the second on 31 January 1632 and subsequent days. No information has come down to us about the special subject he dealt with during his first series of public lessons. In his second he demonstrated the existence of the *valvula coli* [28]. Such demonstrations always took place in the coldest months of the year,

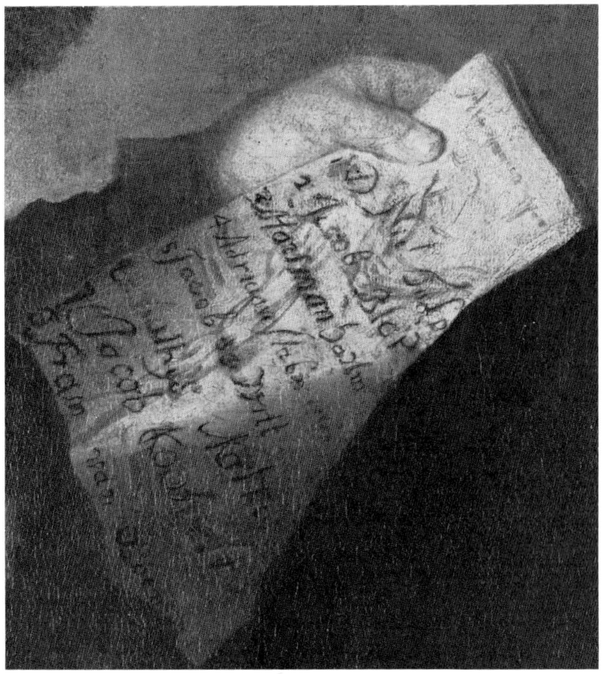

71. The numbered list of names of the prelector and the surgeons.

since it was then that the corpses remained in a reasonable state of preservation for the longest time.

I.H. van Eeghen has rightly pointed out that it is improbable that Dr. Tulp's first public lesson served as the starting point for Rembrandt's painting [29]. That his commission was presumably concerned with the prelector's second public lesson may not only be deduced with a degree of probability from Monnikhoff's notes but it may follow too, from the positions in the picture of Jan Jacobsz. de Witt and of Adriaan Cornelisz. Slabberaen, both wardens of the Surgeons' Guild, the former since September 1630, the latter since September 1631 [30]. Neither had formerly been included in an anatomy piece. De Witt and Slabberaen are both placed close to the head of the corpse, opposite Dr. Tulp. The former is seen bending very attentively over the body; the latter is seated to his right in the foreground and appears to be looking out of the picture at the spectator as he listens. At all events, they occupy the two most prominent places, even if this is not apparent from the numbers (4 and 5) they have been allotted in the list of those portrayed, entered on the page of the sketch-book Hartman Hartmansz. (No. 3) is holding in his hand (Fig. 71). A sketch of a dissected arm was all that was originally on this page—the subject of the lesson depicted in the painting. The way in which the arm has been drawn is reminiscent of a woodcut in Vesalius' famous book [31]. The names of the surgeons portrayed were added to this page later. This must in fact have taken place when there was a risk of their being forgotten. The names are preceded by figures which correspond with those placed next to each surgeon.

When Caspar Commelin was writing about this work of Rembrandt among other things, he confused the persons portrayed. We must assume that, even by that time, the painting had been covered with one or more coats of varnish so that the names on the page of the sketch-book had become illegible, or that they had yet to be added [32]. It is likewise not impossible that the names were painted on to this page when the work underwent thorough restoration in 1732 and were accordingly first mentioned by Monnikhoff in the order shown on it, although the dates have been added below:

1. *D Nicl Tulp* (1593-1674) (Fig. 63).
2. *Jacob Blok* (Block) (1600/01-1664) (Fig. 64).
3. *Hartman Hartm...* (Hartmansz.) (1590/91-1659) (Fig. 65).
4. *Adriaan Slabr...* (Slabberaen) (1597/98-1661) (Fig. 66).
5. *Jacob de Witt (de Witt)* (1581/82-1654) (Fig. 67).
6. *Mathijs Kalko...* (Calkoen) (1590/91-1653) (Fig. 68).
7. *Jacob Koolvelt* (Colevelt) (1595?-1649) (Fig. 69).
8. *Frans van Loenen* (1591/92-1662) (Fig. 70).

Thanks to the research done by I.H. van Eeghen in the Municipal Archives of Amsterdam more has become known of the careers of the surgeons portrayed [33]. The names entered on the page of the sketch-book, which are either no longer complete or slightly damaged, have undoubtedly suffered during the repeated restorations of the canvas (see *Appendix IIIc*).

Dr. Nicolaas Tulp is naturally first to be named (Fig. 63). Claes Pietersz., who called himself Tulp (1593-1674) studied medicine at Leiden. After qualifying in 1614 with Pieter Pauw (1564-1617) as his professor, he settled in his birthplace, Amsterdam. On 24 November 1628 the City Council of Amsterdam appointed him prelector, which meant that he was entrusted with the task of giving the surgeons lessons in anatomy and surgery. He assumed this office on 29 January 1629, holding it until 27 January 1653, after which he devoted himself exclusively to administrative matters for his native town [34].

As has been said, in 1632 Slabberaen (No. 4) and De Witt (No. 5) were already wardens of the Surgeons' Guild. Of the other five, all, except Frans van Loenen (No. 8), were in later years to hold office on the board of the guild. Jacob Block and Jacob Colevelt were closely connected with the theatre. The former was associated with the Amsterdam city theatre for some years both as barber and as a director or governor. The latter wrote various plays and songs [35].

Since we assume that the public lesson given at the end of January 1632 served as the basis for this painting, it is probable that the corpse is that of Adriaan Adriaansz. 't Kint, a criminal who was executed on 31 January 1632 [36]. One notices that the neck of this man—who was condemned to die by hanging—is not visible. The chest is lying on the dissecting table in a slightly raised position, probably on a block placed beneath the shoulders, so that the head has fallen slightly backwards (Fig. 72) [37]. Had the executioner's rope left marks on the neck and has this realistic detail been deliberately concealed? There is also the possibility that, having certainly been present at several other anatomy lessons, Rembrandt may have portrayed some other dead body here.

The corpse is practically intact—there is no sign of the chest and abdominal cavity having been opened up, the process with which public lessons and dissections customarily began, since the organs most subject to rapid decay are located there.

Before proceeding to discuss Dr. Tulp's portrait, something should first be said about the folio volume lying open at the corpse's feet (Fig. 73). In the earlier literature it was assumed without more ado that this book was Vesalius's *Fabrica* and the 1555 Basle edition of that work [38].

Heckscher does not agree, considering a Dutch manuscript in folio format more likely [39]. Others have said they supposed it to be Adriaen van den

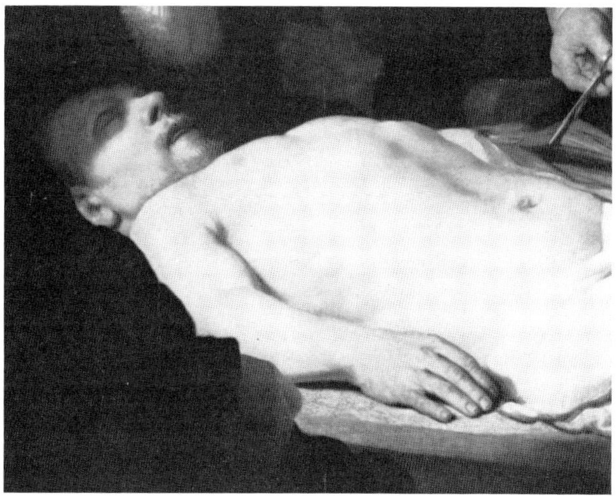

72. The corpse (Adriaan Adriaansz 't Kint?).

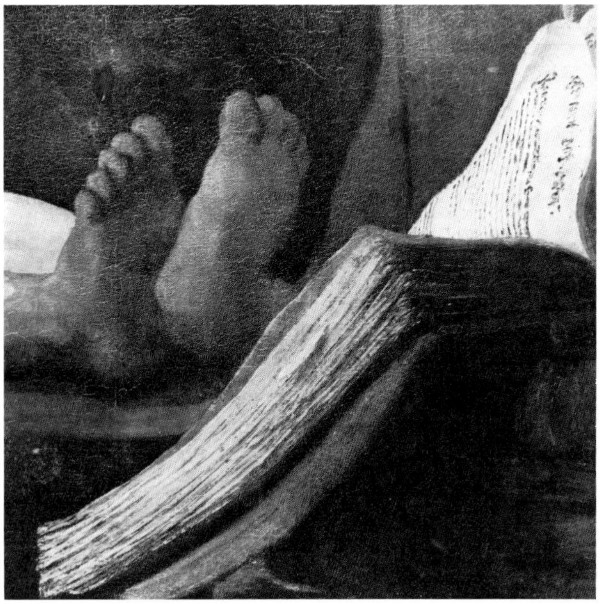

73. The open volume in the lower right-hand corner.

Spieghel's book, published in 1627 and in which one of the engravings by Giulio Casserio shows a dissected arm [40]. Whatever the identity of the work, a book was a traditional attribute of the officiating anatomist [41]. The pages at which the large volume lies open offer no solution since the text they bear is illegible [42].

In view of the subject being taught, it is nevertheless quite possible that the painter intended to suggest Vesalius's *Fabrica.* This would, moreover, be in line with the portrayal of Dr. Tulp as *Vesalius Redivius.* Moreover, it is obvious that the book has a part to play in the composition of the work.

With the forceps in his right hand, Dr. Tulp is shown demonstrating the operation of the muscles of the dissected lower left arm and hand, while making an eloquent gesture with his left hand, the *Quibusdem* (... *dam*?) *orbitur* which may be interpreted as he started his oration by setting out several points (Fig. 74) [43]. Thus Dr. Tulp is painted in his dual function, that is, as practitioner in dissecting and teacher in anatomy.

74. J. Bulwer, *Chirologia...*, 1644. Canon IV. Fig. 6B "*Quibusdem orditur*".

The theme was both topical and traditional. In 1630, in his *Verhandelingh der spieren,* Dr. Vopiscus Fortunatus Plemp had treated this same subject, among others (see note 27), while there is also an unmistakable connection with the woodcut of 1542 by Jan Stephan van Calcar (Fig. 75), where Vesalius is represented as an anatomist with a dissected lower arm and hand. On a table a sheet of paper is lying which describes the subject as "De musculis digitos moventibus..." [44].

75. Jan Stephan van Calcar (?). Portrait of Andreas Vesalius, 1542. Woodcut for the 1543 edition of *Fabrica...*

It is noticeable that Dr. Tulp has had himself portrayed as *Vesalius Redivivus,* a fact stressed by Heckscher, although W. Hastie, Hans Jantzen (see note 38) and Hubert Schrade had already established the connection with Vesalius [45].

In this way, moreover, the prelector emphasized his task as Vesalius's successor, the man who had worked to see that the surgeons of Amsterdam received their charter of privilege from King Philip II in 1555.

Heckscher was indeed the first to have drawn special attention to the conch or shell-motif in the niche behind Dr. Tulp's head. This he interprets as a reference to the high office the prelector had been called on to fill [46].

The role in which Dr. Tulp and the board of the Surgeons' Guild apparently wished to see the prelector portrayed, the subject of this lesson and the dissection which it involved, all cause us to wonder to what extent Rembrandt's version of the occasion is the result of actual observation. Did the painter rely on a prepared specimen, aided possibly by a print, or did Dr. Tulp actually give a lesson on the muscles of the lower arm and the way the fingers operate, perhaps on one of the days subsequent to 31 January 1632? And was it this lesson Rembrandt has represented in this work?

It was, in any case, customary for almost the entire human body to be dissected at the annual public lesson, which lasted for some days, and this was done even if some special theme had been chosen as the main subject. The *pentimento* which has come to light in the X-ray photograph above the under-arm at least permits the hypothesis that Dr. Tulp dissected the lower arm himself during one of his lessons, since the painter could not otherwise have observed this detail and then corrected it (see *Technical data* and Fig. 54).

There has been much argument about the accuracy, or inaccuracy, of the dissected arm and hand as Rembrandt has depicted them [47].

The authors of this study are not in a position to discuss this medical detail. It seems doubtful, to begin with, whether the left arm has indeed been turned outwards through 75°, which operation would have pulled the muscles out of position. Should it be so, however, we have three possibilities to choose from:

1. Rembrandt worked from "life" and made a mistake, either in the way he has attached the arm to the corpse or in direct observation [48].
2. Rembrandt worked from an illustration and then attached the arm to the body incorrectly [49].
3. Rembrandt worked from an illustration which contained the same mistake [50].

M.P. Carpentier Alting and Tj.W. Waterbolk are, by the way, of the opinion that Rembrandt rendered the arm correctly, working from a prepared specimen [51].

One final iconographical detail: the document hanging on a rod on the rear wall eludes deciphering. It is possible that the illegible text contains the examination questions put to the surgeons in the dissecting chamber [52].

The authors have felt that they would do well to confine themselves almost exclusively to what one sees in the painting. They do, however, accept the doubtlessly intentional connection with Tulp's great 16th century predecessor, Andreas Vesalius (1514/15-1564), the founder of modern anatomy. That Tulp should have had himself portrayed as *Vesalius Redivivus* must almost certainly be due to a wish, perhaps even an instruction, the prelector communicated to Rembrandt—the board of the Surgeons' Guild and the other surgeons also portrayed in the work gladly giving their consent and approval, in view of the privilege granted to them in 1555 (see note 23).

It goes without saying that some scholars who have studied this painting have sought to clarify its possible backgrounds. Here, first of all, we would again mention Hubert Schrade's essay [53]. He was the first to point to Dürer's drawing *The Lamentation of Christ* and the relationship between its composition and iconological background and Rembrandt's anatomy piece. The question is, of course, whether Rembrandt can have known this drawing. More significant from the iconological viewpoint, however, is whether Rembrandt, perhaps influenced by Tulp, looked upon medicine as the *ars sacratissima,* as Vesalius had done, although, according to Schrade, this particularly sacred art had been founded on the *nova scientia.*

Schrade also investigates how far Calvinism had made it possible for anatomy to become the subject-matter of art. Among other remarks, he writes: "Sie [the Protestant Netherlands, that is to say] waren im Begriffe, sich eine Kunst zu schaffen, die auf dem mittlerlosen, dem unmittelbaren Verhältnis der Künstler zur Wirklichkeit beruhte".

Heckscher expresses himself differently, yet actually takes Schrade's exposition a step further. In this painting he sees a "Triumph of Sapientia over Malitia", thereby emphasizing that all the persons portrayed, the dissected criminal included, enjoy immortality as a result of scientific research in the public interest [54].

Attention should also be drawn to A.G.H. Bachrach's essay *"Holland and Britain in the Age of Observation"* [55]. Reznicek recently raised the question —immediately terming it a "speculation"—whether, in his composition of the *Anatomy Lesson* Rembrandt had transformed the figure of Christ in Rubens's *The Tribute Money* (Fig. 76) into Dr. Tulp, for symbolic reasons, the intention being to see medicine as the holiest of the arts [56].

The prelector and the surgeons were not only concerned with the dead man's anatomy and the lessons to be drawn from it in a purely medical sense; their religious and philosophical ideas about man and his

76. P.P. Rubens. The Tribute Money, C. 1614. *San Francisco, M.H. de Young Memorial Museum.*

relation to God and/or Creation in general must also have played their part.

As will be apparent from the foregoing, we stand by our opinion that what Rembrandt had done here, in accordance with his commission (see *Historical data*) was, first and foremost, to paint a group portrait. Nevertheless it cannot be denied that this *Anatomy Lesson* also includes several characteristics of historical painting (see below, p. 108) [57].

The technical investigation, however, provides no grounds for assuming that the visible *pentimenti* and the one addition—the figure of Colevelt (No. 7), done moreover by another hand—point to the execution of the work in two separate phases. Such a supposition was not corroborated in any way whatever by the X-ray examination (see *Technical data,* p. 86) [58]. It can, however, be assumed that since the composition was required to be of dimensions unusual for Rembrandt, the young artist was presented with great problems. The *pentimenti* bear clear witness to this. One of these showed that he shifted the position of Hartman Hartmansz. (No. 3) to the right by at least several inches. There are other changes of varying importance to be noticed: Van Loenen's hat (No. 8), which has been painted over; the hat of Dr. Tulp, originally somewhat taller; the head and chest of the corpse, which were slightly lowered; the *pentimento* above the dissected arm (see *Technical data).*

Even though it has been said and written countless times that Rembrandt broke away from the traditional composition of the group portrait, this fact should be stated yet again and categorically. If we compare his work with the Amsterdam anatomy pieces which preceded it and with that of the Delft painters Michiel and Pieter Van Mierevelt (1617), and also with some of the group portraits of governors (*regenten*) painted before 1632, the truth of this cannot be denied [59].

Another remark may be made here on the borderline between iconography and criticism of style: Aloïs Riegl—and later Heckscher—have suggested that "the public" ought to be seen as involved, when contemplating this painting. This they deduce from various attitudes adopted by those portrayed, their variety of gestures, the different directions in which they are looking, and also from the public nature of the annual demonstration. We do not share this view [60].

We see this composition as a successful attempt by an artist seeking to portray a number of persons concerned in an anatomical lesson and dissection in such a way that both the event itself and the individual portraits of all participants are grouped to form a convincing and surprising whole. Rembrandt understood himself to be working like a stage director, giving his "audience" a convincingly realistic picture in which tradition and innovation were combined.

To this extent, one may indeed think of the public, but then only indirectly, in the same way as a stage

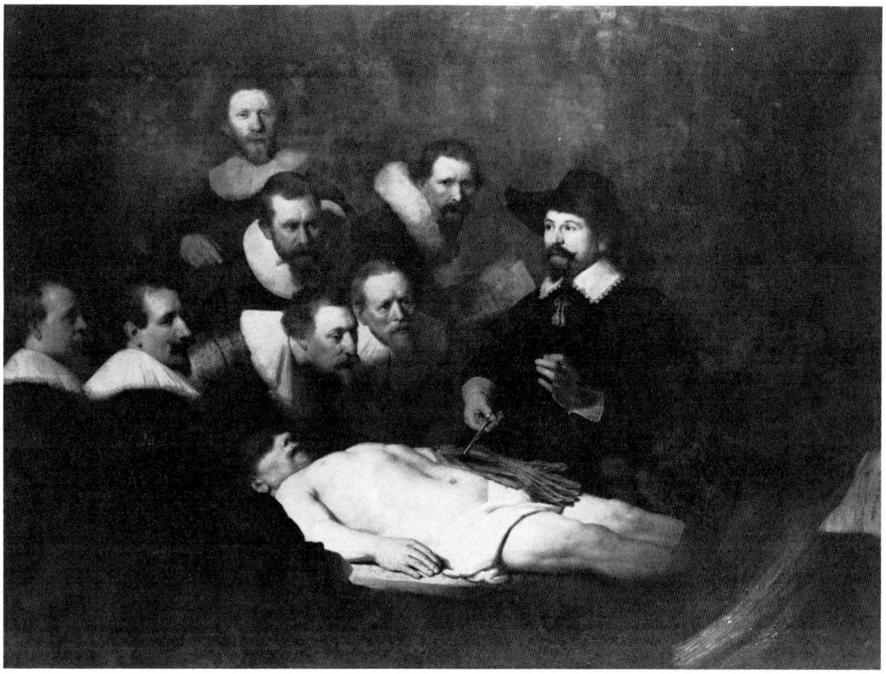

77. Dr. Nicolaas Tulp's Anatomy Lesson. The painting before the 1951 restoration.

director bears his audience in mind. But we encounter the relation between the persons portrayed and the spectator so often as a feature of 16th century portrait painting, that there is really no need at all to see "the public" as an "invisible party" in this anatomy lesson [61].

Reverting to the composition of the painting, it must be stressed that no preliminary study, sketch or drawing, either for the whole piece or for any part of it, has been preserved.

In this respect it should be said that little is yet known about Rembrandt's working methods. In this group-portrait, all the heads except that of Colevelt, have been carefully prepared. This has been made clear by the X-rays particularly (Figs. 52, 53). Did each of the surgeons, and Dr. Tulp, sit as models in the artist's workshop? It may very well be, although the idea that Rembrandt might possibly have conceived the composition of this great work and completed it, working more or less straight on to the canvas amazes one. It is true that several *pentimenti* are visible to the naked eye or have become so in the X-ray and infra-red photographs, but they do not explain how Rembrandt went to work when painting a large group portrait such as this.

The exceptional character of the composition is determined by its pyramidal structure, which Riegl was the first to note. He wrote of "eine strenge Pyramidalkomposition mit gleichmässig absinkenden Schenkeln" [62]. This is so even though Colevelt (No. 7) (Fig. 69) seen in profile and crammed in on the far left, does not appear to have formed part of Rembrandt's original design. We shall be returning to this.

Dr. Tulp occupies a strikingly off-centre position. He is sitting apart from the surgeons and dominates the corpse, which, lying diagonally, forms the link with the surgeons as they listen and observe. This group of six (Colevelt excluded) consists of an inner and an outer group of three, which form two pyramids within the overall pyramid. The inner pyramid is made up of De Witt (No. 5), Block (No. 2) and Calkoen (No. 6), all three of whom have their gaze fixed on the corpse and what the prelector is doing. The outer group consist of Slabberaen (No. 4), Van Loenen (No. 8) and Hartman (No. 3), who appear to be listening to Dr. Tulp's discourse, while their gaze is fixed on the spectator.

After the restoration performed in 1951, it became possible to take account of the factors of space and light in this painting's composition. The heavy layers of varnish had hitherto reduced the background to an opaque uniform surface, with which all the highlighted parts of the corpse and the persons portrayed, however yellowed they may have become, formed a sharp contrast. As a result, the *chiaroscuro* effect was intensified (Fig. 77).

By means of his surprising arrangement of the figures, Rembrandt has succeeded in achieving an effect of depth, suggesting the room or hall in which the demonstration is taking place. This room eludes identification, although the blocks of stone and the large iron ring (of a door?) to the right, behind Dr. Tulp's chair, might possibly be details taken from real life [63].

The painter has shown us no visible source of light. However, in view of the fall of light on the faces of those portrayed, on the corpse and here and there on the clothes, and also taking into account the shadows, we may say that this canvas was undoubtedly painted in strong studio light coming from above left, and there is no reason whatever to assume that the artist painted it by artificial light. The concentration of the light on the dissected body, that is to say, on the upper part of the legs, the torso and the lower half of the face, may reflect a memory of the actual scene witnessed in 1632. The anatomy theatre where the lessons and dissections took place and where the corpse was laid ready, was usually provided with extra lighting from a chandelier or candlesticks [64].

It has already been remarked that in the course of Rembrandt's evolution as an artist, his *chiaroscuro* gained in subtlety [65]. The commission or subject he was engaged on must also be taken into account, however. Compared with many of his Leiden portraits or character studies, the contrasts in this work are less marked, the transitions from light to dark more fluid. It is true that the light areas, corpse, flesh tones, ruffs and Dr. Tulp's hands form important functional elements in the composition, which help to suggest space. But what the *chiaroscuro* particularly does is to determine the sitters' individuality and the variety of expression the artist was seeking.

There can be little doubt that the portraits of the surgeons and of Dr. Tulp himself are good likenesses. Even if the prelector's appearance has been somewhat enhanced by restoration, a comparison with the portrait by Nicolaes Eliasz., called Pickenoy (Fig. 78), shows that Rembrandt must have achieved a good likeness here.

It is noticeable, however, that before the restoration (presumably that of 1732, see *Appendix IIIc*), Tulp had a more prominent moustache and may have been rather rougher and more masculine in appearance (Fig. 79). The restorer seems to have been familiar with Pickenoy's portrait, which corresponds in many respects—expression and also such details as moustache, goatee and collar—with the Dr. Tulp we know today.

In view of the striking differences in the facial expressions and gestures of the surgeons and also the

78. Nicolaes Eliasz. (called Pickenoy). Portrait of Dr. Nicolaas Tulp, 1634. *Amsterdam, Six Collection.*

79. X-ray photograph. The head of Dr. Nicolaas Tulp.

fact that the painting immediately joined the other anatomy pieces in the *Nieuwe Waag* in 1632 (see *Historical data)*, we may assume that the portraits of the others were also regarded as good likenesses.

The new element which Rembrandt introduced into this anatomy piece is the contrast between the almost static figure of the prelector (although he is at work) and the animated appearance of his audience. There is a clear distinction between Dr. Tulp and the others present, the speaker appearing thoughtful as though mediating the next stage in his lecture.

Stylistically, some of these portraits show resemblances to those the artist executed to commissions in 1631-1632. Thus the portrait of Nicolas Ruts (Br.-G., No. 145) (Fig. 24) is not unlike that of Dr. Tulp, and must have resembled it still more closely before the latter was thoroughly restored in 1732. The not very exciting appearance of Maerten Looten (Br.-G., No. 166) is comparable with that of Frans van Loenen (No. 8) and there is also a similarity in the brushwork. In a more general way see also the portrait of Aelbert Cuyper (Br.-G., No. 165).

Returning to the difficulties the artist encountered in deciding upon the composition, attention should also be drawn to the perspective and dimensions of the armchair in which Dr. Tulp is seated. The chair appears to be falling over backwards while the depth of the seat and the length of the arms seem to be out of proportion.

It is not known for what reason Colevelt (No. 7) was added to the company of master-surgeons. Did he announce his wish to be included only when Rembrandt was already too far advanced with his work? However this may have been, during the 1951 restoration it became quite evident that this figure, squeezed into the corner, there being no other place left for him, differs considerably from the others in the manner of painting, colouring and expression (Fig. 53). This observation was confirmed by the X-ray photograph taken in 1968 (Fig. 52). Whereas all the other six surgeons strike us by the variety of expression of their eyes and, in most cases, by the intensity of their gaze, Colevelt is staring at the prelector or rather at the back of Slabberaen's head. The name of Jacob Backer, the first pupil to work in Rembrandt's Amsterdam studio, was already suggested in the restorer's workshop in 1951 as the probable painter of this portrait, which constitutes a weak and uncertain element in the whole [66].

This is by no means the case with Frans van Loenen (No. 8) who is essential to Rembrandt's design. The radiograph (Figs. 50 a, b) and infra-red photograph (Fig. 51) show clearly that Van Loenen was originally wearing a large hat that has been painted over. The areas left blank as revealed in the X-ray photo indicate that the artist included Van Loenen in his composition and most likely finished his portrait (see *Technical data*) [67]. It is difficult to explain why the hat had to disappear. Perhaps for reasons of protocol? Since this surgeon towers above all the others, he must be standing on a platform. He is certainly not one of the more interesting figures of the surgeons.

It is Jacob de Witt who attracts our attention first of all by the way he is bent over the corpse and following the prelector's demonstration intently. Exercising great ingenuity, Reznicek has detected a direct relation between this figure and the bald Pharisee seen leaning over forwards in Rubens's painting *The Tribute Money* (1614) [68]. The young painter from Leiden may well have seen this painting and would almost certainly have been aware of Vorsterman's print made after it. Reznicek rightly points out that Rembrandt has made a surgeon of Amsterdam, with moustache and goatee, of this Leonardesque figure. We feel less at ease regarding the photo-montage which, by inserting the corpse in the *Anatomy Lesson* into the composition of *The Tribute Money* by

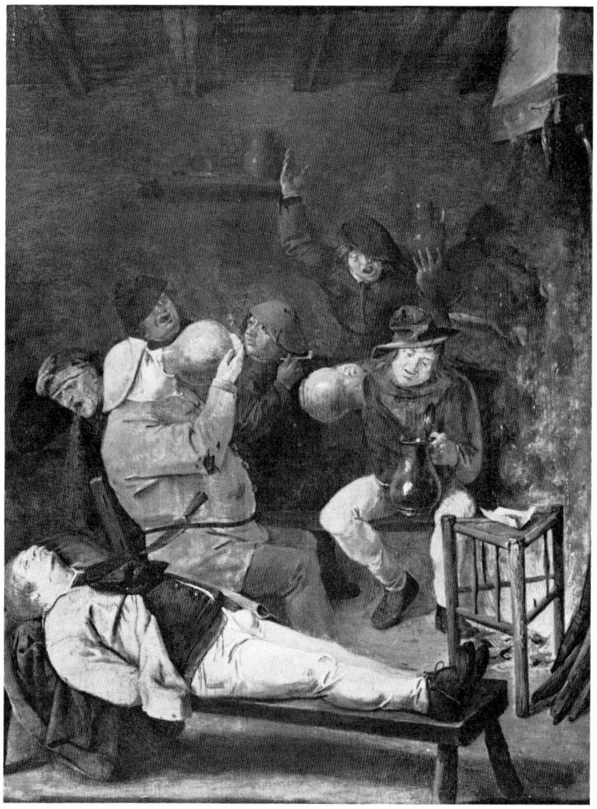

80. Adriaen Brouwer, The Drunken Peasant in an Inn. *Rotterdam, Museum Boymans-van Beuningen.*

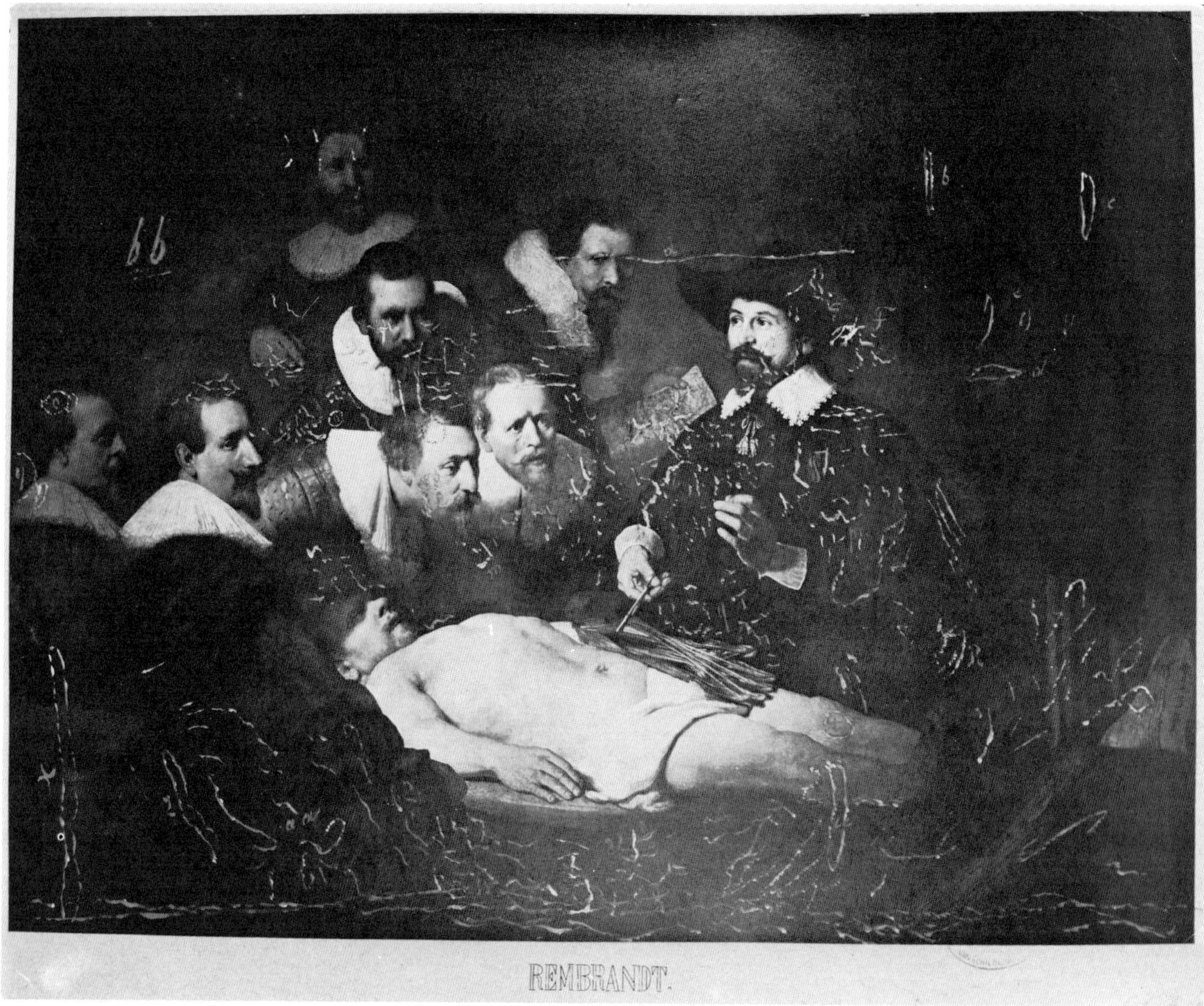

81. Photograph with indications of the damaged areas by the restorer W.A. Hopman, *The Mauritshuis Archives.*

Rubens is designed to demonstrate that Rembrandt's group portrait was based on that painting [69].

As far as the composition of the corpse is concerned, it seems more obvious to us to think of the drunken peasant lying on a threstle in Adriaen Brouwer's painting in the Boymans-van Beuningen Museum in Rotterdam (Fig. 80). The correspondence was pointed out as early as 1926, and this information was taken over by Heckscher [70].

It is far from unlikely that Rembrandt took certain details from various sources and adapted them to his purpose. Both Brouwer and Rubens were artists whose work he was familiar with. As regards the shell above the Pharisee on the far left in Rubens's work, see note 46. For the rest, Reznicek was probably right in a general sense, in so far as, besides borrowing the leaning-over motif, Rembrandt was especially impressed by the variety of attitudes and expressions among the Pharisees in Rubens's painting. He also sought to transform the liveliness of this

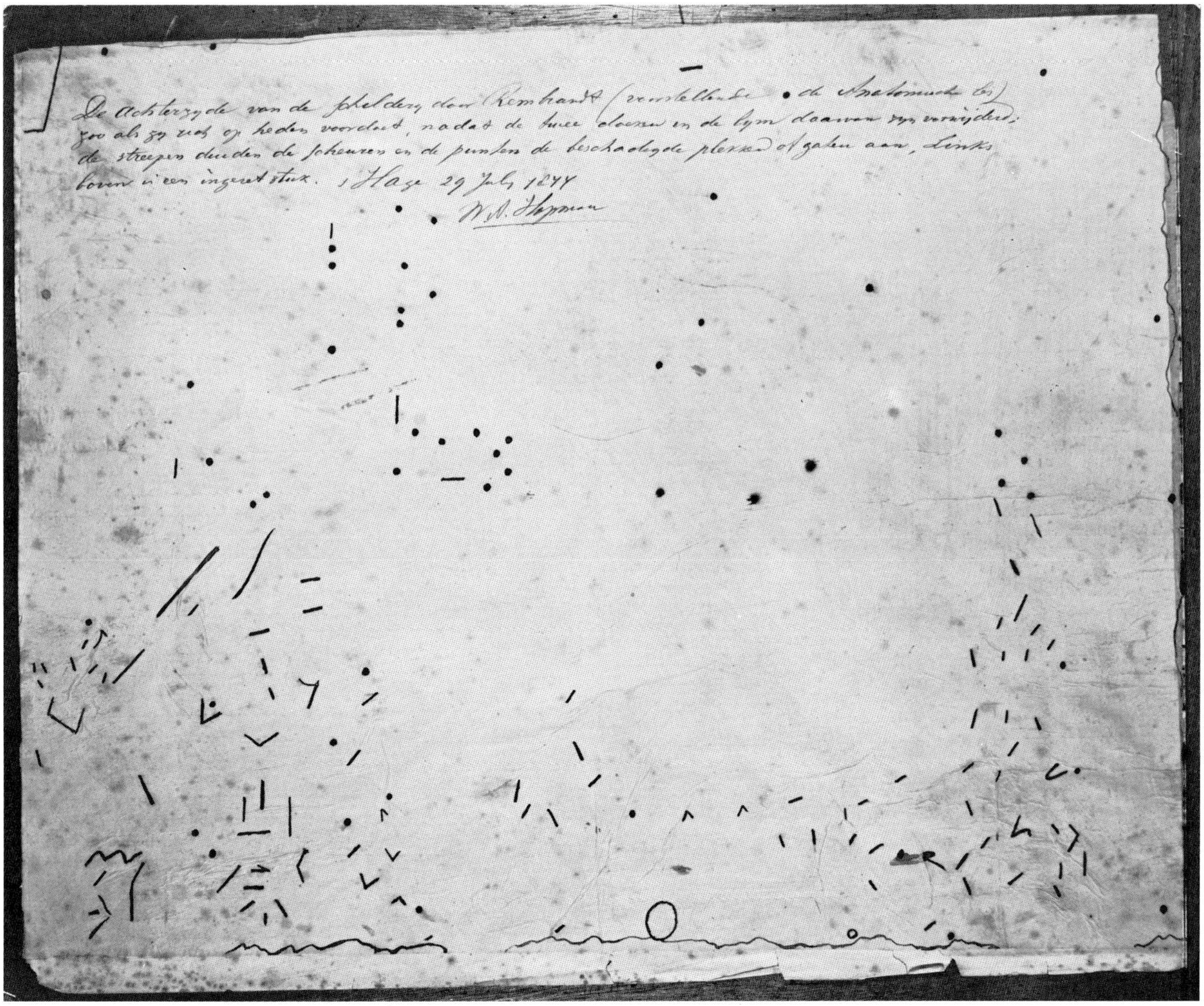

82. Verso of Fig. 81 with a note by the restorer W.A. Hopman (The Hague, 29 July 1877).

group into that of the surgeons gathered together in the presence of Dr. Nicolaas Tulp.

The dominant tone in the colour of the corpse came as a great surprise in 1951. When the various layers of varnish had been removed, the colour proved to be far less "realistic" than had been assumed. The artist must have deliberately avoided painting the body in a repulsive corpse-like colour, and adapted the flesh tones to the tonality and lighting of the painting as a whole.

Flesh tones and black dominate, with some colour here and there. Apart from the white of the ruffs, De Witt's slit-tunic (No. 5)—a detail of costume borrowed from the 16th century—has been painted in shades of violet, Slabberaen's (No. 4) knee stocking is red and Van Loenen's (No. 8) coat is a reddish-brown.

Naturally, in the course of almost 350 years, this painting has undergone repeated restoration, touching up and cleaning (see *Appendix IIIc).* The informa-

83. Chs. Binger. Rembrandt's Anatomy Lesson. Lithograph (1860), with indications of damages and some repaint by the restorer E. Le Roy, Brussels (see *Appendix IIId*). *The Hague, Mauritshuis Archives.*

tion we have does not, in general, tell us much. The X-radiograph shows old damage fairly clearly (Figs. 50 a, b). The lower part of the painting, up to about as far as the edge of the dissecting table, suffered heat and fire damage in 1723. This fairly broad strip was probably painted afresh, on a new chalk ground, in 1877 by W.A. Hopman, (Figs. 81, 82). After this paint was removed in 1951, it became clear that Slabberaen was seated on a chair and his red knee-stocking became visible too.

Heckscher has advanced the view that the *Anatomy Lesson* is based on the aesthetic theory of Franciscus Junius and that its aim is "to teach, delight and move" [71]. It is not excluded that this very general and by no means new doctrine may have penetrated to Leiden and Amsterdam via Vossius, Barlaeus and possibly Tulp as well, and that young Rembrandt had heard of it. It is accordingly regrettable that Heckscher should have stressed that the artist had consciously sought to give expression to Junius's ideas without indicating, except in one instance, where Rembrandt has applied them. Generally speaking, Junius's views did not penetrate the world of North Netherlandish art until later [72].

Finally, the question as to the extent to which this *Anatomy Lesson* is a "realistic record" cannot be ignored. I.H. van Eeghen has hardly a word to say on the matter; Heckscher, on the contrary, devotes an entire chapter of his book to it and feels he can detect a demonstrable realism in a number of details, among them the hall where the demonstration took place and also the lighting. On the other hand, he points to the tradition in painting anatomy pieces according to ideas about death in the past and in Rembrandt's day, while discussing ideas underlying the scene we see in the picture—ideas which, of course, have little to do with realism [73]. Gerson and Reznicek regard this group-portrait also—or above all—as an historical piece immediately conferring a different emphasis on its realism (see note 57).

It would seem to us that there is little point in

raising the question of realism in the analysis of the *Anatomy Lesson*. In so far as one can speak at all of realism, it has mainly to do with the faces of the lecturer and the surgeons.

Seen as a whole, the painting displays a remarkable mixture of realistic observation, pictorial tradition, possible borrowing of details from, and influence by, the work of contemporaries, and, finally and most important of all, of *invention* by Rembrandt himself. It was precisely in his blending of all these elements and the use he made of them that he showed himself to be an exceptional young artist who, confronted with a traditional subject, conferred on it an entirely new form and content.

NOTES

1. The X-radiograph of this *pentimento* was also submitted to Professor A. Querido of Amsterdam, who in the past has already endeavoured to provide an explanation of the supposed anatomical inaccuracies in this painting (see *Iconography and style,* notes 37, 40, 47). He was able to agree with our findings with regard to this *pentimento* and was of the view that it could all be explained by the slightly collapsed attitude in which the corpse is lying (information by word of mouth). The sagging of the left shoulder during the course of the dissection could, he felt, explain the original sketching in of the dissected arm at a rather higher level. The faint *pentimento* showing the outline of the chest a little higher than in the finished work would tally with this.

2. Similar holes are present in the paint-film of the *Self-Portrait* in the Frick Collection in New York (Br.-G., No. 50) as is apparent from an enlargement (x 3) of part of the face (Fig. 56). This painting, too, is said to have been exposed to high temperatures in earlier days.
The photograph in the Frick Collection (New York) records relating to the restoration of this *Self-Portrait* was kindly placed at our disposal by the director.

3. During the thorough restoration carried out in 1951 by J.C. Traas, when many old layers of varnish were removed, the signature and date then visible were at first left intact. It was clear to the naked eye that these could not be the original version. This had, moreover, been known for some time of the facsimile signature in the 1935 catalogue (Cat. M. (1935), p. 277). It was only after some hesitation, therefore, that it was finally decided to remove the old layers of varnish from this signature and dating. The result was surprising: an old, almost undamaged and legible signature and date came to light, rather paler in colour, presumably touched up long before, but possibly the original version.

4. We have no ordinary photograph of the signature and date as these existed on the work in 1935 until their removal in 1951.

5. Heckscher held that he could distinguish the letters *H* and *L* in the space between the present signature and the *f*. No trace of these can be seen on the painting or on the ordinary photograph. On the infra-red photograph of 1950, which Heckscher apparently had at his disposal, however, one can indeed see two letters which, with some stretch of the imagination, can be identified as an *H* and an *L*. In fact, however, these are the letters *n* and *t* of the signature then present, as illustrated in the facsimile. Heckscher was apparently unacquainted with this facsimile or omitted to compare it with the infra-red photograph.
Referring to the facsimile of 1935, Gerson has pointed out that a few illegible "traces" are apparently present underneath the present signature. He remarks, however, that he was unable to confirm Heckscher's interpretation with the naked eye.
This is all correct, in so far as the characters *H* and *L* mentioned by Heckscher are not, as we have said, visible to the naked eye or to be seen on the ordinary photograph of the present signature, and do not even exist. However, the illegible characters in the facsimile to which Gerson refers are not the *H* and *L* as read by Heckscher but, as already explained, the still visible characters in the old, overpainted signature (see Heckscher, p. 11; Br.-G., No. 403).

6. I.H. van Eeghen, *De Gilden, Theorie en Praktijk,* Bussum 1974², p. 99.

7. I.H. van Eeghen, *ibid.,* p. 101.

8. Letter dated 14 November 1828 in the Mauritshuis Archives.

9. The correspondence appertaining to this purchase has been published in F.D.O. Obreen, *Archief voor Nederlandsche Kunstgeschiedenis,* 7, Rotterdam 1888-1890, pp. 195-244; E. van Biema, "De verhuizing van 'de Anatomische Les' naar Den Haag", *De Gids,* 14, 1896, pp. 560-564; for supplementary information see Th. H. Lunsingh Scheurleer, "Rembrandt en het Rijksmuseum", *Bulletin van het Rijksmuseum,* 4, 1956, pp. 27-41; see also A.B. de Vries, "Koninklijk Kabinet van Schilderijen", in *150 Jaar Koninklijk Kabinet van Schilderijen, Koninklijke Bibliotheek, Koninklijk Penningkabinet,* The Hague 1967, pp. 55-56.

10. Heckscher, p. 112; C. Barlaeus, *Antwerpiani Poematatum Pars II, Elegiarum et Miscellaneorum Carminum,* Amsterdam 1646, p. 537. In 1691 this same epigram was displayed in gold letters in the anatomy theatre in the *Nieuwe Waag,* although without the two lines quoted, referring to Dr. Tulp. These lines were no longer topical and were replaced by two lines from another of Barlaeus's poems from the same volume (*In mensam Anatomicam,* p. 207; see also Thijssen, p. 18).

11. It cannot be excluded that Barlaeus's lines on Dr. Tulp were inspired by his image of Rembrandt's *Anatomy Lesson.* It would, after all, be strange if Barlaeus had never seen this painting between 1632 and 1639, since as we know from what Monnikhoff tells us, that it was added to the other paintings in the Surgeons' Guild Room in 1632 (see note 15).

12. It is to be regretted that in his Appendix II B Heckscher did not follow Orlers' description of the anatomical theatre in Leiden by the 17th century descriptions of the anatomical theatre in Amsterdam, such as Melchior Fokkens, *Beschrijvinge Der Wijdt-vermaarde Koop-Stadt Amstelredam,* Amsterdam 1662², p. 161, pp. 240-241; O. D[apper], *Historische Beschryving der Stadt Amsterdam...,* Amsterdam 1663, p. 450; T. van Domselaer, *Beschrijvinge van Amsterdam* 4 (by Isaac Commelin), Amsterdam 1665, p. 197, p. 201.

13. Caspar Commelin, *Beschryvinge der Stadt Amsterdam...,* Amsterdam 1693, p. 651 (published after Commelin's death).

14. It is difficult to deduce with certainty from Commelin's description of the Surgeons' Guild Room whether he is referring to the new situation after the reconstruction work of 1690. He was not, apparently, familiar with the names of the surgeons portrayed, or else these had become illegible. He was in any case mistaken in describing them as the "wardens in office". Only two of the seven surgeons were wardens in the administrative year September 1631 - September 1632, whereas the eight surgeons in the painting of 1656 were indeed wardens or had their names on the nomination list for such appointment for the years September 1655 - September 1656 and September 1656 - September 1657 (See also note 15). The description of the Surgeons' Guild Room very closely resembles that given by his father Isaac (see note 12).

15. Johannes Monnikhoff, *Aanteekeningen op Privilegiën, Willekeuren en Ordonnantiën, betreffende het Collegium Chirurgicum Amstelaedamense,* Amsterdam 1736. To this book, kept in the Amsterdam University Library, is added *inter alia* a handwritten *Na-reeden en Naamen der Overmannen van het Chirurgijns Gilde binnen Amsterdam, volgens de Tijd en ordere van hun bestier met derzelver nominatie, zedert het Jaar 1596.*
Monnikhoff (1707-1787) was admitted as a master-surgeon in 1730 and in 1752 became Amsterdam's official *"stadsbreukmeester"* (hernia surgeon). In his *Na-reeden* Monnikhoff mentions as his source the *Groot Memoriaal Gildeboek,* which has unfortunately been lost. For further particulars of the lives of the surgeons portrayed, see I.H. van Eeghen, 1969, pp. 7-10.

16. Jan Wagenaar, *Amsterdam in zyne opkomst, aanwas, geschiedenissen...,* Amsterdam 1765, vol. 3, book 5, p. 385. Wagenaar was the first to mention that Frans van Loenen never became a guild official. But his statement that the two *oldest* paintings in the Guild Room were painted by Rembrandt is incorrect.

17. Z.C. von Uffenbach, *Merkwürdige Reisen durch Niedersachsen, Holland und Engelland,* 3, Ulm 1754, pp. 545-546.

18. E. Malone and J. Farington, *The literary works of Sir Joshua Reynolds,* 2, London 1819⁵, pp. 356-358: "Above stairs is another Rembrandt, of the same kind of subject; Professor Deeman standing by a dead body, which is so much foreshortened, that the hands and the feet almost touch each other: the dead man lies on his back with his feet towards the spectator. There is something sublime in the character of the head, which reminds one of Michael Angelo; the whole is finely painted, the colouring much like Titian" (Fig. 59). It is stated, incorrectly, that the painting is dated *1672.*

19. Thijssen (1881); Nuyens (1928); Heckscher (1958); R.H. Fuchs, *Rembrandt en Amsterdam,* Rotterdam 1968, pp. 25-31; and in particular I.H. van Eeghen (1969).

20. J.J. Orlers, *Beschryvinge der Stad Leyden* 1641², p. 375: "Dewijle dat zijne Konst ende arbeyt de Borgeren ende Innewoonderen van Amsterdamme ten hoochsten behaechde ende aengenaem was ende dat hy veeltijden versocht werde omme 'tzy Conterfeytselen ofte ander Stucken aldaer te maecken zoo heeft hy goet ghevonden hem van Leyden te transporteren naer Amsterdamme ende is dienvolghende van hier vertrocken omtrent den Jaere 1630". It is not clear at first sight whether Rembrandt's father or Rembrandt himself is referred to in the phrase "zoo heeft hy goet gevonden" (and so he agreed) in the latter part of the final sentence. Houbraken, I, p. 256, interprets this as follows: "En dewyl hy, zoo om 't schilderen van pourtretten als andere stukken, dikwijls genoodzaakt was tot Amsterdam te komen, vond hy goed......zig met 'er woon daar na toe te begeven". We may assume that Houbraken's interpretation, *viz.,* that Rembrandt is the subject of the sentence, is correct, as we were kindly informed by H. Miedema, Amsterdam.
On 25 March 1638, the guardians of Isaac de Jouderville, an orphan and Rembrandt's pupil in the period 1630-31, made up a statement of accounts on the occasion of their ward's coming of age. According to this settlement and the six receipts from Rembrandt which have been preserved, the artist received 50 florins from the guardians on 1 May and 15 November 1630 and on 1 May, 1 August and 19 November 1631 25, 25 and 50 florins respectively.
The receipt in which Rembrandt declares he had received 200 florins since the death of Isaac's mother, in December 1629, (adding up all the sums received once again) has also been preserved. All the receipts but for the first one, dated 1 May 1630, have been signed *"Rembrant Harmensz van Ryn".* Isaac enrolled as a student at Leiden University on 26 April 1632. He married Maria le Fevre (whose family

had first emigrated from Antwerp to Amsterdam) in Leiden on 4 March 1636. The couple settled in this town. The items referring to Isaac's journeys to Amsterdam are most likely concerned with his family affairs and not directly with Rembrandt. See A. Bredius, Künstler-Inventare, 6, The Hague, 1919, pp. 1947-1949, 1951-1956 and 1962; J.G.C.A. Briels, *De Zuidnederlandse immigratie in Amsterdam en Haarlem omstreeks 1572-1630,* Utrecht, 1976, p. 111.

21. H.d.G., *Urkunden,* pp. 19-21, nos. 19, 20 and 25: nos. 19 and 25 relate to a *tontine, viz.,* a sort of mutual savings bank insurance, which 100 persons, Rembrandt included, had taken out on their lives. Since Rembrandt was no longer living in Leiden, a check had to be made in Amsterdam to see if he were still alive. See also: A. Bredius, *Künstler-Inventare* 5, The Hague, 1918, pp. 1685-1686; S.A.C. Dudok van Heel, "Claes Moyaert en zijn familie", *Jaarboek Amstelodamum,* 68, 1976, p. 28.

22. E. Schlumberger, in "Rembrandt célèbre à vingt-six ans", *Connaissance des Arts,* Dec. 1976, p. 106, wrote that each of the surgeons paid 100 florins for his portrait and Tulp 300. Later, it appeared that this information was based on a misunderstanding. The archives contain no mention of any sums of money.
According to I.H. van Eeghen (1969, pp. 1-11), the fact that surgeons who were not wardens were portrayed in Rembrandt's *Anatomy Lesson* can be explained by the circumstance that the other board members had already appeared in the earlier anatomy pieces. According to Monnikhoff, the paintings done by Aert Pietersz. (1603) and Nicolaes Eliasz., called Pickenoy, (1625) were commissioned by the guild, the wardens and the oldest members of the guild. (See also Thijssen, p. 19; Nuyens, p. 57.)

23. Nuyens, pp. 48-49; the Habsburg Court used the Julian calendar, so the actual date of the prerogative was 13 March 1556. The illustrated books will be a reference, *inter alia,* to the works of Vesalius (Andries van Wezel, 1514/15-1564), private physician to the Emperor Charles V in 1543 and from 1555 on to his son King Philip II. The *Epitome,* the abbreviated version of *De Humani Corporis fabrica Libri septem,* was dedicated to young Prince Philip on 13 August 1542.

24. I.H. van Eeghen, *Inventarissen der archieven van de gilden en van het brouwers-college,* Amsterdam 1951, No. 229; Thijssen, pp. 33-35; Nuyens, pp. 55-56. The additions below the articles are of later date (I.H. van Eeghen, *ibid.* 1951, No. 230).
See also, for example, the exhibition cat. *Leidse Universiteit 400,* Amsterdam (Rijksmuseum), 1975, B 12 - B 17.
Professor Pauw also used both human beings and animals for his dissections. See Nuyens, p. 64, regarding a resolution dated 25 February 1631, which mentions the presence of sons of the guild's officials while their fathers performed dissections on corpses in the presence of the prelector.

25. N.P. Tulp, *Observationum Medicarum Libri Tres,* Amsterdam 1641; Thijssen, Chapters II and IV; A. Querido, "Nicolaas Tulp en zijn manuscript", *Spiegel Historiael,* 5, 1970, pp. 304-311. Dr. Tulp performed autopsies on the corpses of various well-known citizens of Amsterdam, who are mentioned by name. Among them was the little daughter of the painter Nicolaes Eliasz., called Pickenoy, and also the wife of the painter Govaert Flinck. Doctors and surgeons in the hospital had also long been allowed to perform autopsies to ascertain the cause of death. These dissections were performed in the "Anatomihuysken, in 't welcke gestorve lichamen (wegens vreemde toevallige ziekten) veelmaals geopent werden, om anderen in toekomende daarvan te genezen" - see G. Hellinga, "De beteekenis van het Amsterdamsche St. Pietersgasthuis voor het ontleedkundige onderwijs in ons land, in vroeger tijden", *Bijdragen tot de geschiedenis der geneeskunde,* 13, 1933, pp. 158, 160, and note 1, referring the reader to T. van Domselaer, *Beschrijvinge van Amsterdam,* 4, Amsterdam, 1665, p. 114. So in Amsterdam a great deal of medical research was performed by way of autopsies. Thijssen even points out (p. 27) that in the 17th century fewer objections were raised to the dissection of corpses than in our very enlightened century. This was in 1881! It does not accordingly appear correct to state that only the bodies of executed criminals might be dissected.

26. Thijssen, p. 107.

27. Vopiscus Fortunatus Plempius, *De fundamentis Medicinae libri sex,* Louvain 1638, p. 218; J. Banga, *Geschiedenis van de geneeskunde en van hare beoefenaren in Nederland,* Leeuwarden 1868, p. 234; Thijssen, pp. 48-49, quoting from the 3rd edition of Dr. Plemp's book, 1654. Also described by Dr. Tulp himself in his book *Observationum...* (see note 25). Dr. Plemp studied at Leiden in 1621, left for Padua in 1622 and obtained his title in Bologna in 1624. Thereafter he was a physician in Amsterdam from 1624 to 1633. In 1630 he published *Verhandelingh der Spieren...,* Amsterdam 1630. In this text-book, dedicated to Tulp, the muscles of the hand are also treated in connection with lateral wounds which involve the loss of movement in hand and fingers. See also J. van Beverwyck, *Alle de Wercken, Soo in de Medecyne als Chirurgye.* 2, Utrecht 1651, Chapter II, fol. 48-49. Plemp, who would probably also have liked to have been considered for the post of prelector, appears to have attended the public anatomy lesson of 1632. He does not, however, say a word about the dissection of the arm during these lectures (Thijssen, pp. 48-49). It is possible that the subject of the anatomical lesson of 1632 was a reaction to Plemp's publication. In 1634 Plemp, a Roman Catholic, was appointed professor in practical medicine at the University of Louvain, being the first to hold this post.

28. Tulp described this "*darmclap*" (intestinal valve) exhaustively in his book (see note 25). In doing so, he was at variance with Professor Pauw, who denied the existence of this valve (*valvula*); Thijssen, pp. 45-48.

29. I.H. van Eeghen, 1969, pp. 5-6.

30. Heckscher, pp. 188, 190 (information from I.H. van Eeghen).

31. Heckscher, p. 70, ill. 11b.

32. Monnikhoff (c. 1750) and Wagenaar (1765) mention the surgeons in the same order as they appear on this page (see *Historical data*); these names were also recorded by Reynolds when he saw the painting in 1781 (see *Historical data*). According to I.H. van Eeghen, the handwriting is 17th century, but we would not exclude the possibility of a first half of the 18th century dating (1732?).

33. I.H. van Eeghen, 1969, pp. 7-10. The author gives a good account of the functions and the social standing of the surgeons portrayed.

34. Thijssen, pp. 1-4; Nuyens, p. 64; A. Querido, "Nicolaes Tulp en zijn manuscript", *Spiegel Historiael,* 5, 1970, pp. 304-311.

35. M.M. Tóth-Ubbens, "De barbier van Amsterdam", *Antiek,* 10, 1975, pp. 381-411.

36. Thijssen, p. 51, was the first to identify the corpse as that of Adriaan Adriaansz.; many other followed suit. See also Heckscher, p. 115.

37. A. Querido, "De Anatomie van de Anatomische Les", *Oud Holland,* 82, 1967, p. 130.

38. A. Vesalius, *De Humani Corporis Fabrica. Libri septem.* Basle 1555. See W. Hastie, Rembrandt's Lesson in Anatomy, *Contemporary Review,* 60, 1891, p. 276. This author seems to be the first to assume that the open folio volume was meant to be Vesalius's book (information kindly provided by William Schupbach, London); Hans Jantzen in "Rembrandt, Tulp und Vesal", *Kunst und Künstler,* 24, 1926, p. 314.

39. Heckscher, p. 67.

40. C.E. Kellett, review of W.S. Heckscher, "Rembrandt's Anatomy of Dr. Nicolaas Tulp", in *Burlington Magazine,* 101, 1959, p. 152; A. Querido, "De Anatomie van de Anatomische Les", *Oud Holland,* 82, 1967, pp. 135-136; Adriaen van den Spieghel, *De Humani Corporis fabrica. Libri Decem,* Venice 1627.

41. Heckscher, p. 41.

42. Heckscher, p. 67. Here, as elsewhere, the author stands by the realism of the representation which in other cases he rightly ignores.

43. See Dr. John Bulwer, *Chirologia or the Naturall language of the Hand,* London 1644, Canon IV, p. 95, Fig. 6B. It seems to be very likely that *Quibusdem* is a misprint and should be read as *Quibusdam.* Professor A.G.H. Bachrach kindly gave this information. See also Heckscher, p. 40 and note 47, where he expresses the less convincing opinion that the gesture is based on Franciscus Junius; A. Querido, "De Anatomie van de Anatomische Les", *Oud Holland,* 82, 1967, p. 136.

44. This woodcut was included in the editions of the *Fabrica* dated 1543 and 1555. Heckscher, p. 73; G.A. Lindeboom, *Andreas Vesalius and his opus magnum, a biographical sketch and an introduction to the Fabrica,* Nieuwendijk, 1975, p. 13.

45. Heckscher, pp. 65-76; H. Jantzen, see note 38; H. Schrade, "Rembrandts 'Anatomie des Dr. Tulp' ", *Das Werk des Künstlers,* 1, 1939-1940, p. 88. One should not overlook Pieter Pauw's edition of *A. Vesalii Epitome Anatomiça,* Leiden 1616 (in 4°), subtitled *Opus redivivum...*

46. Heckscher, pp. 40, 118-120. The conch motif was already in use in the days of classical antiquity. In early Christian art a conch was sometimes placed behind the head of a scholar or philosopher. The motif is also encountered during the Renaissance in scenes with biblical figures such as the Virgin Mary and John the Baptist.
The shell motif also occurs in the portraits of an unidentified married couple (1518) by C. Engelbrechtsz., Brussels, Musées Royaux des Beaux-Arts, Nos. 570 and 571.
It is quite possible that Rembrandt borrowed the shell motif behind Dr. Tulp's head from Rubens. The motif is frequently found in the latter's work; e.g. in *The Tribute Money* (Fig. 76). See also E.K.J. Reznicek, "Opmerkingen bij Rembrandt. De anatomische les van Dr. Tulp", *Oud Holland,* 91, 1977, pp. 86-87). This shell also occurs in Rubens's painting *Justus Lipsius and his pupils* in the Palazzo Pitti in Florence (c. 1610); in this work a bust, formerly said to be of Seneca, is seen standing in a niche with a shell, behind Lipsius. The portrait of Philips Rubens, elder brother of the artist, a town clerk and humanist († 1611), engraved after Rubens by Cornelis Galle (1615), also has a shell in a niche. See F. Baudouin, *P.P. Rubens,* Antwerp 1977, ill. 236 and 5.

47. J.G. de Lint, *Rembrandt,* The Hague 1930, pp. 44-46; Heckscher, pp. 66-67; C.E. Kellett, review of W.S. Heckscher, Rembrandt's Anatomy of Dr. Nicolaas Tulp, in *Burlington Magazine,* 101, 1959, p. 152; G. Wolf-Heidegger and A.M. Cetto, *Die Anatomische Sektion in bildlicher Darstellung,* Basle 1967, pp. 308-310; A. Querido, "De Anatomie van de Anatomische Les", *Oud Holland,* 82, 1967, pp. 130-136; *Nederlands Tijdschrift voor Geneeskunde,* 119, 1975, pp. 1561-1566 (J.A. Los), pp. 1867-1868 (J. Smeulers), pp. 1868-1869 (J.A. Los), pp. 1869-1870 (G.A. Lindeboom) and 120, 1976, pp. 71-73 (G.A. Lindeboom); M.P. Carpentier Alting and Tj. W. Waterbolk, "Nieuw licht op de ontleedkundige fouten in Rembrandt's 'Anatomische Les van Dr. Nicolaas Tulp' ", *ibid.* 120, 1976, pp. 1900-1902.

48. *Inter alia:* G. Wolf-Heidegger and A.M. Cetto, *Die Anatomische Sektion in bildlicher Darstellung,* Basle 1967, pp. 308-310.

49. *Inter alia:* Heckscher, p. 67.

50. A. Querido, "De Anatomie van de Anatomische Les", *Oud Holland,* 82, 1967, pp. 130-136.

51. M.P. Carpentier Alting en Tj. W. Waterbolk, "Nieuw licht op de ontleedkundige fouten in Rembrandt's 'Anatomische Les van Dr. Nicolaas Tulp' ", *Nederlands Tijdschrift voor Geneeskunde,* 120, 1976, pp. 1900-1902; we do not consider their argument that "in view of the colours it seems impossible that Rembrandt copied the anatomy from a black-and-white illustration" is tenable.

52. A guild order of 1597 laid down that questions to be asked at the masters examination had to be hung up on display each year in the Guild Room (Nuyens, p. 54). Heckscher, p. 11, assumes that this document may possibly bear the announcement of the public anatomy lesson of 1632.

53. H. Schrade, "Rembrandts 'Anatomie des Dr. Tulp' ", *Das Werk des Künstlers,* 1, 1939-1940, pp. 60-100.

54. Heckscher, p. 120.

55. Exh. cat. "*The Orange and the Rose*", London (Victoria and Albert Museum), 1964, p. 14 and cat. no. 58.

56. E.K.J. Reznicek, "Opmerkingen bij Rembrandt. De Anatomische les van Dr. Tulp", *Oud Holland,* 91, 1977, p. 87, note 27. The author and the secretary of the board of editors of *Oud Holland* provided us kindly with a proof of this article prior to its publication. See also W. Hastie (note 38), pp. 274-275.

57. See Br.-G., no. 403 and the literature quoted there; E.K.J. Reznicek, "Opmerkingen bij Rembrandt. De Anatomische Les van Dr. Tulp", *Oud Holland,* 91, 1977, p. 83.

58. There does not seem to be sufficient reason to speak of two phases in the painting of the *Anatomy Lesson* (E.K.J. Reznicek, "Opmerkingen bij Rembrandt. De Anatomische Les van Dr. Tulp", *Oud Holland,* 91, 1977, pp. 84-86). There are, it is true, several *pentimenti* (see *Technical data*), but these more likely indicate alterations made while the work was in progress. The figure of Colevelt must, indeed, be seen as an addition by another hand.

59. For example, see B. Haak, Exh. cat. "*Regenten en Regentessen, Overlieden en Chirurgijns*", Amsterdam (Historisch Museum) 1972, ill. 21, 22, 30, 31 and 50: also published in *Antiek,* 7, 1972, pp. 81-116, 287-302.

60. A. Riegl, *Das holländische Gruppenporträt* (editor Ludwig Münz), 2 vol., Vienna 1931, vol. 1, p. 182; Heckscher, pp. 22, 26.

61. H. van de Waal, "The Syndics and their Legend" in *Steps towards Rembrandt,* Amsterdam 1974, pp. 254-256.

62. A. Riegl, *ibid.,* p. 185.

63. Contrary to Heckscher, who accepts that the room shown is a faithful depiction of the dissecting chamber in the *Nieuwe Waag,* we believe that this room should be taken as imaginary (see Heckscher, p. 14).

64. Heckscher, p. 37 and ill. IX-12.

65. H. van de Waal, "Rembrandt and Chiaroscuro" in *Steps towards Rembrandt,* Amsterdam 1974, pp. 13-18.

66. A. Jordan, in "Bemerkungen zu einigen Bildern Rembrandts", *Repertorium für Kunstwissenschaft,* 7, 1884, pp. 185-186, was the first to express the view that Colevelt and Van Loenen may not have formed part of the original composition. This article came to our knowledge only after the 1951 restoration by J.C. Traas.

67. The technical data show that it is incorrect to suppose that Van Loenen did not form part of the original composition, as Heckscher, among others, thinks (Heckscher, pp. 18, 40 and note 48, ills. I-Ic).

68. E.K.J. Reznicek, "Opmerkingen bij Rembrandt. De Anatomische les van Dr. Tulp", *Oud Holland,* 91, 1977, pp. 80-88.

69. E.K.J. Reznicek, *ibid.,* fig. 9.

70. Heckscher, pp. 17 and 36. Reference to this correspondence has been made before: W. Drost, *Barockmalerei in den germanischen Ländern,* Potsdam 1926, pp. 106-107, ills. 86, 87; H. Schrade, "Rembrandts 'Anatomie des Dr. Tulp' ", *Das Werk des Künstlers,* 1, 1939-1940, p. 85; A. Heppner in "Brouwer's influence upon Rembrandt", *The Art Quarterly,* 4, 1941, p. 42, denies this possible relationship most emphatically. We are of the view that Heppner is too categorical here: what was involved, after all, was a compositional idea.

71. Heckscher, p. 4; see also Judson, p. 306.

72. J.A. Emmens, *Rembrandt en de regels van de kunst,* Utrecht 1968, pp. 55-57, 150. Emmens, too, felt it was unlikely that Franciscus Junius's book could have had any influence on the *Anatomy Lesson.* H. Miedema shares this opinion, as we were informed by word of mouth.

73. Heckscher, pp. 37, 67 and 97.

VII

Self-Portrait in a Plumed Hat TECHNICAL DATA

Plate IX; Fig. 84

Panel, 62.9 x 46.8 cm. Signed *Rembrandt.f.;* 1636-37.

Cat. Br. (1895), No. 149; Valentiner, p. 146; H.d.G., No. 545; Cat. M. (1935), No. 149; Br., No. 24; Bauch, No. 311 (not as a self-portrait); G., No. 189 (not as a self-portrait); Br.-G., No. 24; Cat. H. (1977), No. 149.

84. Self-Portrait in a Plumed Hat.

The panel has been bevelled on all four sides. A crack runs down the oak panel from top to bottom and approximately in the middle. It has been repaired with a glue containing white lead with the result that important details are not visible in the X-radiograph. The X-ray photograph corresponds with the surface view of the picture, where comparison proved possible (Fig. 85).

Examination using ultra-violet radiation and by means of infra-red photography revealed no special information. An infra-red reflectogram showed more details in the hat (Fig. 86).

The paint of the background is thin and smooth and almost devoid of *craquelure*; in many places the texture of the wood is visible through the paint-film. The paint is thicker in the light areas of the face and the coat; here, too, there are but few cracks. In the darker parts of the head—in the blackish-brown of the hair and hat—on the other hand, we find pronounced *craquelure* with very wide and irregular cracks in various places; these, however, are lacking in the dark areas of the eyes.

The ground consists of chalk, and some white lead was also found, which may have come from an apparently thin intermediate layer in white lead in some places, or from a layer containing white lead. In the darker areas, such as the eyes and hat, the white lead underpainting is absent.

There is a blackish-brown underpaint, consisting of Cologne earth, bone black and brown ochre, under the light areas of the face and collar. The flesh colour is composed of white lead mixed with a little red and yellow ochre and partly glazed with a crimson-coloured lake pigment. The yellow of the ornamentation on the collar consists partly of yellow ochre but the bright yellow pigment which is also present appears to be lead-tin yellow. The earring has been painted in this old colour too. The brownish-black of the hair and hat is made up principally of Cologne earth and ochres. Lighter touches have been painted in over this dark paint in yellow and brown

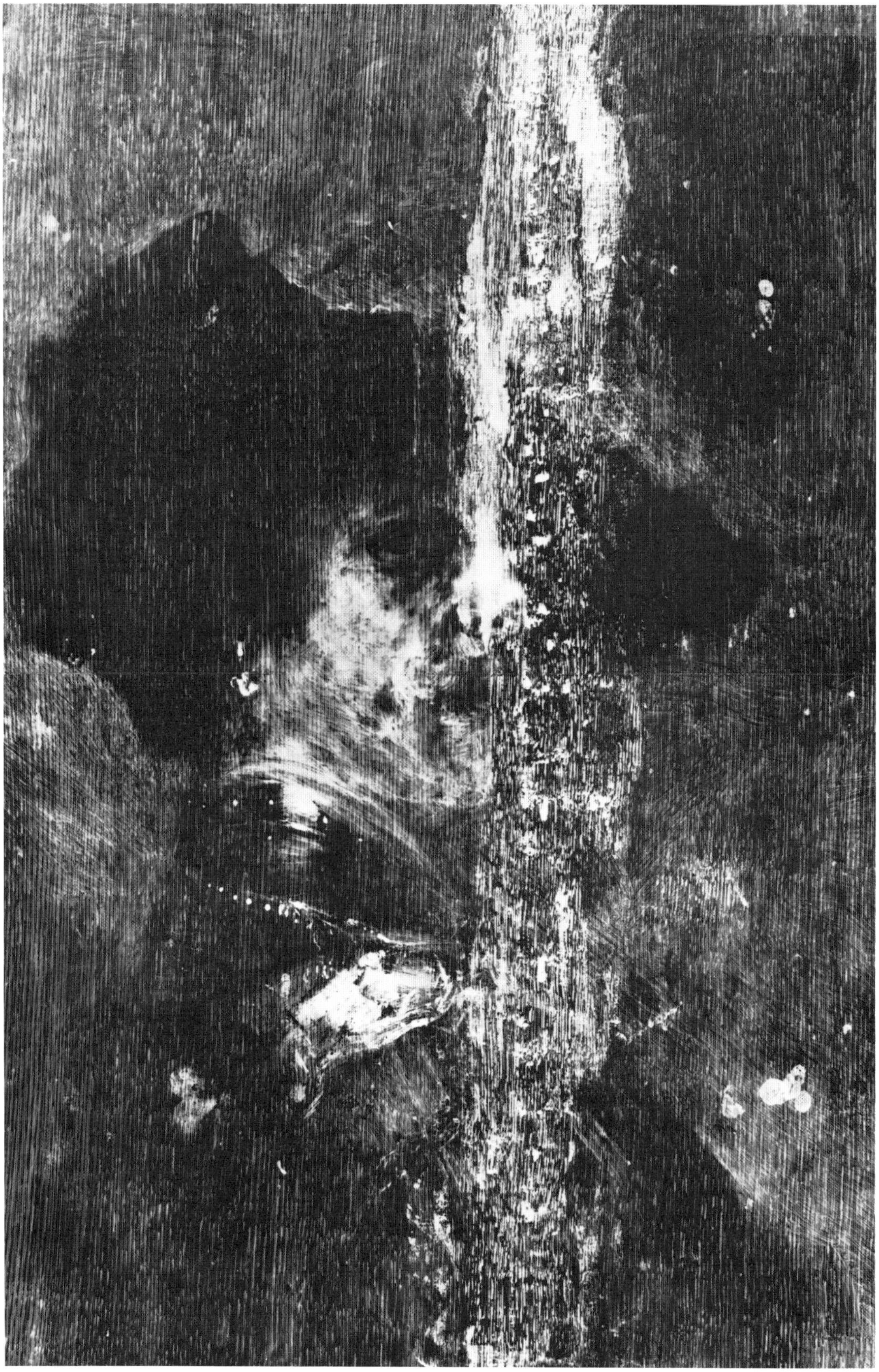

85. X-ray photograph.

86. Infra-red reflectogram.

ochre. Yellow and red ochre were found in the background, mixed with bone black and white lead. In the white lead of the collar and neckcloth, the trace elements copper, silver and tin, were found.

The signature *Rembrandt.f.* has been painted in dark grey; some letters have more relief than is usually found in Rembrandt's signatures (Fig. 87). The paint in this signature is of the same structure

87. Signature.

as that of the top layer of the picture itself and has been applied with a certain dash. Examination produced no evidence to cast doubt on its authenticity. That is to say, in so far as one can speak with assurance here (see *Introduction*).

HISTORICAL DATA

This *Self-portrait* comes from the collection of Mr. Govert van Slingelandt, Seigneur of De Lindt and West-IJselmonde (1694-1767) at The Hague (see also Nos. I and VIII). In 1752 the painting was described by Gerard Hoet as follows: "Een Mans Kop levens grooten, door *Rembrant van Ryn,* H. 1 v. 11 d., br. 1 v. 6 d." [1]

Pieter Terwesten, in describing Stadhouder William V's collection did not identify the subject either, as a self-portrait by Rembrandt: "Een Mans Pourtrait, levens groote, zynde een Borst-stuk, ongemeen schoon, kragtig en natuurlijk geschildert, door DENZELVEN [= Rembrandt van Rijn]; op *paneel,* 1 (V) 11 (D) 1 (V) 6 (D)" [2].

Sir Joshua Reynolds (1723-1792) made a commendatory, if brief entry in his travel diary, after visiting William V's collection in The Hague in 1781: "A portrait of a young man by Rembrandt, dressed in a black cap and feathers, the upper part of the face overshadowed: for colouring and force nothing can exceed it" [3].

This painting was also carried off to Paris in 1795, returning to The Hague in 1815 [4]. In 1816 the collection was transferred to the State's keeping and from 1822 was opened to the public in the former residence of Johan Maurits von Nassau-Siegen (1604-1679), known after him as the "Mauritshuis" (see also Nos. I, V and VIII).

Collections

Mr. G. van Slingelandt, The Hague, 1752-1768
Stadhouder William V, The Hague, 1768-1795
The Louvre, Paris, 1795-1815
King William I, The Hague, 1815
Royal Collection of Paintings, The Hague, 1816
"The Mauritshuis"—Royal Collection of Paintings, The Hague, 1822

Dimensions quoted

1752 1 ft. 11 in x 1 ft. 6 in = approx. 57.5 x 45 cm
1770 1 ft. 11 in x 1 ft. 6 in = approx. 57.5 x 45 cm
1874 62.5 x 47 cm
1977 62.9 x 46.8 cm

Head and shoulders portrait of Rembrandt, turned to the right. The painter is looking out at the spectator over his right shoulder. He is wearing a moustache and a goatee. On his head is a hat with a scalloped brim and three ostrich feathers. He has an earring in his right ear, and is dressed in a cloak with a bandolier. He has an iron ring-collar round his neck, and a neckcloth hangs out of it (Fig. 84).

During the 18th century this painting was described as a "Man's Head" and a "Man's Portrait" (see *Historical data*) and during the 19th as "A man's portrait. This portrait represents a warrior, having a cap with black plumes..." [5]. It was not until De Stuers compiled his catalogue in 1874 that it was called a "Portrait of Rembrandt van Rijn as an officer" [6]. After this it was for many years accepted as being a self-portrait, until Glück expressed doubts on the matter in 1933—in our view erroneously. Bauch and Gerson share Glück's opinion [7].

The set of the eyes, the glance and the facial expression as a whole, however, argue in favour of identification as a self-portrait.

The question does, however, remain whether this panel should be regarded as a self-portrait in the strictest sense of the word or whether it is also open to another interpretation. Has Rembrandt dressed himself up as an officer or nobleman here? None of the accessories (hauberk, bandolier, plumed hat, earring(s)) would contradict such a view.

It is striking that Rembrandt used a feathered hat repeatedly and in a variety of forms [8]. We may accordingly assume that there was a hat of this kind amongst the accessories in his studio. Head gear of this sort was normal stage property as well. In the *commedia dell'arte* we find the character known as the *Capitano* or *Amoroso* wearing the same kind of hat. A little later on, the *Amant* in the "*Troupe Royale*" is similarly attired. There is a character dressed in this fashion in Jan Steen's *Garden Party* of 1677 too and in his book *The Comedians in the Work of Jan Steen* S.J. Gudlaugsson identified him as a *Capitano* [9]. This makes it all the more understandable that in his double portrait known as *Rembrandt with Saskia,* or *The Prodigal Son in the Tavern* (c. 1636; Br.-G., No. 30), Rembrandt should be wearing a similarly ostentatious hat and simultaneously acting the amorous cavalier and the prodigal son with great verve [10].

Although the manner in which he is attired in this self-portrait might prompt us to identify Rembrandt with the *Capitano* or *Amoroso* in the *commedia dell'arte,* it should nevertheless be stressed that such an identification is not borne out either by his actual dress or by the serious expression on his face. There is a clear distinction in this respect between this work and the above mentioned painting of c. 1636 in Dresden. Whether a self-portrait or not, *The Standard-Bearer* (c. 1636; Br.-G., No. 433), in which the character portrayed is not only shown dressed in a kind of Burgundian costume but is also wearing a sword, is a more suitable candidate for identification as a Captain or Nobleman than is this Hague self-portrait.

88. J.P. de Frey. Etching. 1795.

The panel is signed but not dated. The brushwork is fluent and sure of touch; the play of light on the face and in the shadow of the hat on the forehead and under the eyes is subtler than in his portraits of the early Amsterdam period. In view of its affinity with the Dresden *Rembrandt and Saskia* painting already mentioned and rightly dated at c. 1636, and particularly in view of the stylistic relationship to the *Man in a Polish Costume* (1637; Br.-G., No. 211) [11], this work must have been painted about 1637, thus somewhat later than the date quoted since 1935 in the Mauritshuis catalogues.

It has already been observed that during the first half of the sixteen-thirties Rembrandt must have had frequent occasion to see works by and after Rubens and in many a respect sought to compete with him [12].

We feel there is a certain affinity with Rubens in this self-portrait and that this is especially evident in the sure and convincing brushwork, the flesh tones, and also in the firmness of form, which compete with the great Flemish painter's exceptional qualities. It is, however, noticeable that those features which appear completely natural in Rubens's mature works, that is to say, the panache of the nobleman, the extravert manner and the inquiring eyes, tend in Rembrandt's case to come across as deliberate, so that we may even speak of self-assurance [13]. In this self-portrait we are made aware of a rather probing and almost haughty glance.

Two prints should be mentioned in connection with this self-portrait: an etching by Joh. P. de Frey (1760-1834), dated 1795, after this painting (Fig. 88) and an engraving made by Fr. Rosaspina (1762-1842) after a drawing by Jean-Honoré Fragonard (1732-1806), based on the painting [14].

Many copies of this work are known: Holburne of Menstrie Museum of Art, Bath, probably painted by Thomas Barker of Bath (1769-1847) (canvas, 57 x 44,5 cm); Mischel Collection, Elberfeld (in 1901); Art market (Vollmüller), Coblenz (1950), formerly in the Fr. Lauffs Collection, Bonn (canvas, 55.5 x 44 cm, signed and dated *Rembrandt ft. 1635*; judging by the photograph, a 19th century copy); Russel Hartley collection, San Francisco; Nationalmuseum, Stockholm, No. 346.

NOTES

1. Hoet, II, p. 404.

2. Terwesten, 709. This description tallies in the main with that in the catalogue compiled by F. ten Dall "uit de Aantekeningen van den Overleden Heer Directeur T.P.C. Haag" and published in Drossaers-Scheurleer, III, pp. 202-242; see also "Self-portrait as a Young Man" (No. I, note 10).

3. The original manuscript is in the collection of the Custodia Foundation at the Netherlands Institute, Paris. E. Malone and J. Farington, *The Literary Works of Sir Joshua Reynolds* 2, London, 1819[5], p. 346; E. Malone, *Joshua Reynolds, The Works,* Hildesheim, 1971 (reprint of the London 1797 edition, p. 69). See also W.R. Juynboll, "De reis van Sir Joshua Reynolds in de Nederlanden", *Varia historica aangeboden aan Prof. Dr. A.W. Byvanck,* Assen, 1954, pp. 177-185.

4. No. 131 in General Pommereul's list (see Scheurleer, p. 32 and note 76).

5. J. Steengracht van Oost-Capelle, *De Voornaamste schilderijen van het Koninklijk Kabinet te 's Gravenhage,* The Hague, 1826-1830, No. 26.

6. V. de Stuers, *Notice historique et descriptive des tableaux et des sculptures exposés dans le Musée Royal de La Haye,* The Hague, 1874, p. 124, No. 118.

7. G. Glück, "Rembrandts Selbstbildnis aus dem Jahre 1652", *Aus drei Jahrhunderten Europäischer Malerei,* Vienna, 1933, p. 296; Bauch, No. 311 and p. 16; G., No. 139.

8. See *inter alia:* Br.-G., Nos. 23, 30, 81 and 433.

9. S.J. Gudlaugsson, *The Comedians in the Work of Jan Steen and his Contemporaries,* Soest, 1975 (English edition of the original Dutch version, The Hague, 1945, pp. 44-46, ills. 38 and 42). Regarding the suitor's dress, Gudlaugsson writes (p. 44) that this costume evokes associations which are to be found both in Rembrandt's self-portaits and in the romantic costumes worn by members of the Orders of Knighthood of the time. See also H. Kindermann, *Theatergeschichte Europas,* 3, Salzburg, 1959, p. 348; and 4, 1961, p. 68; exh. cat. *Jan Steen,* The Hague (Mauritshuis), 1958-1959, cat. No. 58 with illustration.

10. Exh. cat. *De schilder en zijn wereld,* Delft (Het Prinsenhof), 1964-1965, No. 95; I. Bergström, "Rembrandt's Double-Portrait of himself and Saskia at the Dresden Gallery. A Tradition Transformed", *Nederlands Kunsthistorisch Jaarboek* 17, 1966, pp. 143-169; C. Tümpel, "Ikonographische Beiträge zu Rembrandt. Zur Deutung und Interpretation seiner Historien", *Jahrbuch der Hamburger Kunstsammlungen,* 13, 1968, pp. 95-126 (Tümpel's opinion that "Rembrandt differentiates between history and portrait", p. 123, cannot be shared in all instances); see also A. Mayer-Meintschel, "Rembrandt und Saskia im Gleichnis vom Verlorenen Sohn", *Jahrbuch Staatliche Kunstsammlungen Dresden,* 1970-71, pp. 39-57.

11. Regarding the self-portrait in The Hague, see also F. Erpel, *Die Selbstbildnisse Rembrandts,* Vienna, 1967, p. 166, Cat. No. 62, ill. 31; Erpel puts the painting's date at c. 1636; B.P.J. Broos in "Rembrandt's portrait of a Pole and his horse", *Simiolus,* 7, 1974, p. 210, ill. 19, identifies this Pole as Andrzej Rej, governor of Libusza, who was in Amsterdam in 1637.

12. H.K. Gerson, "Rembrandt and the Flemish Baroque: His Dialogue with Rubens", *Delta* 12, 1969, pp. 7-23; H.K. Gerson, "Rembrandt en Rubens", *Handelingen van het 31ste Nederlandse Philologencongres 1970,* Groningen, 1971, pp. 24-32.

13. Compare Rubens's self-portrait (Windsor Castle, 1622-23). See Frans Baudouin, *P.P. Rubens,* Antwerp, 1977, pp. 215 and 326, ill. 170.

14. See H.d.G., No. 545.

89. Bathsheba

VIII

Bathsheba

TECHNICAL DATA

Plate X; Fig. 89

Panel, 47.2 x 38.6 cm. Signed and dated *Rembrant f.f. 1636.*

Cat. Br. (1895), No. 147; Valentiner, p. 180; H.d.G., No. 57; Cat. M. (1935), No. 147; Br., No. 505; Bauch, No. 18; G., No. 84; Br.-G., No. 505; Cat. H. (1977), No. 147.

A strip of oak wood, 4 cm wide, has been added to the oak panel down the right-hand side. The join is visible here and there in the paint. A piece of linen has been attached to the reverse side in this place with a paste containing white lead. This was temporarily removed when the X-ray photographs were taken. The additional strip of wood differs in structure from the original panel and according to J. Bauch it has come from a different tree [1]. The present dimensions of the painting correspond with those quoted in 1758 so that it is reasonable to assume that this addition had already taken place before that year.

Examination under ultra-violet light yielded no special information (Fig. 90). In the infra-red photograph (Fig. 91) and on the reflectogram especially (Fig. 92), the added strip of wood shows up as a dark band, while fairly clearly defined, dark, arc-shaped segments are visible in the left and right top corners of the original panel. This last feature indicates that the composition was originally rounded off at the top. It is, however, noticeable that these segments are not quite symmetrical; the one on the left is rather longer at the top and runs rather lower down than the one on the right. Since we may assume that they were originally equal and symmetrical, a simple reconstruction shows that when these curved sections were painted, the original panel must have been ½ to 1 cm wider on the right-hand side than it is where the join is now visible. On the reverse of the panel, along the join, one can still see the original bevelled right edge, which, compared with the bevelled left edge, has been cut down by the same ½ to 1 cm. One can only guess why the panel was cut down by more than ½ cm, and then widened with a strip of wood 4 cm broad. However, it seems plausible that before the new strip of wood was glued on, about ½ cm of the bevelled right-hand edge had first to be planed away, to achieve a better join. The examination (see below) revealed also that the added

90. Ultra-violet fluorescence photograph.

91. Infra-red photograph.

92. Infra-red reflectogram.

93. X-ray photograph.

strip differs considerably from the original panel as regards the ground and underlying paint layers.

The X-ray photograph does not indicate any noticeable changes in the original composition, yet there are a few small differences between the radiograph and the painting (Fig. 93). Thus, in the radiograph, the left breast is rather larger than in the painting but in the latter the left forearm has been made rather plumper than it was originally. In the painting, the left shoulder, which protrudes further forward in the X-ray photograph, is less pronounced. Only very little of the white garment behind the figure, painted afterwards on the added strip, is to be seen in the X-ray photograph. Unlike the original part, it has been thinly painted, with no white lead underpainting. The radiograph also creates the impression that the figure was inclined further forward than the one we see in the painting. This difference is only apparent and is due to the fact that the hair covering the upper part of the back in the painting does not show up in the X-ray photograph.

In various places in the background, the texture of the wood can be seen through the thin paint-film. In the figure of Bathsheba, the red and white garment, and the vegetation in the background, the paint has been applied rather thickly.

In most places, and in the light areas particularly, the *craquelure* consists of the normal fine network of cracks. As frequently found in layers of paint which have been applied thinly to a panel, the *craquelure* is less pronounced in the foreground and background. There are some places where the paint displays a network of "drying" cracks of the crow's foot type. This structure of cracks is found, for instance, in the shadows under the nose and in the hair on the left, under the head, and near the left hand, where the painting has been done in yellow or brown ochres over a dark reddish-brown underpaint. Hardly any differences can be observed between the *craquelure* in the paint on the original panel and that on the additional strip. In those places where the paint has not cracked along the join, the cracks run quite normally, from left to right.

The original panel possesses a chalk ground, occurring chiefly in the irregularities of the wood. Besides the chalk, in or on, the thin ground, as the case may be, a little white lead was found, which also shows up in the structure of the wood in the X-radiograph. Both at the top and the bottom edge of the panel, a thin pale brown layer—presumably the *imprimatura*—was encountered on the white ground. As has already been said, a dark reddish-brown underpainting is to be found in the areas of shadow of the figure of Bathsheba herself and the garment.

The layer-structure of the paint on the added strip is quite different from that on the original panel. Here the ground is a dark grey-brown and composed of umber, bone black, chalk and white lead. It was the last-mentioned ingredient which produced the white wood-grain structure in the radiograph [2]. On to this dark ground, a thin intermediate layer of coarse black pigment (bone black) has been applied and here and there a thin layer of a red lake pigment in addition. The presence of the thin black (carbon) layer explains the dark effect obtained in this area in both the infra-red and the ordinary photograph.

The fact that the ground and underpainting on this strip are quite different from those on the original panel, together with other technical findings, also suggests that some time elapsed between the painting of these two parts of the work. It is not, however, possible to say how long this period was. The structure of the *craquelure* and of the composition of the white lead on the old and newer sections, as far as trace elements show (see below), support the assumption that the addition was made prior to 1758 (see *Iconography and style*).

Where the dark, arc-shaped segments appear in the infra-red photographs, there is dark grey paint underneath the top paint layer, containing a quantity of carbon black and some white lead. This dark layer was not found elsewhere on the original painting and was apparently used only in the curved sections. No other layers of paint were found underneath this dark layer, apart from the ground.

Investigation into the composition of the white lead in the original painting and of that on the added strip did not reveal any differences. Traces of copper, silver and tin characteristic of old white lead were found in both. The yellow of the beads in the bracelets and necklace was identified as lead-tin yellow. The other yellow pigment in the painting proved to be yellow ochre and the red and brown pigments mainly consists of ochres and umber. Vermilion was also detected in the red parts (robe). These have been underpainted with yellow and red ochre, white lead and carbon black, and richly glazed with a red lake pigment. The flesh tones consist of a mixture of white lead, yellow and red ochre, while a red lake pigment has been applied here in the form of a thin glaze.

No green pigment was detected in the background vegetation; here the paint is composed of umber and brown and yellow ochres, containing coarse white and black grains of pigment.

Apart from the differences as regards the ground and underlayer, few differences were found in the pigments, structure and texture of the top paint layer on the original panel and those of the upper layer on the added strip, although some difference was noticeable as regards the coarseness of some of the pigments.

The signature and date (Fig. 94) are to be found at the bottom, right. The characters *R, e, m, b* and *r*

94. Signature and date.

lie entirely on the original panel, the *a, n, t* and *f* on the added strip, right of the join. Only part of the last figure in the date, read by many as a *7* but by us as a *6*, has been painted on the added strip of panelling.

The first thing to be considered in judging the signature is that the panel was, taking the join into account, originally ½ to 1 cm wider than it is now. This means that the first five characters in the signature could not have been there *before* the panel was widened, since there would have been no more room left for the other letters on the ½ to 1 cm then remaining. The entire signature must, therefore, have been added after the panel had been enlarged. Since we are unable to determine when this enlargement took place, except that it must have been before 1758, uncertainty also remains as to the signature's age. If we accept that the added strip dates from after Rembrandt's day (see below), the signature cannot be original.

These considerations do not apply to the date, which could very well have been painted in before the panel was widened. Both signature and date bear the signs of age. Thus the cracks in the top layer of the picture run through into the paint of the letters and figures. The edges especially of these letters and figures are worn away where particles of paint have been dislodged. These features do not, however, enable us to make even a rough estimate of the age of the signature and date.

HISTORICAL DATA

This panel is probably identical with the painting auctioned in Antwerp on 23 May 1758 as item No. 39 (collection of P.J. Sneijers). It was described as: "Een zeer schoon Kabinet-Stukje, verbeeldende Susanna aan de Fontein in den Hof met een Boef die door het hout ziet, door *denzelven* [Rembrandt]; hoog 18, breet 15 duimen. 157-0" [3]. Pieter Jan Sneijers (1696-1757) was a painter and art dealer of Antwerp. We know that he maintained contacts with art dealers in The Hague. His name appears in the stocklist of Willem Lormier, an art dealer in The Hague [4].

The painting next formed part of the collection of Govert van Slingelandt, which Stadhouder William V acquired *en bloc* in 1768. As a result, the number of Rembrandts in the Stadhouder's collection rose to four (see also Nos. I, V and VII).

The description given by Terwesten (1770) corresponds fairly closely with that of 1758, although it mentions more than one "scoundrel": "Een dito extra fraay Stukje, zynde Susanna, die, by 't Bad zig praepareerende om te Baden, door de [twee] Boeven bespied wordt; in alles niet minder schoon, kragtig en uitvoerig als het vorige, door DENZELVEN [Rembrandt]; op *paneel.* 1 (V) 6 (D) 1 (V) 3 (D)" [5].

Sir Joshua Reynolds noted this painting when he visited Stadhouder William's collection in 1781, recording: "A study of a Susanna, for the picture by Rembrandt, which is in my possession: it is nearly the same action, except that she is here sitting. This is the third study I have seen for this figure. I have one myself, and the third was in the possession of the late Mr. Blackwood. In the drawing which he made for this picture, which I have, she is likewise sitting; in the picture she is on her legs, but leaning forward. It appears very extraordinary that Rembrandt should have taken so much pains and have made at last so very ugly and ill-favoured a figure; but his attention was principally directed to the colouring and effect, in which it must be acknowledged he has attained the highest degree of excellence" [6].

In the catalogue compiled by F. ten Dall "from the Notes of the late *T.P.C. Haag,* former director", this painting was described as follows: "Bathseba bij het Bad, zig preparerende om te baden, op Paneel, in een dito Lijst 1 v 6 d, 1 v 3 d door *Denzelven* [= Rembrandt]" [7].

In 1795 this painting was removed to Paris with the greater part of the Stadhouder's collection. After the fall of Napoleon, in 1815, 120 items were returned to The Hague, including this work (see also I, V and VII).

Collections

P.J. Sneijers, Antwerp, 1758
Mr. G. van Slingelandt, The Hague, 1758-1768
Stadhouder William V, The Hague, 1768-1795
The Louvre, Paris, 1795-1815
King William I, The Hague, 1815
Royal Collection of Paintings, The Hague, 1816
"The Mauritshuis"—Royal Collection of Paintings, The Hague, 1822

Dimensions quoted

1758	18 in x 15 in = approx. 45 x 37.5 cm
1770	1 ft. 6 in x 1 ft. 3 in = approx. 45 x 37.5 cm
1977	47.2 x 38.6 cm

Price

1758 157 florins

ICONOGRAPHY AND STYLE

An almost completely naked young woman, with her left foot still in her one slipper and her right foot placed over the other, is preparing to bathe in a spring. Behind her, in the bushes, the profile of an old man or woman can be distinguished. In the background, a palace with a square tower and balustraded terrace. Beside the young woman, who is leaning forward, a bowl is seen on a console, with a pot of ointment in it and an ornament. Behind her lie cast-off garments (Fig. 89).

Reynolds spoke scornfully of this female nude of Rembrandt's, thereby falling into line with a century of criticism of the artist's work (see *Historical data* and note 6) [8]. Nevertheless, he himself owned 14 works attributed to Rembrandt [9].

Jonkheer Johan Steengracht van Oost-Capelle, the Mauritshuis's first director, wrote in similar vein about this work in 1827: "One searches in vain in this Susanna for the attractions with which other painters have usually endowed her; the figure is very vulgar, and even were it not Rembrandt's work, one would say it is badly drawn. These faults are not unusual in a master who was not very fastidious in the choice of his subjects. He employed the coarsest women for the purpose, painting them as they were, without embellishing their shapeless figures. The effect of light and brown and the powerful treatment alone make the small painting noteworthy. Mr. Jochem (*sic*) Reynolds speaks of this in his description of the Stadhouder's Collection..." [10].

This painting is known in the Rembrandt literature as "Susanna at the Bath", but there is far more reason to identify the naked woman as Bathsheba. In early descriptions of the work, this woman bathing is frequently identified as Susanna (see the sale catalogue of 1758; Terwesten 1770; Sir Joshua Reynolds 1781). T.P.C. Haag, however, the director of the Stadhouder's collection from about 1760 to 1795, rightly identified her as Bathsheba [11]. In the first draft of a catalogue of the paintings in the Royal Collection which he compiled but which never saw print, Steengracht van Oost-Capelle, listing it as the second item, had originally described the work as "Bathsheba preparing to bathe" [12]. This was in 1818. When selecting 100 paintings in the Royal Collection at The Hague (1826-1830) for print, he spoke of a "Susanna". Thus Steengracht revised his opinion subsequently to 1818, presumably after learning of earlier views (the sale catalogue of 1758, Terwesten 1770 and the edition of Reynold's writings, first published in London in 1797) [13].

The anxious and startled expression worn by this young woman at the bath, which has so often been remarked upon and which would be in keeping with the Susanna story, seems nevertheless to owe more to interpretation than to actual observation. Bathsheba's looking up at the spectator is comprehensible, quite unaware though she is of King David observing her from his palace yet himself invisible. There are, moreover, other illustrations of the story of Bathsheba and King David in which David is not visible [14].

The head seen in the foliage, referred to as the "scoundrel" and associated with the Susanna story (see *Historical data*), may be meant to be the messenger (generally represented as an old woman-servant), who is approaching with David's missive. No such letter is mentioned in the Bible story, but this detail was presumably borrowed from some other literary version of the story of David [15]. This profile, the greater part of which lies on the added strip, is exceptionally weakly done and has certainly not been painted by Rembrandt's own hand (Fig. 95). Furthermore, in the original composition there was scarcely sufficient room for a head or a figure. It is not inconceivable that an attempt was made to alter the *Bathsheba* into a *Susanna* by adding this head, after the *Susanna and the Two Elders* had been auctioned in Amsterdam in 1737 (now in Berlin-Dahlem; dated 1647; Br.-G., No. 516) [16] (Fig. 99). The strong resemblance between the attitude of this female figure and that of the figure in the painting, then possibly in the Sneijers collection, may have been noticed and have suggested this change.

Three prints by Buytewech (1591-1624) have had

95. The profile in the bush.

97. Willem Buytewech. An Old Woman brings Bathsheba the Letter of King David, 1615. Etching.

96. Willem Buytewech. Bathsheba Combing her Hair, 1615, Etching.

98. Willem Buytewech. Bathsheba reading King David's Letter, c. 1616. Etching.

99. Rembrandt. Suzanna surprised by the Two Elders 1647. *Berlin-Dahlem, Gemäldegalerie*

100. X-ray photograph. Suzanna. See note 18.

101. Bathsheba (Detail).

102. Pieter Lastman. Bathsheba at her Toilet. *Leningrad, The Hermitage.*

some influence on the iconography and composition of The Hague Bathsheba. They are: *Bathsheba at her toilet, Bathsheba receiving David's message* (dated 1615) and *Bathsheba reading David's letter* (Figs. 96-98). The Bathsheba in the first of these prints, in which the young woman is seen all but naked and combing her hair, has had a special influence on Rembrandt's version. The foliage to the right, the well to the left, the bowl with the pot of ointment and the architecture of the palace in the background can all be traced back to the three prints by Buytewech [17].

In the third of these Buytewech prints, an inscription, *VANITAS,* is to be read along the rim of the bowl. It is no longer possible, however, to ascertain whether Rembrandt's Bathsheba was also intended to symbolize Vanity.

What is clear is that in painting this work, Rembrandt was more interested in rendering the naked model than in illustrating the biblical text [18] (Fig. 101). Using Buytewech's motifs and also borrowing from Lastman [19] (Fig. 102) he arrived at his personal version of the theme.

Rembrandt does not seem to have found painting his model's attitude an easy task. The posture in the Berlin work is far more convincing. The style of painting in the Hague nude is certainly more fluent and the conception less emphatically realistic than in his *Andromeda* (No. IV); yet there is no lack of folds of skin round the belly and rings round the legs, under the knees, left by garters. There is definitely more sensuality in the rendering of the skin than in earlier works of his, yet not the pictorial richness we find in his later nudes (*Danaë,* dated 1636 (?), but reworked circa 1650, Br.-G., No. 471; *Bathsheba,* 1654, Br.-G., No. 521).

Mention has already been made of the rounding off of the upper corners [20]. No difference in the painting in these two places can be detected with the microscope, so that one may assume that Rembrandt himself overpainted both segments, but the reason for this remains obscure.

The painting of the palace in the background and of the trees and foliage in the original composition, i.e. before the 4 cm wide strip was added on the righthand side, corresponds to a high degree, as regards execution and tones of colour, with Rembrandt's work in the period around 1636-1637 (see, for example, *Tobias and the Angel,* Paris, The Louvre, 1637, Br.-G., No. 503).

The reader is referred to the *Technical data* for information regarding the signature and the date.

A copy of this painting was formerly in the collection of Dr. L.D. van Hengel, Arnhem (auctioned at Ellecom, 19-21 May 1953, No. 390).

NOTES

1. The dendrochronological investigation made by J. Bauch was unsuccessful in determining the age of the wood. The wood of the added strip is of the same period as that of the original panel but has come from another tree. This, too, would suggest that the repair to or alteration of the panel was carried out prior to 1758 (see also *Appendix I,* 2f).

2. H. Kühn, "Untersuchungen zu den Malgründen Rembrandts", *Jahrbuch der Staatlichen Kunstsammlungen in Baden-Württemberg,* 2, 1965, p. 200, mentions a dark-brown ground of chalk and ochres (umber) and not a white one in this painting. According to our examination, this dark-brown ground is present only on the added strip of wood and in restored areas along the upper edge of the panel.

3. Terwesten, p. 202, No. 39.

4. Manuscript in the keeping of the Netherlands Institute for Art History, The Hague; see, for example, Lormier's note on No. 337 (a landscape by Philip Wouwerman): "Van Jan Peter Sneijers Antwerpen".

5. Terwesten, p. 709; the author probably wanted to see *two* "scoundrels" to substantiate the identification of the subject matter. Even Martin is still found writing of two heads in the undergrowth (Cat. M. (1935), No. 147).

6. E. Malone and J. Farington, *The Literary Works of Sir Joshua Reynolds,* 2, London, 1819[5], pp. 344-345. The first edition had appeared in 1797. The painting in his collection to which Reynolds refers, illustrating the Susanna story, is now in the Museum in Berlin-Dahlem (Br.-G., No. 516); the work referred to as a study is presumably the *Susanna* in

the Louvre, Paris (Br.-G., No. 518); the drawing is at present in the Berlin Kupferstichkabinett, Benesch, III, Cat. No. 590, ill. 721.

7. See No. I, *Self-portrait as a Young Man,* note 10.

8. J.A. Emmens, *Rembrandt en de regels van de kunst,* Utrecht, 1968, pp. 63-95.

9. See the sale catalogue of Sir Joshua Reynolds' collection, London (Christie's), 13-17 March 1795 (Lugt, I, No. 5284); "Sir Joshua Reynolds' Collection of Pictures", *Burlington Magazine,* 86, 87, 1945, pp. 133-134, 211-217 and 263-273.

10. *De Voornaamste schilderijen van het Koninklijk Kabinet te 's Gravenhage,* The Hague, 1826-30, No. 27.

11. See No. I, *Self-Portrait as a Young Man,* note 10. In Ten Dall's copy a description only of the *Bathsheba* is given, so that we do not know on what grounds T.P.C. Haag referred to the work as a *Bathsheba* (see Drossaers-Scheurleer, III, p. 202; "Catalogus van het Kabinet Schilderijen van Zijne Doorl.:Hoogheid den Heere Prince van Orange en Nassau in 's-Gravenhage", *Antiek* 11, 1976, p. 171, No. 130).

12. Catalogus van het Koninklijk Kabinet van Schilderijen in 's-Gravenhage, bevattende de Schilderstukken der oude Meesters, thans in de Groote Gallerij ten toon gestelt, benevens de Levensbeschrijvingen der Schilders door den Directeur J. Steengracht van Oost-Capelle (Mauritshuis archives).

13. See notes 3, 5, 6 and 7.

14. E. Kunoth-Leifels, *Ueber die Darstellungen der "Bathsheba im Bade". Studie zur Geschichte des Bildthemas 4. bis 17. Jahrhundert,* Essen, 1962, p. 70, also refers to the Hague painting as a *Susanna.* It is probable that she adopted the generally accepted title, without checking its accuracy. C. Tümpel in *Rembrandt legt die Bibel aus,* Berlin, 1970, No. 35, also interprets the Hague painting as a depiction of Susanna. See also C. Tümpel, *Rembrandt,* Amsterdam, 1975, p. 19, for the same. In our view no "Herauslösung" (elimination)—concentration on the main event in the story and elimination of the subsidiary character(s), such as the "scoundrels" in this painting, according to Tümpel—is involved here nor is there any question of fright being the main theme. In our view, the palace in the background clearly points to a representation of the Bathsheba theme here and should there be any question of "Herauslösung" (elimination) this would refer to the invisible figure of King David.
E. Kunoth-Leifels, p. 48, lists examples of Bathsheba scenes in which, as in this Hague version, David is not present. It is not excluded that David might have been visible earlier, and that the figure has been wiped out in the course of time, as the result of cleaning or restoring. There is no indication whatever of any figure in the X-ray and infra-red photographs, or in the macro-photographs, which could be identified as David.

15. See also E. Kunoth-Leifels, *ibid.,* p. 69.

16. Assuming the Hague painting to be a *Susanna,* Benesch mistakenly associates drawings of Orientals with the work (Benesch, I, Cat. Nos. 155, 156, 157 and 159, ills. 168, 169, 170 and 177).

17. Exh. cat. *Willem Buytewech 1591-1624,* Rotterdam (Boymans-van Beuningen Museum), 1974-1975, Nos. 111, 112 and 113; ills. 6, 7 and 8. See also E. Haverkamp Begemann, *Willem Buytewech,* Amsterdam, 1958, VG 20, p. 172, ill. 7; ms. annotation at the back of a print in the Rijksprentenkabinet, Amsterdam: "Susanna en de boef" (18th century handwriting; information kindly given by the staff of the Print Room). This reference to one scoundrel is very remarkable. May it be assumed therefore that the unknown owner of the print in the 18th century had some knowledge of Rembrandt's painting, sold in 1758?

18. The *Susanna* in Berlin-Dahlem (Cat. 1975, No. 828E; Br.-G., No. 516) is probably a composition of approximately the same period as the *Bathsheba,* probably circa 1635, but it was altered and completed by Rembrandt in 1647 (see H. Kaufmann, "Rembrandts Berliner Susanna", *Jahrbuch der Preussischen Kunstsammlungen,* 45, 1924, pp. 72-80; A. Burroughs, "New Illustrations of Rembrandt's Style" *Burlington Magazine,* 59, 1931, pp. 3-10) (Fig. No. 102).
This painting also illustrates Rembrandt's interest in the nude model. The pose is nearly the same as that in the *Bathsheba.* See also the commentary in Br.-G., Nos. 505 and 516.

19. It should be remembered that Rembrandt also studied Lastman for certain details. See K. Freise, *Pieter Lastman. Sein Leben und seine Kunst,* Leipzig, 1911, p. 251, ill. 21: *Bathsheba at her Toilet,* St. Petersburg, Zabielsky collection (now in the Hermitage, Cat. 1958, No. 5590), and also P. Lastman's *Susanna,* dated 1614, in the Museum at Berlin-Dahlem (inv. No. 1719).

20. H.d.G., No. 57; Cat. M. (1935), No. 147.

103. Portrait of a Man with Grey Curly Hair.

IX

Portrait of a Man with Grey Curly Hair

Plate XI; Fig. 103

Canvas, 79.5 x 66.0 cm. Signed and dated *Rembrandt. f. 1650.*

Cat. Br. (1895), no. 560; Valentiner, p. 334; H.d.G., No. 384; Cat. M. (1935), No. 560; Br., No. 130; Bauch, No. 400; G., No. 304; Br.-G., No. 130; Cat. H. (1977), No. 560.

TECHNICAL DATA

The original canvas of this painting has a weave of 11 warp and 13 weft threads per sq. cm. There is one relining canvas.

The many places where the painting had been damaged and repaired are clearly visible in the fluorescence photograph and also in the infra-red photograph (Figs. 106 and 107).

In the X-ray photograph the damage sustained by the canvas and the paint is also clearly discernible (Fig. 104). The image of the portrait recorded by radiography corresponds with the surface view of the painting. The head has not been underpainted in white lead; even in the details of the brush strokes, the lighter areas in the X-radiograph correspond with those in the painting (Figs. 104, 105). The same applies to the light areas of the shirt and jerkin. No *pentimenti* were detected.

In the background there are some places—for instance, to the right of the head—where the texture and *craquelure* of the paint are those characteristic of old paint. The paint-film has clearly worn off in these areas. As a result, the texture of the old linen is visible through the surface paint. One can even see the old bare linen itself. Large sections of the background, however, appear to have been thinly overpainted with a semi-translucent brown paint, through which the wide cracks and flakes of paint of the old top layer are visible.

There is a great deal of overpainting in black on the coat and no *craquelure*. The same applies to large areas of the jerkin, which has only been slightly retouched in its uppermost parts. Age cracks occur here in what is probably the original brown, red and grey paint. These cracks continue into the white paint of the shirt. In the light areas of the head one finds a normal, fine network of age cracks. The white paint, mixed with yellow and red ochre, has been applied so thinly in places to the dark-grey and brownish underpaint that in these places the flesh tone is of a greyish tint. In the left temple, left cheek and chin, this dark layer comes to the surface, deter-

104. X-ray photograph.

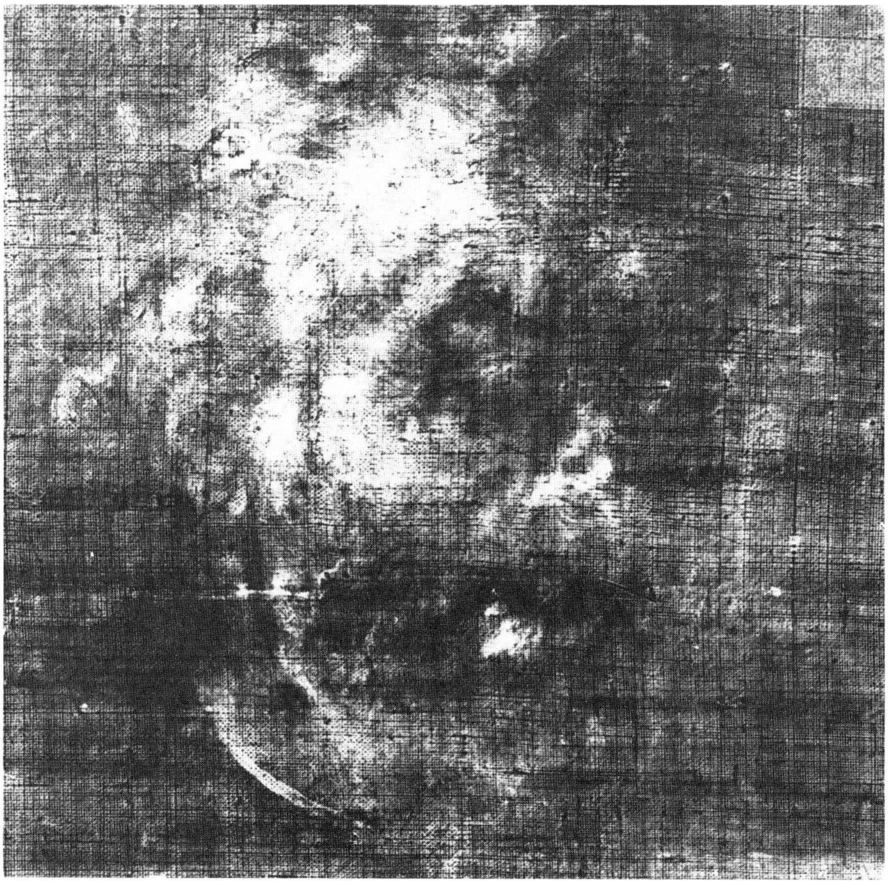

105. X-ray photograph. Detail.

106. Ultra-violet fluorescence photograph.

107. Infra-red photograph.

mining the colouring of the dark areas of shadow in this half of the face.

The canvas has been primed with a thin layer of red ochre, mixed with a little yellow ochre and chalk, only slight remains of this layer being present in various places [1].

To this first ground layer a dark brownish-grey second layer of ground, made up of a coarse granular mixture of white lead, chalk, carbon black, umber and red ochre, has been applied. As has been said above, this dark layer of paint comes to the surface in the shadows on the face.

To the layer of dark-grey in the background, behind the head, red ochre has been applied and largely covered, during restoration, with brown paint. The flesh tone is white lead, blended with yellow and red ochre, then glazed with a red lake pigment. The red above the right eyelid is vermilion, thinly glazed with red lake. The dark, purple-red colour of the mouth consists of a grey underlayer on which a crimson-red lake pigment has been applied. The red-brown of the jerkin is brownish red ochre; the red streak on it consists of red lake applied to a white lead underpaint, while the white of the collar has been painted on to a black underpaint. Trace elements of silver, copper and tin were found in the white lead.

108. Signature and date.

To the left, next to the shoulder, the painting is signed *Rembrandt. f. 1650* (Fig. 108). This signature is on a part of the background which the fluorescence image shows to have been less thoroughly restored than the other parts. Here, too, the paint layer shows some *craquelure*, part of which continues into the thinly applied brownish-black paint of the signature. This signature has clearly been retouched and is lighter in colour than the date, which looks rather more reliable. Although we detected no convincing evidence to doubt authenticity, we feel it would be appropriate to adopt a certain reserve as regards the authenticity of signature and date especially in view of the far-reaching restoration the painting has undergone.

The reason for fairly drastic restoration was that the painting seems to have been rolled up at some time; consequently paint layers and linen have sustained severe damage in the form of horizontal fractures (see infra-red photograph, Fig. 107 and X-ray photograph, Fig. 104).

HISTORICAL DATA

In 1809 this portrait of a man formed part of the collection of the art dealer Jean-Baptiste-Pierre Lebrun (1748-1813). The paintings Lebrun had assembled had come from Spain, Southern France and

109. Etching after the Portrait. From a J.B.P. Lebrun stock catalogue, Paris (1809).

Italy. An etching based on this portrait is reproduced in the exhibition catalogue of 1809. Under the etching we read: «Rembrandt van Ryn, P.xit hauteur 29 pouces, largeur 25 pouces, sur Toile» (Fig. 109). In the catalogue, this painting is paired with another of the same dimensions, a portrait of a girl. Both paintings were praised: «Les deux têtes ici représentées sont de sa plus belle manière, et la jeune fille peut être regardée comme un chef-d'œuvre» [2].

On 20 March 1810, Lebrun held an auction in Paris at which item No. 57 was this *Man with Grey Curly Hair*: "Un grand Buste d'homme à cheveux et barbe courte, sur toile". In a note in the copy of the catalogue in the keeping of the Netherlands Institute for Art History in The Hague, we read: "mise sur table et retirée" and a sum of 1,000 francs [3].

The painting then entered the collection of Sébastien Erard (1752-1831), the celebrated builder of pianofortes and harps, whose collection was auctioned in Paris on 23 April 1832. In the lengthy description of this portrait of a man, it is said in the catalogue that "cette tête sur laquelle ne tombe que peu de jour, et qu'environnent de grandes ombres, n'a point ce brillant qui fait une vive impression sur la vue. Mais elle est remarquable par cette profondeur, cette fusion de teintes harmonieuses et transparentes par cette magie, pour m'exprimer suivant l'usage, que le célèbre Rembrandt découvrit le premier dans les couleurs de sa palette, et qui est encore un secret pour beaucoup de peintres d'un grand mérite. Ajoutons à cette qualité une exécution large, un modelé savant, et nous n'aurons rien dit de trop à l'éloge de ce portrait. On croit que c'est celui du père de Rembrandt. Sa tête est nue, son visage, vu de trois quarts, est caractérisé par des traits fortements prononcées, son expression, d'accord avec la simplicité de son vêtement, indique un homme du commun" (Cat. No. 120) [4].

The painting next made its way to England, where it was auctioned in London on 23 May 1885 (Cat. No. 482) as a portrait of the "Artist's Father", and said to come from the collection of Sir William Wellesley Knighton, Bart. It also mentioned that the work was signed and dated, although no particulars are given. The dimensions quoted were 31 x 26 inches. Accompanying the description was a photograph made by the firm of F. Hanfstaengl, in Munich (Fig. 110). In the copy of the sale catalogue kept at the Netherlands Institute for Art History the following note has been added in ink: "Lesser 162.15.0"; with a pencil note, added later and reading: "Lesser £162/15/ musée de la Haye 1890". The word *Father* has also been struck through in pencil and *Brother* substituted. After having spent some time in the collection of Sir Charles J. Robinson, in London, this so-called "Father", now referred to as Rembrandt's "Brother", arrived back in Paris, at the art dealer's Ch. Sedelmeyer, from whom A. Bredius purchased it for the Mauritshuis in 1891 for 30,000 francs.

110. The reproduction in the sale catalogue of 1885 (Photograph by Hanfstaengl).

Collections

Unknown collection in Spain, Southern France or Italy
J.-B.-P. Lebrun, art dealer, Paris, 1807/1808-1810
S. Erard, Paris, 1832
Sir William Wellesley Knighton, Bart., Blendworth Lodge, Hampshire, England, 1885
Lesser, art dealer, London
Sir Charles J. Robinson, London, 1889
Ch. Sedelmeyer, art dealer, Paris, 1890-1891
"The Mauritshuis"—Royal Collection of Paintings, The Hague, 1891.

Dimensions quoted

1809	29 pouces x 25 pouces = approx. 78.3 x 67.5 cm
1832	29 pouces x 24 pouces, 3 lignes = approx. 78.3 x 65.45 cm
1885	31 in x 26 in = 78.74 x 66.4 cm
1895	78 x 66 cm
1977	79.5 x 66.0 cm

Prices

1810	1,000 francs
1885	£162.15*s*. 0*d*
1891	30,000 francs

111. Rembrandt. The Man with the Golden Helmet. *Berlin-Dahlem, Gemäldegalerie.*

112. Rembrandt. "Rembrandt's Brother" (1654?). *Moscow, Pushkin Museum.*

ICONOGRAPHY AND STYLE

A half-length portrait of a man, elderly in appearance, and turned threequarters to the right. He has grey curly hair and is wearing an almost black coat over a white shirt and a brownish-red jerkin (Fig. 103).

Owing to the fairly simple clothing the man is wearing and presumably also on account of his rather shaggy head, he was identified in 1832 as Rembrandt's Father (see *Historical data*). In 1891, Bode thought he recognized the painter's brother in the portrait, pointing out the resemblance to the *Man with the Golden Helmet* (Berlin-Dahlem; Br.-G., No. 128) (Fig. 111) and the *Rembrandt's Brother* (Moscow; Br.-G., No. 131, dated *1654*?) (Fig. 112) [6]. A certain likeness was also noticed to the servant at the back in the *The Centurion Cornelius,* a painting originating in Rembrandt's circle, but of authorship not yet identified [7]. Since Rembrandt's brother died in 1652, it is highly improbable that the painter would have made another portrait of him two years afterwards, although the possibility cannot be ruled out altogether. In view of the existing uncertainty, we would not ourselves identify the portrait as Rembrandt's brother.

Summarizing the results of the technical investigations, we can state that this portrait had suffered badly in the course of time (see Figs. 104 to 107) and that horizontal damage—fractures in the paint and canvas—indicates that at some stage the painting must have been rolled up.

The attribution of the work to Rembrandt has been questioned on more than one occasion, whereas the accuracy of the dating has, as far as we are aware, been accepted. Rightly? It is no easy task to place the impressive head (which has been more daringly painted than the rest of the work) among the portraits Rembrandt produced around the year 1650. If the figure *5* in the date is original, and correct, although retouched, we wonder by what figure it was followed. There is, in any case, a close resemblance between this head and the portrait of the same model in the Museum of Moscow (Br.-G., No. 131) (Fig. 112).

Striking features of the Hague painting are the

summary treatment of the clothing and the broad and firm way in which the head has been painted, even though it has suffered from old folds in the linen. Thus, before restoration, the contrast between the well preserved and thickly painted areas of the head and the damaged areas had become more pronounced, the dark underpainting being visible in the latter parts. Yet the painting cannot be regarded as wholly completed even where the head is concerned and especially not as regards the treatment of the hair. The X-ray photograph also conveys the impression of a sketchily painted portrait (Fig. 104).

It is not surprising at all that the name of Carel Fabritius has been mentioned more than once in connection with this painting [8]. These references did not, however, amount to more than suggestions. We should also refer the reader to the remarks made by Daniel Pont, who supposes that Carel Fabritius assisted the unidentified painter of the picture in the Wallace Collection (see note 7). We are not much wiser as a result of all these suppositions.

If one judges by the technical examination and what one can see for oneself, one would be very inclined to assume that Rembrandt never completed this work. The head had been boldly conceived, with strong accentuation here and there, but the final, finishing layers are lacking (cf. *The Man with the Golden Helmet*) (Fig. 111) (Br.-G., No. 128). The man's clothing is merely suggested. It is not clear, for instance, whether Rembrandt intended to paint a left arm, which the man would hold up in front of his chest and which, in the etching in Lebrun's catalogue of 1809 (Fig. 109), has apparently been taken to be a kind of muff.

It would seem to us that Rembrandt planned this painting as a study of an interesting head which he painted more elaborately on several occasions (see also *The Man with the Golden Helmet*). Did the artist make this study with a view to some painting (for instance, Br.-G., No. 131) or was he painting this particular model once more, possibly *after* having painted the work in Moscow, later putting the work aside, unfinished? We do not know.

NOTES

1. According to H. Kühn, "Untersuchungen zu den Malgründen Rembrandts", *Jahrbuch der Staatlichen Kunstsammlungen in Baden-Württemberg* 2, 1965, p. 200, a white ground consisting of chalk and white lead.

2. *Recueil de gravures au trait à l'eau forte, et ombrées, d'après un choix de tableaux de toutes les écoles, recueillis dans un voyage fait en Espagne, au midi de la France et en Italie, dans les années 1807 et 1808,* Paris, 1809, 2, pp. 53-57, Nos. 152 and 153. This portrait of a girl is also reproduced. Its present whereabouts are unknown. It was auctioned on 15 May 1953 as item No. 83 at Christie's, London (Br.-G., No. 393). One of us (De V.) saw this painting in 1950, in the Goekoop collection at The Hague, at the time noting: "definitely not a Rembrandt". There is nothing to justify the assumption that this portrait of a girl and the *Portrait of a Man with Grey Curly Hair* are companion pieces or are in any way connected.

3. Lugt, I, No. 7727.

4. Lugt, II, No. 12962.

5. Lugt, III, No. 44957.

6. W. Bode, "Das Bildniss von Rembrandt's Bruder Adriaen Harmensz. van Rijn im Mauritshuis", *Oud Holland,* 9, 1891, pp. 1-6. K. Bauch also published this painting (as he did the *Man with Golden Helmet,* Br.-G., No. 128) as a portrait of Rembrandt's brother Adriaen, though questioning the identification (K. Bauch, *Der frühe Rembrandt und seine Zeit,* Berlin, 1960, pp. 168-169, ills. 150 and 149).

7. Catalogue of the Wallace Collection, London, 1968, pp. 259-262, with ill., Inv. No. P 86. In this catalogue the work is attributed to Rembrandt, with a note to the effect that others attributed the painting to Barent Fabritius, to Rembrandt's studio, and to Barent and Carel Fabritius together. See also: D. Pont, *Barent Fabritius, 1624-1673,* The Hague, 1958, dissertation, Utrecht, appendix 4, pp. 151-153.

8. J.Q. van Regteren Altena, by word of mouth, circa 1952; G., No. 304, p. 500; Victor de Stuers's opinion is quoted in F.J. Duparc, *Een eeuw strijd voor Nederlands cultureel erfgoed,* The Hague, 1975, pp. 122-123: In the second place, I ask myself whether it is a Rembrandt. I acknowledge that a photograph does not provide a sufficient basis for arriving at a definite opinion. But I cannot conceal that my first impression was that it is *not* a Rembrandt, but a Carel Fabritius... Here it should be noted that De Stuers and Bredius took pleasure in disagreeing with each other.
The Mauritshuis archives contain a correspondence of December 1890 and January 1891, among Bredius, Bode, Von Tschudi (Berlin) and Obreen (at the time director of the Rijksmuseum in Amsterdam). The subject of this correspondence was the painting known as "Rembrandt's Brother", which had just been purchased from the Paris art dealer Sedelmeyer, and which was restored by Hauser on Bode's recommendation. Apparently, Bredius was seeking support from the others for his purchase—a support they granted generously.

113. Two Negroes.

X

Two Negroes

Plate XII; Fig. 113

Canvas, 77.8 x 64.5 cm. Signed and dated *Rembrandt f 1661*.

Valentiner, p. 495; H.d.G., No. 336; Cat. M. (1935), No. 685; Br., No. 310; Bauch, No. 539; G., No. 390; Br.-G., No. 310; Cat. H. (1977), No. 685.

TECHNICAL DATA

The original canvas has 12 warp and 14 weft threads per sq. cm. There is one relining canvas.

Examination under ultra-violet light and by means of infra-red photography revealed no special features.

The X-ray photograph shows a thinly painted canvas with a ground containing white lead (Fig. 114). As a result the light areas of the figures do not on the whole show up very well in the radiograph, especially since relatively little white lead has been used in the few light areas of the two heads.

Whereas the head of the foremost negro is clearly recognizable in the radiograph, that of the negro behind him appears mainly in darker outlines only, within which outlines the essential light areas are only poorly defined.

As regards the *pentimenti* or alterations in the original painting which show up in the radiograph, it can be said that these are, in general, far from clear and therefore difficult to interpret. The most obvious alterations are to be found in the cloth or shawl draped over the shoulders of the first negro, which, it seems, originally fell down to the right, across his chest [1].

Although deliberately painted thinly, the thin layers of paint on this work have worn off and been restored in many places; the profile of the linen is even visible through the paint in the grey background above the heads. There are also numerous small splitting cracks in the paint in this place. In the old layer of grey paint fairly coarse white, black and red pigments were found, but this layer has been overpainted in many places in a neutral, greyish-brown shade of umber. To the left of the head of the first negro the grey background, containing white lead, has been painted rather more thickly, this also being evident in the X-ray photograph (Fig. 114). In various places to the right of this head, the paint appears to be of more recent origin. To the left of the other negro, the paint of the background contains strikingly coarse pigments and may, for this reason, be original.

114. X-ray photograph.

115. Infra-red photograph (detail).

Below, to the left, the work presents a clear picture of the damage sustained by the original paint; here a network of cracks is scarcely recognizable any longer.

Both heads have a *craquelure* which suggests age, especially in the light areas. Here and there in the darker areas, one doubts, however, whether the uppermost layer of paint is still the original one. In the clothing of both negroes there are dark areas, which have clearly been restored. Scratches have been made in the wet paint in the outline of the right shoulder of the negro at the back, in that of the forearm of the other negro and that of the balustrade on which his arm is resting. Here, that is to say, parallel light and dark scratches can be seen in the paint, yet these have a far less pronounced pictorial effect than those we found in similar places on early paintings we have examined, e.g. in the moustache of the *Study of a Man Laughing* (No. II) and in the cloak worn by Simeon (No. V). Here, the underlying grey and yellow must have been well dried, for only the very thin upper layer of brown paint (possibly added later) was removed when this scratching in the paint took place. In the region of the forearm the scratches even run across the old cracks and must therefore be of later date.

The ground is pale red and consists of red and yellow ochre with a good deal of chalk and a smaller amount of white lead. On top of this first layer a second of greyish-brown has been added. This is of varying thickness and even entirely absent in places. It is made up of white lead, chalk, umber, red and yellow ochre and also quite a lot of carbon black. As is evident, especially on the left side of the painting, this layer is rather heterogeneous in its composition, large white, yellow and red grains of pigment being present in a greyish-brown mass. The white in the top layer is white lead, blended with yellow and black pigments. An analysis of the grey intermediate layer revealed traces of copper, tin and silver, all of which must have come from the white lead.

The pattern in the garment worn by the foremost

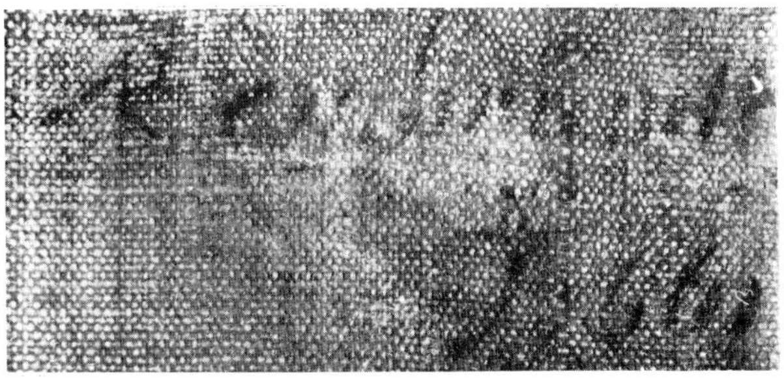

115a. Signature and date.

negro has been painted in yellow ochre as has also the mouth.

Nowhere has a red lake pigment been employed—neither as a glaze nor in areas of shadow. Besides bone black. Cologne earth was detected in the black (brown) areas. Parts of the faces and the clothing have been painted in greyish-brown tints in which grains of yellow ochre, bone black and white lead are present.

The signature *Rembrandt f 1661* (Fig. 115a) has been painted in the top right-hand corner, in a place where the paint is bare and worn away but where it has also been partially restored. (Concerning this signature see also *Iconography and style.*) Another capital letter *R* can be vaguely discerned preceding the signature and this may have been part of an earlier one (Fig. 115).

HISTORICAL DATA

This painting came from the De Montribloud collection, which was auctioned in Paris on 9 February 1784 and the ensuing days. The description in the sale catalogue reads as follows: "no. 43. Par le même (= Rimbrandt Van Rhyn). Un sujet de deux figures vues à mi-corps: il représente des têtes de nègres; l'un d'eux est ajusté d'une robe doublée de rouge, & une espece de manteau formant une draperie. Ce Morceau est d'une touche savante, & d'une grande force de couleur: hauteur 30 pouces, largeur 24. T.". According to a note made in the copy of the sale catalogue kept at the Netherlands Institute for Art History in The Hague, the work fetched 72 pounds and 1 shilling [2]. Its new owner was Lord Berwick, resident at Attingham Hall, near Shrewsbury, Shropshire. Later, the painting came on the London art market (Ch. J. Wertheimer and G. Donaldson). It was from the latter that A. Bredius acquired the canvas in 1902. The year after, he loaned it to the Mauritshuis, bequeathing it in 1946.

This painting is possibly identical with the work *Twee mooren, in een stuck van Rembrandt* as mentioned in the inventory of Rembrandt's possessions, dated 1656 (see, also, *Iconography and style*).

Collections

De Montribloud, Paris, 1784
Lord Berwick, Attingham Hall, Shropshire, England
Ch. J. Wertheimer, art dealer, London
G. Donaldson, art dealer, 1902
Dr. A. Bredius, The Hague, on loan to the Mauritshuis, 1903-1946
Bredius Bequest, 1946

Dimensions quoted

1784 30 pouces x 24 pouces = approx. 81 x 64.8 cm
1914 77.8 x 64.4 cm
1977 77.8 x 64.5 cm

Price

1784 72 pounds 1 shilling

ICONOGRAPHY AND STYLE

Two figures of negroes, standing, the nearest looking to the left and the other to the right and downwards, over the other figure's right shoulder. Both are wearing costumes (Fig. 113).

According to W. Ch. Dusée, formerly keeper of the Ethnological Museum in Leiden, two different types of negro have been portrayed here. The figure on the right is apparently a North-West African, originating from Morocco, from the region bordering on South-West Mauretania [3]. Dusée also pointed out that negroes from these regions were not traded as slaves by the Dutch but, after capture, were often carried off to be exchanged with Dutchmen who had been taken prisoner. There is no reason to assume, as Hamann does, that these are two "negro princes" on a visit to Amsterdam [4].

According to the inventory of Rembrandt's goods and chattels drawn up on 25 and 26 July 1656, a painting was to be found in the large *schilderkamer* on the first floor of his house in the *Breestraat* which was listed as follows: *Twee mooren, in een stuck van Rembrandt* [5]. It is possible that this painting is the same as the *Two Negroes* discussed here. Among a series of classical heads in the *Kunst Caemer,* there was "Een moor nae 't leven afgegooten" [6]. It is probable that this head later found its way into the collection of an unidentified sculptor. In his travel diary, Zacharias Conrad von Uffenbach wrote as follows concerning his visit on 2 March 1711 to "ein Bildhauer auf dem Brettermarkt": "Er hatte einen Mohrenkopf, den Rembrandt nach dem Leben abgeformet haben soll, den er aber gar hoch hielte" [7].

116. Detail.

117. Old Copy. *Bucarest, Museum of Art of the Romanian Democratic Republic.*

118. Old Copy. *Present location unknown.*

Een Moor by Rembrandt originating from the collection of the art dealer Johannes de Renialme was valued in 1657 at 12 florins [8].

It is apparent from these sources that prior to 1656 Rembrandt made a number of studies of negroes' heads.

In Rembrandt's work, we find the negro appearing on many occasions in religious scenes, in conformity with tradition [9]. As far as is known, he did not paint any young negroes as status symbols (i.e. pages) of prominent families [10].

One of the questions which arises from this painting of two negroes, each glancing in a different direction, is whether they might not have posed for part of a large composition of which we have no knowledge.

Two negroes appear as minor figures in *The Fury of Ahasuerus* by Jan Steen (in the Barber Institute of Fine Arts, Birmingham), a composition strongly influenced by the stage [11]. Thus The Hague painting could be a preparatory study for a picture representing a biblical or historical scene. The costumes might also suggest that the artist had seen these two young negroes in a procession or perhaps on the stage [12].

The technical data show that this canvas has sustained damage with the passage of time and has undergone fairly extensive restoration. Even bearing this in mind, we are struck by the thinness of the paint, which the painter will have chosen, particularly to achieve the many nuances in the shades of colour —more especially in the dark flesh tones in each figure. The painting is, indeed, built up of a limited number of colours which offer only slight contrast with one another.

The striking features lie in the play of light, which once again draws our attention to the splendid painting of the two dark heads. The lips of the negro on the right are slightly parted and he is looking upwards; the figure on the left, on the contrary, has his lips closed and is looking downwards. Rembrandt has painted these two figures, conspicuous in their day in Amsterdam, with such sensitivity that we could not point to any comparable work painted during the 17th century [13].

The signature and date in the top righthand corner give rise to questions. The name *Rembrandt* has been painted in very clumsily and has presumably been superimposed on an older signature, formerly visible. The remnants of an earlier, rubbed-off signature, of which an *R* is just faintly visible, point to this (see *Technical data*) (Figs. 115, 115a). Whether, at the time, the date, which was possibly present too (*1661*), was correctly read before being painted in again is more than doubtful.

It is no easy matter at all to place this painting in Rembrandt's œuvre on stylistic grounds alone. Even if we disregard the entry "Two Moors" in the inventory of 1656 (see above and Br.-G., No. 310), a dating before 1661 and even before 1656 seems plausible. We find nothing in the master's œuvres shortly before or shortly after 1660 which could lend more plausibility to the 1661 dating. We know of no other paint-film of this same period so thinly done as this, whereas this particular characteristic can be traced among some of the works painted during the first half of the fifties, e.g. the portrait of Nicolaes Bruyningh (1652; Br.-G., No. 268); compare also the portraits of Clement de Jonghe (?), c. 1652, Br.-G., No. 265) and Titus (c. 1655; Br.-G., No. 122).

Two old copies of the painting are known to us (Figs. 117 and 118) [14]. Both appear to be the work of a far less skilled hand. No names of pupils can be mentioned with any conviction in this respect. The fact that these copies, made in the 17th, if not 18th, century, exist, does, however, indicate that the Hague painting enjoyed a certain renown or at least aroused interest.

NOTES

1. In the X-ray photograph, to the right of the head of the foremost negro, one can, with a little ingenuity, construc a third (overpainted) head, in which two eyes (the white and the dark pupils) have been indicated, the nose (with a point of light and dark nostrils) and also the shape of a mouth and chin.
We would not, however, exclude the possibility that an optical illusion may be involved here, resulting from the chance interplay of dark and light spots, difficult to interpret individually. These are of a kind encountered more than once in the radiographs of old paintings which have been restored, and about which it is difficult to draw unequivocal conclusions.

2. Lugt, I, No. 3673. It is not clear to us where the red lining mentioned in this catalogue was observed.

3. Communicated by word of mouth.

4. R. Hamann, *Rembrandt,* Berlin, 1948, p. 396.

5. H.d.G. *Urkunden,* p. 209, No. 344; R.W. Scheller, "Rembrandt en de encyclopedische Kunstkamer", *Oud Holland,* 84, 1969, p. 88, note 37.

6. H.d.G. *Urkunden,* p. 198, No. 161.

7. Z.C. von Uffenbach, *Merkwürdige Reisen durch Niedersachsen, Holland und Engelland,* 3, Ulm, 1754, p. 582. The sculptor is not mentioned by name. According to a written communication from Dr. I.H. van Eeghen, this artist may have been Cornelis van Thiel (1677 - after 1742), who lived along the Binnen Amstel, between Reguliersbreestraat and Watersteeg. It was along this stretch of canal that the (Dood)kistenmakersgracht (Coffin-Makers Canal) lay, which could be translated by "Bretter" (Bretter = planks).

8. A. Bredius, *Künstler-Inventare,* 1, The Hague, 1915, p. 234. The valuers were the painter Adam Camerarius and the art collector Martin Kretzer. This *Moor* was formerly associated with the *A Young Negro Archer,* now in the Wallace Collection (Cat. 1968, p. 112, No. P 238), attributed to Govaert Flinck (1615-1660). See J.W. von Moltke, *Govaert Flinck, 1615-1660,* Amsterdam, 1965, p. 103, No. 180, ill. 29.
The estate left by Johann Jacob Sandrart (1655-1698) of Nuremberg, great-nephew of the painter Joachim Sandrart (1606-1688), also included a painting with two figures of negroes referred to as "Zween Mohren, in einer verguldten Rahm, umb 1 (Gulden) 30 (Creuzer)". Unfortunately the painter's name has not come down to us. See R.A. Peltzer, "Sandrart-Studien", *Münchner Jahrbuch der Bildende. Kunst,* N.F. 2, 1925, p. 155, No. 79. Joachim Sandrart and his pupil, Mattheus Merian, stayed in Amsterdam from about 1637 to 1642.

9. Paintings: *The Baptism of the Eunuch,* Utrecht, Rijksmuseum Het Catharijne-convent, dated 1626 (See exh. cat. *"Geschildert tot Leyden anno 1626"*, Leiden (De Lakenhal), 1976-1977, No. S 25 with ill.); *Samson Threatening his Father-in-law,* Berlin-Dahlem, Gemäldegalerie (Br.-G., No. 499), dated 163(5); *Landscape with the Baptism of the Eunuch,* Hanover, Landesmuseum, on loan (Br.-G., No. 439), dated 1636; Etchings: *Christ before Pilate* (B. 77 = Münz, No. 204 = Hollstein, Vol. 18, p. 42, Vol. 19, p. 71), 1635/36 and *The Baptism of the Eunuch* (B. 98 = Münz, No. 211 = Hollstein, Vol. 18, pp. 53-54, Vol. 19, p. 95), 1641; Drawings: *Portrait of a Negro in a Turban* (Benesch, II, Cat. No. A4, "attributed to Rembrandt", ill. 593); *Two Negro Drummers mounted on Mules* (Benesch, II, Cat. No. 365, ill. 412); *A Negro Band* (Benesch, II, Cat. No. 366, ill. 413).

10. See, for example, the portrait of the Marchese Elena Grimaldi by Anthony van Dyck, Washington, National Gallery, Cat. 1975, No. 688, with ill. See also O. ter Kuile, *A. Hanneman,* Alphen aan de Rijn, 1976, p. 15 and note 103.

11. Exh. cat. *Jan Steen,* The Hague (Mauritshuis) 1958-59[2], No. 49, ill. 51.

12. Mr. Dusée is unable to attribute the clothing to any particular region, which could point to its being theatrical costume.

13. For example, cf. the *Studies of a Negro* in Brussels, Musées Royaux des Beaux-Arts (Cat. 1971, No. 53), which was often attributed to Van Dyck, but which was re-identified, rightly, we feel, as a work by Rubens (see J.S. Held, "The Four Heads of a Negro in Brussels and Malibu", *Miscellanea in memoriam Paul Coremans. Bulletin Koninklijk Instituut voor het Kunstpatrimonium,* 15, 1975, pp. 180-192); G. Dou, *Study of a Negro,* Hanover, Landesmuseum, Cat. 1954, No. 81 and *Negro Head,* Copenhagen, Statens Museum for Kunst, Cat. 1951, No. 183; Albert Eckhout, negro studies (see Th. Thomsen, *Albert Eckhout. Ein niederländischer Maler und sein Gönner Moritz der Brasilianer,* Copenhagen, 1938, ills. 12-14).

14. Bucharest, Museum of the Romanian People's Republic, canvas, 83.4 x 59.2 cm (mistakenly attributed to Ferdinand Bol); W. Clifford Duits, art dealer, London, 1968, panel, 25.4 x 27.9 cm (present whereabouts unknown). Both pieces differ from one another and also, especially as regards clothing, from the painting in The Hague.

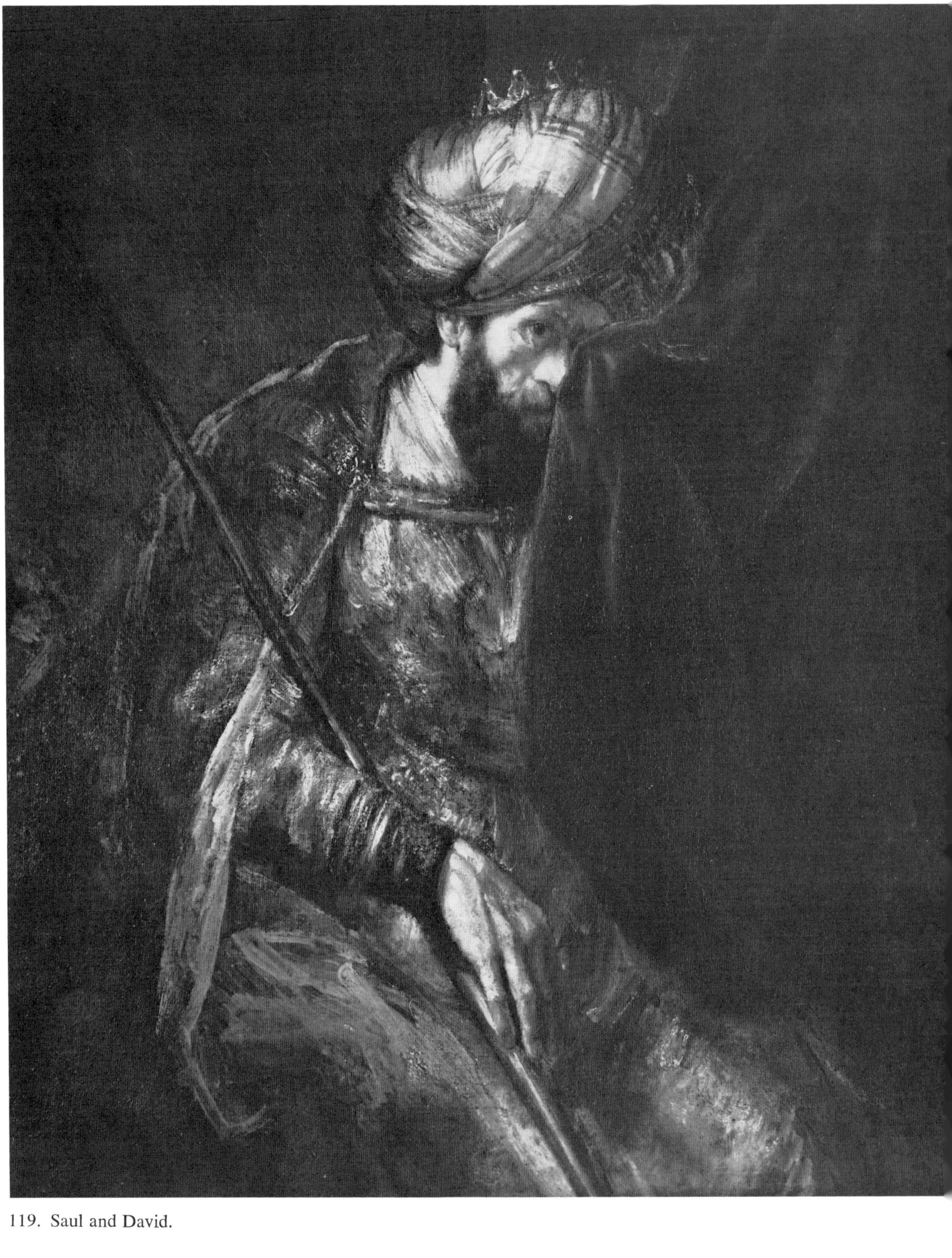

119. Saul and David.

XI

Saul and David

Plates XIV-XVI; Fig. 119

Canvas, 130.0 x 164.3 cm. Unsigned, undated; c. 1655 and c. 1660-1665.

Valentiner, p. 470; H.d.G., No. 36; Cat. M. (1935), No. 621; Br., No. 526; Bauch, No. 35; Br.-G., No. 526 (rejects the attribution to Rembrandt); Cat. H. (1977), No. 621 ("the attribution is not accepted by all Rembrandt scholars") [1].

TECHNICAL DATA

The original canvas has 13 warp and 15 weft threads per sq. cm and is made up of two sections, sewn together along their entire length, the seam running across the work 7 cm below the centre line.

It can be seen from the painting itself, and better still from the X-ray photograph (Fig. 120), that this work was cut in two at some time in the past, one piece bearing the figure of Saul and the other, smaller, piece David and the harp. With a view to the composition, the upper part of this second piece must have been cut off. The two main pieces were put together again later, the section then missing above David's head being filled in with a fragment from some old painting. The X-ray photograph shows how the three pieces have been put together with notched edges [2]. It did not prove possible to ascertain from the technical investigation how much of the height and width of the painting has been lost as a result of its dismemberment and later re-assembly.

According to the X-radiograph, no more than a few centimetres need have been involved in the centre, but the photograph does not permit greater precision.

The painting has been relined, using glue. Strips of linen applied during earlier restoration are also to be found along the edges. Along the whole of the right edge there is a strip approximately 5 cm wide, and narrower strips, some 4, some 3 cm wide, along the top edge and along the entire bottom edge, with a few, here and there, along the left edge.

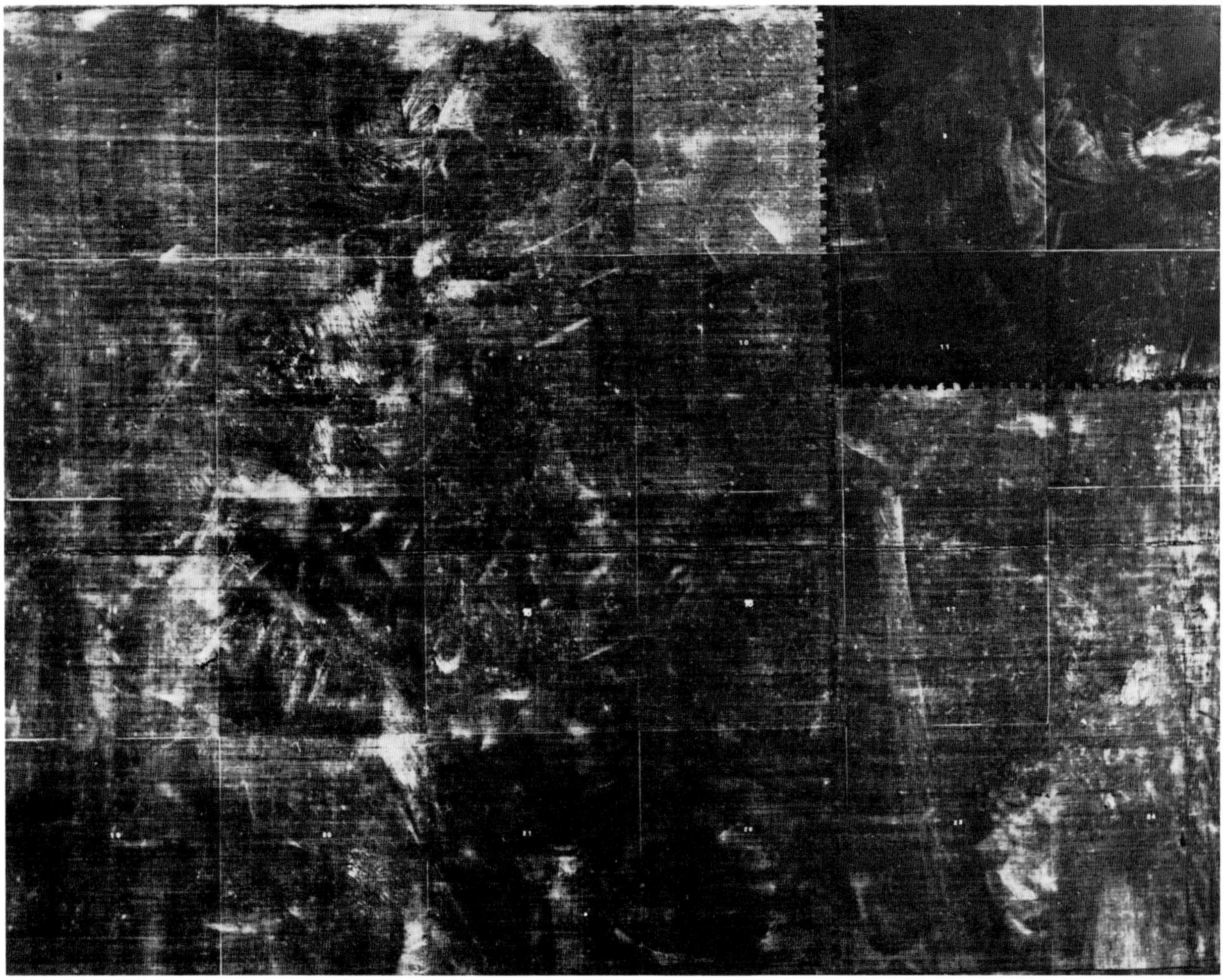

120. X-ray photograph.

Owing to marked interference from the strongly fluorescent layers of varnish, examination under ultra-violet light did not produce any special information. Examination by means of infra-red photography did, however, yield some interesting material (Fig. 121). Thus the infra-red image shows that the upper part of the right sleeve of the tunic was completed before the red cloak was painted over it; this is evident from the now obvious strap and clasp at shoulder height. Moreover, this photograph shows the carved round end of the right arm of the chair on which Saul is seated, more clearly than the painting itself does.

The X-ray photograph confirms that the two parts of the painting did indeed originally form a whole. This is apparent from the horizontal seam which runs right across the work and from the uniform weave. By contrast the fragment added in the top right-hand corner differs considerably, being far darker than the two main parts in the radiograph. Details (a sleeve and hand) of the original picture on this fragment can also be discerned (Fig. 122). The very evident difference in density on the radiograph between this added fragment and the two pieces belonging to the original picture results from the absence of white lead in the ground of the added fragment, whereas a fair quantity of white lead was mixed into that applied to the original canvas.

In the X-ray photograph, the figures of Saul and David are comparatively weak and lacking in contrast, which makes it difficult to discern details. This is due to the relatively strong absorption of the X-rays by the fairly thick layers of priming containing white lead as compared with the only slight absorption by the more thinly painted figures, where, in the red, black and brown areas, little or no white lead has been used. Thus it is only with difficulty that one can distinguish details of the figure of David in the radiograph. The pillar of the harp, into which a larger amount of white lead has been mixed, is more clearly distinguishable.

In Saul's head and turban the lighter details, con-

121. Infra-red photograph. Detail. King Saul.

taining white lead, show up more clearly than the light areas in the figure of David. Here the paint has been applied more thickly and even the brush-strokes can be distinguished in the radiograph. It also becomes apparent that the upper part of the right arm, which is covered by the red cloak, has been painted in the same manner as the forearm, as was already deduced from the infra-red photograph.

In the X-ray photograph remain various light areas of differing density, form and size, e.g. above the head of either figure, in the dark areas between them, (now mainly curtain) and to Saul's left, which are not (no longer) discernable in the painting. However, no clear figures or details can be distinguished in these places. The fact that in some of these light areas, e.g. to the right above Saul's hand, the brush-stroke, or at least the structure of the paint, can still be discerned, strongly suggests that interesting details in this work have been painted out (Figs. 123, 124).

Large areas have been overpainted thinly and evenly during restoration—backgrounds, foregrounds and the space between the two figures—and in these places there is little *craquelure*. In those areas where little or no restoration work has been done—in the two figures particularly—we find the *craquelure* normal for an old painting—for instance, in the old, coarse-grained paint layer of Saul's head and turban.

The tip of the brush has been used to scratch in the wet paint of the beard. The yellow under-garment Saul is wearing also has a network of age cracks and the structure of the paint here is rather worn; the same applies to the hand and javelin. The red lake pigment in which the cloak has been painted, and its edging, which has been painted in yellow and red ochre, bears a *craquelure* which does not differ in structure from that in the old areas of paint mentioned above. Much of the curtain to Saul's right has been thinly overpainted with an umber-coloured paint. In the underlying layer of coarse-grained grey and red paint, it was still possible, however, to distinguish the old *craquelure* of the original top layer. Old layers of grey, red and yellow cracked paint were also discerned beneath the thinly overpainted background, mentioned above, near both figures, and also in the uniformly smooth umber-coloured area between Saul and the harp.

In the figure of David, as in that of Saul, a pattern of old cracks is to be seen in the coarse-grained layers of paint which here and there have worn away. The paint of the face and hands, which is mainly yellow, grey and brown, is old and rather uneven, owing to slightly raised edges of the cracks. The top right-hand area, which does not belong to the original painting, has been overpainted in a smooth, dark tone and displays practically no *craquelure*.

The layers of priming on this work are fairly thick and practically nowhere is the linen or its texture visible on the surface. The ground is grey-brown and consists to a large extent of white lead, yellow and red ochre, and also contains umber, bone black and chalk. The pigments are fairly coarse, the lumpy aggregates of white lead being especially prominent.

In various places, clear indications were found of the ground having been applied in two layers, as in the case of other paintings on canvas too, the lower layer appearing to be darker in tone. In most places, apart from the two figures, a uniformly thin layer of bone-black was found on top of the grey-brown ground. On this black layer—in the background, to the left of Saul, and in the curtain—an uppermost layer of a red lake pigment was found, with the result that the blacks also acquired a deeper tone.

This structure must indeed be the original one, for this black intermediate layer was also detected beneath areas which have been very considerably restored and overpainted, while the red lake pigment was often encountered in such places too.

The grey underpainting in the turban Saul is wearing has been applied straight on to the ground and is made up of coarse-grained white lead and carbon black. This grey is visible in some smaller areas on the surface. No black intermediate layer was detected in the paint layers of the turban.

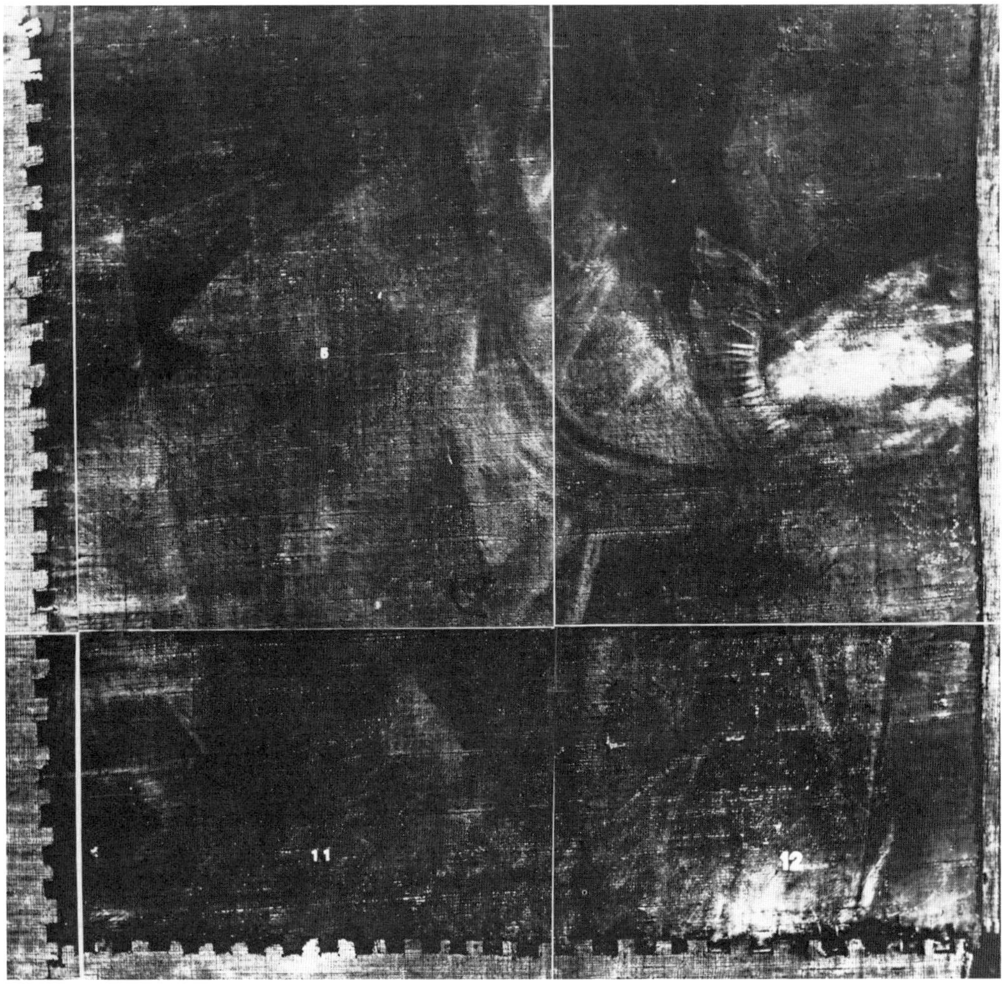

122. X-ray photograph. The added canvas in the upper right corner.

The turban has been painted in white lead, yellow and red ochres, mixed with black, while the blue pigment consists of azurite. Here, on the surface, a few large fragments were also found of a lighter blue pigment and this was identified as smalt. This same pigment was encountered elsewhere on the painting too, e.g. in the heads of Saul and David.

In addition to yellow ochre, the pigment known as lead-tin yellow was detected in the turban. It is remarkable that this pigment was found in the turban only and nowhere in the yellow of Saul's cloak and sleeves, nor in the David figure. The black layer on the ground is also missing in Saul's head, although the grey underpainting is again present here. It is visible particularly in places where the surface paint is thin and worn away and consists of white lead, umber and carbon black, with particles of a red lake pigment too. The flesh colours are composed of white lead mixed with yellow and red ochre and particles of a red lake pigment.

Part of the collar of the cloak has been painted with unblended white lead. The analysis of this white lead revealed traces of silver and copper, which were also found in the white lead of the highlights of the small crown on the turban.

The tunic Saul is wearing under the cloak has been painted chiefly in red and yellow ochres, with the addition of white lead and carbon black. In some places, the grey underpainting forms the dark areas.

The yellow and pale yellow paint of the upper part of the right sleeve of the tunic, covered by the red lake pigment of the cloak, proved to consist of the same pigments as were found in the uncovered lower part of the sleeve, *viz.,* white lead and yellow ochre. This examination of the pigments supports the conclusion drawn from the infra-red photograph, the X-ray photograph and also from scrutiny with the microscope, that the upper arm was originally completed and that the red cloak was painted in over it only afterwards.

123. Detail. King Saul and curtain.

124. X-ray photograph. Detail.
King Saul and curtain.

The cloak has been painted in red lake, partly (i.e. to the left, near the sleeve) on top of a black underlayer in which a fairly large number of coarse white grains of pigment were found. The shoulder-line of the cloak consists mainly of red ochre, while there is yellow ochre, too, in the edge folded back. The structure of this edge is interesting in so far as a layer of red lake is present under the top layer of paint, with here and there a very thin layer of carbon black beneath it. Under the latter a fairly thick intermediate layer of coarse-grained brownish-grey is found, and then the even black layer on top of the brownish-grey ground (as in the curtain and the background to the left of Saul).

The unusual structure of these layers can be explained as a further confirmation of the thesis that the large red cloak with its edging does not form part of the original painting but should be attributed to changes made in the original composition.

Under the right arm, where the cloak falls across Saul's right thigh, a number of red strokes are visible, consisting of red ochre. Closer examination revealed the presence, in places, of a layer of yellow ochre of varying thickness, beneath these red strokes of paint. Practically everywhere beneath this yellow ochre there is another layer of red ochre, with the ground beneath. Here and there, in this ground, remnants of a black layer could still be traced, and also a red lake. This structure also points to changes in the original composition, for in the areas of red beneath these red strokes, one finds only one thin layer of ochre. Here the uppermost red areas are followed by a layer of bone-black and then the ground. In this area there is a great deal of generously-applied red glazing in addition to, and on top of, the red ochre, as there is also over the yellow ochre areas in the edging of the cloak.

It can be said further that, in the background, left, near the figure of Saul, old areas of red and yellow were detected under the extensive retouching in thin umber colours, although it is not possible to deduce any particular detail from these areas.

David's head has the same paint structure as Saul's. Here, too, the grey-brown priming is followed by dark-grey underpainting containing coarse grains of white pigment, bone-black, umber and particles of a red lake pigment. The upper layer is made up of a mixture of yellow and red ochres, carbon black, red lake and white lead. Here, too, no black underlayer was found.

David's collar is composed of white lead and red ochre. Black underpainting can be seen in places where the top layer has worn off, but here and there black has also been applied on the red. There are places, too, where no layer of black was found and here the white and red lie immediately on top of the brownish-grey priming.

David's red garment has been painted principally in red ochre, white lead and yellow ochre. Here, on top of the priming, there is first a rather darker red ochre, but the upper paint layer is lighter in shade, yellow ochre and white lead having been added. No intermediate layer of black was found here either.

There is no signature and no date on the painting, nor were any remnants traced.

HISTORICAL DATA

The provenance of *Saul and David* cannot be traced back further than the year 1830 . In that year the work was in the collection of Victor-Louis-Charles de Riquet, comte de Caraman (1762-1839), which was auctioned in Paris between 10 and 12 May [4]. De Riquet was the French ambassador in Vienna until 1828, when he returned to Paris. In the sale catalogue the *Saul and David* is listed as item No. 76. We read: "David jouant de la harpe devant Saül. Assis et vu à mi-corps, Saül cache derrière un rideau la moitié de son visage; son air sombre indique l'agitation de son esprit. Une tunique de drap d'or et un manteau de velours cramoisi composent son vêtement. Plus bas que Saül, est placé David jouant de la harpe; on ne voit que la partie supérieure de son corps. Tableau capital où l'énergie du pinceau égale la vigueur du coloris, où Rembrandt, on peut bien le dire, a une physiognomie pittoresque qui est toute à lui. T. h. 45 p.—l. 67". The painter is referred to as "Rembrandt (Van Rijn, Paul)" [5]. According to a note in the copy of the sale catalogue kept in the Netherlands Institute for Art History, The Hague, the work was sold on this occasion for 250 francs—a remarkably low price.

The painting then became part of the collection of Didot de Saint Marc. After his death, in 1835, Saint Marc's widow married Abel Vautier, a member of parliament from Caen, and it was then presumabiy, that the *Saul and David* came into his possession; on 9 or 10 December 1863 the *Saul and David* was auctioned as item 31 in the Vautier collection [6]. According to Horsin Déon, who wrote the preface for this sale catalogue, the work was the most important item in the collection and it was accordingly described at great length [7]. In the copy of the sale catalogue in the keeping of the Netherlands Institute for Art History in The Hague, the following notes were added at a later date (c. 1876): "10000? Haro pour Oudry 12000 f à la vente Oudry racheté 29000 f à Durand Ruel par Febure. revendu 40 ou 50000 à

Cologne par Bourgeois". These notes correspond more or less with changes of ownership until about 1876. At this Vautier auction the painting was purchased by Oudry, a very wealthy engineer, for the sum of 10,000 francs. His adviser for the acquisition was the writer and art critic Henri de Rochefort (1830-1913). In his autobiography, entitled *Les aventures de ma vie,* the latter wrote about this purchase and about the doubts which the well-known art collector Dr. Louis Lacaze (1798-1869) had expressed, or heard of, concerning the *Saul and David* [8]. The marked variations in the prices fetched by the work are also, we feel, an indication of the doubts rumoured about regarding the attribution to Rembrandt.

The Alphonse Oudry collection was auctioned in Paris on 16 and 17 April 1869. Item No. 52 in the sale catalogue reads as follows: "Le roi Saül, livré à la plus noire mélancolie, se dérobe à moitié derrière un large rideau; devant lui, le jeune David joue de la harpe afin de chasser les sombres pensées qui obsèdent l'esprit du roi. Cette œuvre magistrale est de la plus belle époque du grand peintre; il y a déployé une puissance dramatique digne de Shakspeare et une incomparable magie de couleur et de clair-obscur. Collection Didot. Toile.—H. 1 m. 31 c., L. 1 m. 64 c." [9].

At this auction, the art dealer Durand-Ruel bought the *Saul and David,* selling it shortly after this to Arthur Stevens in Paris. The painting then came into the possession of the Paris art dealer Bourgeois, who sold it to A. Freiherr von Oppenheim, a banker and collector in Cologne. In that city, the work was put on exhibition in 1876 [10]. On account of doubts which had arisen as to its attribution to the master, Bourgeois took the painting back. After this, it was for some years in the possession of Ph. George in Ay, near Epernay. In 1890, Durand-Ruel purchased the work again, this time from Ph. George, and exhibited it on several occasions, in Chicago in 1893, for instance, and in Amsterdam in 1898 [11]. During the last-mentioned exhibition the *Saul and David* was purchased by A. Bredius for the sum of 200,000 francs [12]. Like his other works by Rembrandt, this painting, too, was bequeathed to the Mauritshuis by Bredius in 1946.

Nothing is known about the painting's vicissitudes prior to the year 1830 [13]. From the description then given of it, it is possible to deduce that the representation was the same as the one we see today. It is noteworthy that in that year, 1830, the dimensions of the canvas were quoted as 121.5 x 180.9 cm; that is to say, approximately 8 cm less in height and approximately 16 cm broader than the dimensions which have been available to us since 1869 (see the Oudry auction in Paris; 131 x 164 cm; note 9). As regards the difference in height, it should be remembered that strips of linen 4 and 3 cm wide, respectively, were added at the top and bottom, the top strip running as far as the piece of canvas which has been inserted in the top righthand corner (see *Technical data*). This is sufficient to explain the overall difference of approximately 8 cm.

The 16 cm difference in width very probably resulted from the entire canvas having been cut into two parts (to have Saul and David as two separate works) and from the restoration performed afterwards. It is understandable that the top right-hand corner should have been lost, since unless this was removed, the proportions of the separate figure of David playing the harp would have been unusual.

Didot de Saint Marc's widow married in 1835 Abel Vautier of Caen and the latter's estate was auctioned in 1863, the *Saul and David* being among the items (although no dimensions were mentioned). The question is: did Didot de Saint Marc, who had purchased the work in 1830, or his widow, take the drastic step of dividing the painting? It is also possible that the wealthy collector Oudry experimented with the painting, since it was precisely in the years between 1863 and 1869 that doubts had arisen regarding its authenticity, partly as a result of the Rochefort-Lacaze controversy (see note 8). Such incomplete information suggests only that the work was cut in two and put together again sometime between 1830 and 1869.

It is possible that prior to 1830 this *Saul and David* had been a taller picture. The picture of David playing the harp will be discussed again, under the heading *Iconography,* but with the original dimensions of the painting in mind, we ought to draw attention to the remarkable manner in which the harp has been sliced off and to David's posture which is difficult to understand.

Since it was not unusual at all for a large canvas to be made up of strips of linen of equal size, we may assume that the lower half was formerly c. 14 cm higher, since the visible join runs across 7 cm below the centre line [14]. However this may be, in view of the height of the painting in 1830, this cutting away from the lower edge must have taken place before that date.

Collections

V.-L.-Ch. de Riquet, comte de Caraman, Paris, 1830

Didot de Saint Marc, 1835

Abel Vautier, Caen, 1863

Alphonse Oudry, Paris, 1869
Durand-Ruel, art dealer, Paris
Arthur Stevens, Paris
St. Bourgeois, art dealer, Paris
A. Freiherr von Oppenheim, Cologne, 1876
St. Bourgeois, art dealer, Paris
Ph. George, Ay near Epernay, 1890
Durand-Ruel, art dealer, Paris/New York, 1890-1898
Dr. A. Bredius, The Hague, on loan to the Mauritshuis, 1898-1946
Bredius Bequest, 1946

Dimensions quoted

1830	45 pouces x 67 pouces = approx. 121.5 x 180.9 cm
1869	131 x 164 cm
1876	129 x 163 cm
1898	130 x 164 cm
1977	130 x 164.3 cm

Prices

1830	250 francs
1863	10,000 francs
1869	12,000 or 12,500 francs
c. 1870	29,000 francs
c. 1876	40,000 or 50,000 francs
1890	140,000 francs
1898	200,000 francs

ICONOGRAPHY AND STYLE

King Saul, seated on a dais, is dressed in a yellow tunic over which he is wearing a broad red cloak. A small crown has been fixed on top of his multi-coloured turban. He has drawn a curtain towards him with his left hand thus covering the left side of his face, in particular his left eye. His right hand is extended but relaxed and rests on a javelin on his right. Opposite him David, a half-length figure, is seen playing the harp (Fig. 119). Saul's dress is of a general historical character and is meant to represent an oriental potentate. His mighty turban with the crown stresses the oriental and biblical personality as well as his rank. David wears a doublet with slashed sleeves which are gathered in at the wrists, a kind of costume worn during the 16th century and often seen in pictures from Northern Italy.

The harp, which David is pressing against his left shoulder, is an "angular", also known as a Gothic harp. The simply-fashioned pillar and neck, carved

125. Rembrandt. David playing the Harp before Saul, c. 1630. *Frankfurt, Staedelsches Kunstinstitut.*

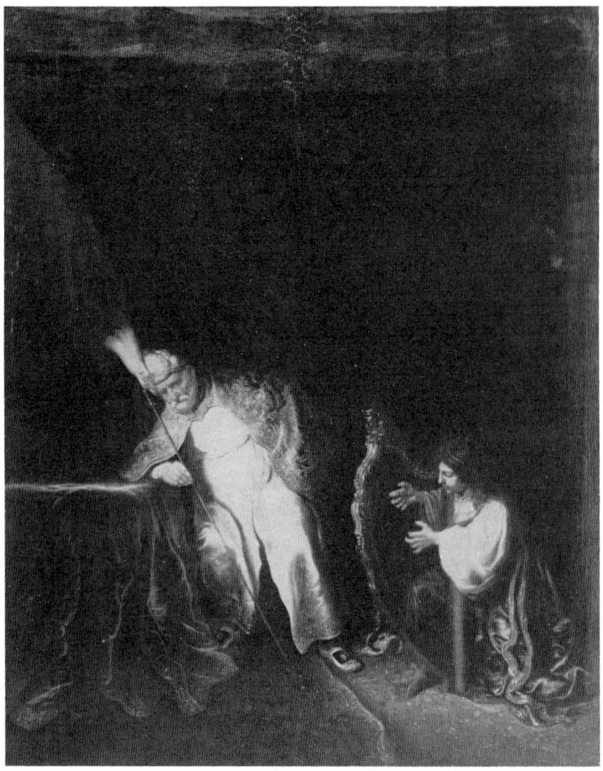

126. Salomon Koninck. David playing the Harp before Saul, 1655. *Schwerin, Staatliches Museum.*

127

128

129

130

131

127. Old copy after Rembrandt (?). David playing the Harp before Saul. Drawing. *Present location unknown.*

128. Old copy after Rembrandt. David playing the Harp before Saul. Drawing. *Paris, Musée du Louvre.*

129. Lucas van Leyden. David playing the Harp before Saul. Engraving, B. 27.

130. After Maerten van Heemskerck. David playing the harp before Saul. Engraving.

131. Frans Floris. David playing the Harp before Saul, 1555. *Chiaroscuro* woodcut.

out of one and the same piece of wood, have a ridge and flutings as their decoration. A harp of this type has twenty-six strings [15].

References to a few other versions of the same theme may prove helpful in visualizing the harp David is using. Among the paintings are: Rembrandt (Br.-G., No. 490) (Fig. 125); Salomon Koninck (1655), Schwerin, Museum (Fig. 126); among the drawings: copy after Rembrandt, Sir Robert Mond's collection, Cat. No. 430 (Fig. 127); copy after Rembrandt, Paris, Musée du Louvre, (Fig. 128). In these works, the harp is placed on the ground while the player is kneeling either on both knees or on one. There is a clear distinction between this instrument and the "hand harp" which we also encounter in the 16th and 17th centuries: *inter alia,* Lucas van Leyden (Fig. 129); Maerten van Heemskerck (Fig. 130); Frans Floris (Fig. 131); Pieter H. Schut (Fig. 132); D. Colijns, Utrecht, Rijksmuseum Het Catharijneconvent (Fig. 133).

Until a short time ago there was no agreement as to King Saul's mood. Many have seen in him a lonely figure, so deeply moved by the music David is playing on his harp that he has grasped the edge of the curtain around his throne to dry his tears on it [16]. As far as we have been able to ascertain, it was Emile Michel who was the first to mention this particular. He and other authors up to and including G. Knuttel (1956), who agreed with him, were of the view that this work was an illustration of the scene in The First Book of Samuel, Chapter 16, verse 23. In the English Authorized Version of the Bible this passage reads as follows: "And it came to pass, when the evil spirit from God was upon Saul, that David took an harp, and played with his hand: so Saul was refreshed, and was well, and the evil spirit departed from him" [17].

In the Dutch Authorized Version of 1637 [18] this passage is explained in the margin as follows: "The terrors and tortures of evil spirits ceased when David played. God, in His providence, has so ordered and disposed these matters that David should be admitted to the court of the King in order that he might open and prepare the way for him to the Kingdom for which he had chosen and already anointed him".

In 1948, however, Jacob Rosenberg wrote: "His uncovered eye, wide open and darkly brooding, betrays his inner torment; so does the slightly suggested movement of his right hand on the javelin" [19]. For this reason, the scene depicted would be The First Book of Samuel, Chapter 18, verses 9-11 [20]. In the English Authorized Version these verses read as follows: "And Saul eyed David from that day and forward. And it came to pass on the morrow, that the evil spirit from God came upon Saul, and he prophesied in the midst of the house: and David played with his hand, as at other times: and there was a javelin in Saul's hand. And Saul cast the javelin; for he said, I will smite David even to the wall with it. And David avoided out of his presence twice".

The annotations to these verses in the Dutch biblical text read as follows: "Hebrew: eyed David. Spied on him and looked for any opportunity to kill him: or from that time forward he looked on him with evil in his eyes and was hostile to him".

The sense is that Saul, being tormented by the evil spirit, fell into transports and acted strangely.

"David played in order to alleviate Saul's unrest and torment and to cheer him in his melancholy" [21].

It would seem from the Bible texts quoted that Rembrandt has not, in any case, portrayed Saul when his peace of mind had been restored. What he has shown is the hostile King in I Samuel 18, who is keeping his eye on David, whom he distrusts, and, half-concealing his face, his hand on his javelin, is waiting for the right moment to slay him. The verses in I Samuel 19 do not differ very much in content from those in I Samuel 18.

Tümpel has pointed out that in his compositions, Rembrandt includes objects of iconographical significance which may bear a reference to episodes preceding or following that depicted [22]. Thus, in this painting the javelin points to what is to follow, according to Tümpel, which would mean that he, too, is of the view that it is not I Samuel 16 but I Samuel 18 that has been illustrated here. (In I Samuel 16 there is no mention at all of the javelin.) The ominous look in Saul's right eye—which many, strangely enough, have overlooked—also corresponds with what we read in I Samuel 18, verse 9: "And Saul eyed David from that day and forward".

Thus we may be certain that in the Mauritshuis painting, it is the text of I Samuel 18, verses 9-11 that Rembrandt has taken as his theme.

The conflicting interpretations are not, for that matter, surprising, although we would not go so far as does Irmgard Smidt-Dörrenberg, who suggests that Rembrandt had not intended to illustrate any particular biblical episode [23]. We do, however, share her view that his interpretation of the story goes far beyond the text found in the Bible, telling the story in his own sensitive imaginative language.

It is strange, too, that so many authors should have written about a Saul who is highly moved and wiping away his tears, since no tear is to be seen in his eye or on his cheek. Owing to this interpretation and owing also to Saul's apparently more or less relaxed

posture—overlooking his facial expression—it is un-
posture—ignoring his facial expression—it is understandable that for so long he should have been taken here for a Saul whose mind was at peace. We should also assess this interpretation in the light of the ideas regarding Rembrandt's evolution generally accepted until a short time ago. In his youthful period, Rembrandt had shown a predilection for baroque features and for the visible expression of emotion (see, for example, his *Saul and David* of c. 1630; Br.-G., No. 490) (Fig. 125); but the older artist, ripe with experience, was more interested in deep feelings and emotions.

Nor should we overlook the iconographic tradition of which Rembrandt was so often aware. In the various 16th and 17th century versions of the "Saul and David" theme, the situation described in I Samuel 18, verse 9, where a suspicious Saul is contemplating revenge, is sometimes the main theme, while at other times it is the situation in verse 10, where Saul, in a fury, is about to pierce David with his javelin.

We do not find anything to go on in the work of Lastman and his contemporaries, neither as regards the *Saul and David* in The Hague nor as regards the *Saul and David* Rembrandt painted about the year 1630 (Fig. 125).

In both the painting by Salomon Koninck (1655) (Fig. 126) and the Hague painting, Saul is shown contemplating revenge, while David is completely absorbed in his playing. Some drawings from the Rembrandt school representing the story of Saul and David have been preserved but they have no connection with the Hague painting [24]. A drawing which may possibly come somewhere near the painting is the one reproduced on page 157 (Fig. 128). Hofstede de Groot, Valentiner and others saw some connection between this drawing—a copy of an unknown drawing by Rembrandt—and the *Saul and David* in the Mauritshuis [25].

Rembrandt had a great admiration for the work of Lucas van Leyden and knew undoubtedly, if he did not own, his engraving illustrating Saul and David [36] (Fig. 129). Although the theme is naturally treated differently, the same text, I Samuel 18, verses 9-11, forms the basis of both works, with the emphasis on verse 9.

In 1555 Frans Floris made a *chiaroscuro* woodcut (Fig. 131). An inscription on the throne reads *Saul 1 REG. Ca. XVI,* yet the scene illustated is to be found in I Samuel 16 [27]. Here, apparently, David has exercised a benign influence on the king, whose servants are endeavouring to calm him down completely.

In contrast to this, two prints illustrate the situa-

132. Pieter H. Schut. David playing the Harp before Saul, 1659. Engraving.

tion in which Saul, with his javelin raised, is about to "pin" David to the wall (with the emphasis on verse 10) [28]. One after Maarten van Heemskerk (Fig. 130), bearing the inscription: *Invasit spiritus malignus Saul, ac lanceam misit, putans et configere posset David cum parete; 1 Re. 18.,* and the other by Pieter H. Schut (from the illustrated Bible of 1659, with an explanatory text below it which reads: "David speelt voor Saul die hem soeckt te dooden. 1 Samuel 18: 10)" (Fig. 132).

Rembrandt probably knew the paintings which David Colijns (1582-1668) had made on canvas and which had been attached to the wings of the organ in the *Nieuwe Zijds Kapel* in Amsterdam (c. 1635-40). These are now in the Rijksmuseum Het Catharijne-

133. David Colijns. David playing the Harp before Saul, c. 1635/'40. *Utrecht, Rijksmuseum, Het Catharijneconvent* (photograph taken during restoration).

convent in Utrecht [29]. On one David is shown with Goliath's head, on the other he is playing the harp before Saul, who is in a fury and raising his javelin to kill him (Fig. 133).

Knüpfer has made a highly emotional and baroque composition of his *Saul and David,* in which Saul's second daughter Michal—who is also David's wife—is also present. In the Bible text, however, she does not appear until the next chapter. Here, after Saul's fury with David has subsided, she helps David to flee (I Samuel 19, verses 9-12). Knüpfer's composition bears no relationship whatever to Rembrandt's painting [30].

Although we have not endeavoured to be exhaustive in this survey, we feel justified in saying that in the painting in The Hague, Rembrandt has gone entirely his own way.

The curtain Saul is tugging towards him (doubtlessly part of the hangings of his throne) is a motif which Rembrandt was, as far as we know, the first to employ and which is of more than superficial significance: it accentuates the gulf between the two figures—a gulf which is emphasized still more by David's complete absorption in his playing, which is another motif found first in Rembrandt. Although David is doing his utmost to bring peace to his master's mind, he is unable to bridge the gap between them, which is stressed by the curtain and Saul's gesture.

We do not know whether there was anything of importance to be seen on the piece of canvas above David's head now lost to us (a piece measuring 60 x 60 cm). It might, for instance, have shown David's wife Michal, Saul's daughter, looking on. We are not convinced there was anything to be seen, however, in view of the spatial factor and the painting's composition and especially as there is no mention of this in the fairly detailed description of the work in the sale catalogue of 1830.

Saul's head has sometimes been compared with that of *A Bearded Man* (Br.-G., No. 284) [31]. This resemblance is not convincing. Moreover, Rembrandt had a wide choice of characteristically Jewish types in his immediate vicinity.

Valentiner has suggested that the drawing *Nathan admonishing David* is directly related to *Saul and David* and that this drawing may have been a sketch for a companion piece [32] (Fig. 134). We do not, in any case, know of any painting illustrating this subject. It should, however, be granted that this drawing and the *Saul and David* show a certain relationship in the grandeur of composition and in mood.

The story of David playing the harp for Saul in order to drive away Jehovah's evil spirit is one of the earliest illustrations of the healing effect of music [33]. Although the commentary in the Dutch Authorized Version of 1637 speaks of David playing the harp "to refresh Saul in his melancholy", and although it is suggested that Saul's gesture, pulling the curtain towards him, is a fairly customary one to express melancholy, we do not, however, believe that Rembrandt was particularly concerned to paint Saul as a melancholic [34].

In 1969 H. Gerson published his rejection of Rembrandt's authorship of *Saul and David.* He attributed the work to pupils in Rembrandt's studio, pointing to the drawing, Benesch, VI, No. C 76 (Fig. 128), and to the *Descent from the Cross* in the National Gallery in Washington (Br.-G., No. 584). Gerson was unfortunately obliged to be brief, yet the arguments he puts forward seem to us anything but convincing. They are, at all events, difficult to refute since they are no less subjective than the view of his predecessors and contemporaries who do accept the attribution to Rembrandt [35].

It is true that since 1947 doubts as to whether this is Rembrandt's own work have been expressed now and then, but, as far as we know, by word of mouth only [36]. The history of this painting shows that even in the 19th century it had been doubted whether this was the work of Rembrandt's own hand (see *Historical data*).

Doubt can often be the first step on the road to truth. We fear, however, that here too, it is not yet possible to say the last word (see *Introduction*) [37].

The dating of the work varies between the middle of the fifties to about the middle of the sixties [38]. This uncertainty was one of the reasons for Gerson's rejection of the attribution to Rembrandt.

The X-ray photographs, the infra-red photograph and the microscopic investigation, too, into the structure of the paint layers have brought facts to light which had previously escaped the naked eye (see *Technical data*). Many years before the technical investigations took place, however, one of us (De Vries), had advanced the opinion to a few of his colleagues that the painting might have been executed in two stages. This was possibly one of the reasons why some of them were uneasy about the attribution to Rembrandt [39]. This opinion has been confirmed to a certain extent by the technical examination of the work.

Stylistic considerations lead us to assume that, after having completed the work about the middle of the fifties, the painter turned his attention to it again at some time between 1660 and 1665. In the second

134. Rembrandt. Nathan admonishing David. Drawing. *New York, The Metropolitan Museum of Art. Bequest of Mrs. H.O. Havemeyer, 1929.*

phase, the red cloak, which had originally fallen from the shoulders down Saul's back (cf. the drawing showing *Nathan admonishing David,* Benesch, V, No. 947 (Fig. 134) and also Benesch, V, No. 948) was much enlarged so that it now fell down over his upper right arm and the armchair on which Saul is seated. The infra-red photograph (Fig. 121) leaves no doubt on this score, and once we are aware of it we can also clearly see that the strap and clasp with which the cloak is fastened originally continued across to the shoulder and also that the entire sleeve of the right arm had been painted in the first stage.

In the X-ray photograph (Fig. 124), to the right, above the hand resting on the javelin, we see old overpainting in white lead, containing a few light dots, as in the right sleeve (see *Technical data*), and these are difficult to interpret. They do, however, indicate that the fall of the curtain was different in the first stage and left more of Saul's tunic visible. Thus these overpainted areas might have had to do with details of this garment.

The rather wild strokes of paint across Saul's thigh, which have prompted cirticism from some quarters, have been painted in over the original arm of the throne; a circular volute at the end of it is still visible under the red of the cloak. This was not noticed until now.

It is possible to conceive that the enlargement of the cloak and the broadening of the curtain in the second phase of the painting are connected. There is a certain compositional balance between these two components. And where the red of the cloak is concerned, this finds its counterpart in the red which is so eloquent in the figure of David.

Investigation has shown that the piece of canvas removed from above David's head was lost, and replaced, when the original composition was restored, by a fragment of an old painting, probably a 17th century work (see the *Technical* and *Historical data*). A portion of a coat, a cuff and a hand can be discerned inthe X-ray photograph (Fig. 122). H.E. van Gelder's opinion that, when this piece was added in the

135. The photograph of the painting taken by T. Sardnal. Durand-Ruel éditeur, Paris, c. 1895.

top right-hand corner, to complete the canvas, it bore a woman's portrait which was replaced by a plain background when the work was restored after Bredius had purchased it, is not tenable [40]. However this may be, the inserted part is certainly not a happy detail in the painting by reason of its unrelieved black and the heavy varnish.

As far as we know, the *Saul and David* has not undergone further restoration since 1898 nor have the layers of old and yellowed varnish been removed. A photograph, kindly made available about 1969 by Ch. Durand-Ruel of Paris, shows the state of the work around the year 1895 [41] (Fig. 135).

It is remarkable that Rembrandt should not have signed so large a work, though in pointing this out, we should remind the reader of the caution with which signatures should be approached (see *Introduction*), when deciding on the authenticity of works said to be by Rembrandt, since they often prove not to be wholly reliable.

There is no means of ascertaining whether a signature did once (before 1830) exist on a rather taller work, perhaps at the bottom or possibly on the lost portion of the canvas in the top right-hand corner.

As regards the date of the work, the figure of David fits into Rembandt's œuvre during the period around 1655—one may think here particularly of his *Titus Reading* (Br.-G., No. 122). The treatment of the light on both faces and the absorption of each character in what he is doing (David playing the harp, Titus reading) support this view and even point clearly to Rembrandt's hand and mind.

A few final remarks. The foregoing makes clear that no part of the investigation (technical, historical or stylistic) has made it possible to decide conclusively as to Rembrandt's authorship. The entire investigation, the technical included, has, however, produced nothing to support the view that the painting is the work of a pupil or pupils. It goes without saying that Rembrandt and his pupils prepared canvases and did the underpainting in his studio in the same manner, using the same paints. We are quite willing to accept that at some stage, or stages, Rembrandt called in his pupils' assistance, but we should be surprised if he allowed them to co-operate in the painting of large compositions, where the interpretation of the theme and the execution were paramount. We should also be surprised, although less so, if he allowed this when important changes were to be made. What we do at least know is that Rembrandt was the

136. Aert de Gelder. David playing the Harp before Saul, 1682. *Bremen, Kunsthalle.*

only Dutch painter of his time to create and imagine a new biblical world, proceeding from a tradition which—and that is what matters—he carried further, enriching it with new possibilities of expression [42]. In this painting, the love-hate relationship existing between the King and his favourite, who was also his foe, is accentuated by a dialogue which does not consist of words but is conjured up by music. This psychological situation is suggested in a way hardly to be expected from any of Rembrandt's pupils.

The *Saul and David* by Aert de Gelder (painted 1682, i.e. many years after he had left Rembrandt's studio) (Fig. 136) shows clearly how a less talented painter approached a composition of the master, presumably known to him: it became no more than a banal interpretation of the same theme [43].

No answer has ever been given to the question as to whether Rembrandt was commissioned to paint this work [44]. Being in difficult financial circumstances, as he was, the artist was not likely to have painted so large a canvas, had it not been commissioned. It is possible that Lodewyck van Ludick, an art dealer for whom Rembrandt painted a *Jonathan and David* about the year 1659, had customers for historical paintings of this importance [45]. Its dimensions were certainly unusual for the average-sized house in Amsterdam. Although no indication has ever been found to suggest as much, it is not inconceivable that Rembrandt painted the work for one of the rich Portuguese Jews in the city, some of whom had art collections and who lived, as we know, in Rembrandt's neighbourhood. It is not excluded either that some other foreigner besides Ruffo commissioned works from the painter in the fifties and sixties (see No. XII, Homer) [46].

As far as the authors are concerned, they are not aware of any sufficient reason to doubt that this is a work painted by Rembrandt himself, although they admit that some questions remain to which they have no answer.

NOTES

1. This painting has already been described in detail by A.B. de Vries in "Nog eens Saul en David in het Mauritshuis", *Album Amicorum J.G. van Gelder,* The Hague, 1973, pp. 347-352.

2. L. Kuiper pointed out that he had never before encountered this manner of joining. He considers it possible that it was a matter of adopting the method of joining wooden panels. He did not, however, wish to commit himself to saying when such a method was employed.

3. See A. Bredius, "Jaarverslag Mauritshuis over 1898", *Verslagen omtrent 's Rijks verzamelingen van geschiedenis en kunst,* 21, The Hague, 1899, p. 69 and note 1; notes in the sale catalogue of the Abel Vautier auction, 9-11 December 1863; The memoirs of M. Paul Durand, published in L. Venturi, *Les archives de l'Impressionisme,* 2, Paris, 1939, p. 168; written communication from the firm of Durand-Ruel & Cie, Paris.
H.d.G. is in error in referring to the A.J. Petit auction of 5-6 July 1826 in Malines, No. 223: "David pinçant de la harpe, tableau capital de ce maître. P.".
According to the note in the copy of the sale catalogue kept at the Netherlands Institute for Art History in The Hague, the work was sold for 110 florins to a certain Pierets (Lugt, II, No. 11227). The painting of David playing the harp was painted on wood.

4. Lugt, II, No. 12364.

5. The painter has also been referred to as Paul in the following sale catalogues: Lugt, II, No. 27580 and Lugt, II, No. 31191 (see notes 6 and 9). Rembrandt was often named Paul during the 19th century. In 1877, C. Vosmaer in his *Rembrandt. Sa vie et ses œuvres,* The Hague, 1877, p. VI, wrote: "It would be as well if we were at last to cease giving him the first name of Paul, a name he never bore". Vosmaer, by the way, made no mention of the *Saul and David,* neither in his 1868 nor in his 1877 edition.

6. These particulars concerning the Didot de Saint Marc collection are quoted in the sale catalogue; Lugt, II, No. 27580.

7. "David jouant de la harpe devant Saül. Ce prince, abandonné de Dieu, se cache derrière un rideau pour écouter les accords mélodieux de la harpe de David, dont le charme chasse de son esprit les pensées furieuses qui ont laissé sur son front leur indélébile empreinte. Le calme de David, sous la douce impression de son chant, forme le contraste le plus heureux entre l'homme maudit et la pure et expansive jeunesse de l'élu, et exprime avec bonheur les différents sentiments qui les animent tous deux. L'entente de cette composition répond à l'illusion que produit son piquant effet. Le costume royal de Saül composé d'un manteau de velours cramoisi, d'une robe de drap d'or, d'un turban de cachemire aussi mélangé d'or, ajoute encore au grand caractère de cette belle peinture. Mais, ce qui la recommande pardessus tout, c'est sa couleur brillante, ses beaux empâtements, produit d'une touche facile, grasse et mœlleuse tout à la fois; ce sont ces clairs obscurs si transparents, c'est l'harmonie de ce tableau qui le classent parmi les meilleurs du maître". It is noteworthy that no dimensions are quoted.

8. H. de Rochefort, *Les aventures de ma vie,* Paris, 1896-98, 1, Chap. VI, pp. 117-118; communicated by Madame S. Béguin of the Musée du Louvre. The text reads as follows: "Vers la fin, le docteur La Caze—à qui je n'ai jamais connu un malade—avait un peu perdu de son infaillibilité artistique. Il achetait à bas prix des rossignols qu'il baptisait à sa façon—Je me rappelle m'être fortement entrepris avec lui au sujet d'une magnifique toile de Rembrandt, représentant *David jouant de la harpe devant Saül,* et dont il contestait l'authenticité. Cet aveuglement m'exaspéra, et je ne pus m'empêcher de lui dire: 'Monsieur Lacaze, vous n'avez pas le droit d'employer votre grande autorité en matière de maîtres anciens pour déprécier un tableau qui n'est pas douteux. Examinez-le de plus près et vous serez de mon avis.' Mais, assez vaniteux, le docteur Lacaze était aussi très entêté. Il s'obstina ou fit semblant de s'obstiner dans son opinion. Le Rembrandt fut acheté dix mille francs seulement, par un ingénieur fort riche, M. Oudry à qui je conseillai de ne pas laisser échapper une aussi rare occasion".

9. Lugt, II, No. 31191. The dimensions quoted agree with the actual measurements.

10. Exh. cat. *Kunsthistorische Ausstellung,* Cologne, 1876, No. 61. The painter was named Paul Rembrandt van Rijn.

11. Exh. cat. *Paintings, Sculptures, and Other Objects Exhibited During the World's Congresses,* Chicago (The Art Institute), 1893, No. 27; Exh. cat. *Rembrandt. Schilderijen bijeengebracht ter gelegenheid van de inhuldiging van Hare Majesteit Koningin Wilhelmina,* Amsterdam, (Stedelijk Museum), 1898, No. 118. According to H.d.G. the *Saul and David* was also for a time in the possession of the collector H.O. Havemeyer. We have not, however, been able to find anything to substantiate this. It may be that Havemeyer had the work "on approval" while it was in the United States. The name Havemeyer is mentioned in notes kept by the firm of Durand-Ruel, but it has not been recorded that he bought it, as is the case with other names noted.

12. A. Bredius sacrificed his horse and carriage for it. Later on he refused a very high offer, many times the price he had paid for the work. This offer was made by J. Pierpont Morgan, the greatest collector in the United States in the years prior to the Great War of 1914-18.
It is highly remarkable that doubts as to the authenticity of the work ceased once Bredius had purchased it. Jan Veth did not express the slightest doubt about Rembrandt's authorship. On the contrary, he was deeply impressed. ("Uit een geannoteerden catalogus van de Rembrandt-tentoonstelling", *De Kroniek,* 16, 23 and 30 October 1898, pp. 13-14). Neither were any further doubts formulated in any of the "Rembrandt literature" after 1898, until Gerson rejected Rembrandt's authorship in 1969.

13. Dutuit, 3, contains a description of a *Story of Saul* by Rembrandt, a work which was auctioned with the collection of the painter and art dealer Jacques de Roore (1686-1747), on 4 September 1747, a fact recorded by Mrs. A. Both-de Brauw in her study on the *Saul and David,* a typed copy of which is in the Mauritshuis files. Further research has shown, however, that the hypothesis we published in 1973, to the effect that this *Story of Saul* might perhaps be identical with the *Saul and David* in the Mauritshuis, cannot be correct. According to a note in the sale catalogue kept in the Netherlands Institute for Art History in The Hague (Lugt, I, No. 672), this painting was purchased by "D'ablin" i.e. Baron d'Ablaing van Giesenburg. When the latter's collection was auctioned in Utrecht on 26 October 1775, item No. 4 in the sale catalogue (Lugt, I, No. 2445; a copy at the Bibliothèque Nationale in Paris) reads as follows: "Een konstig stuk, daar David de tyding van Sauls dood met de Vorstelyke Eerteekenen door de Amalekiet gebragt worden, zeer stout geschilderd door Rembrant van Ryn, hoog 6 voet 4 duim breet 7 voet 4 ½ duim". (This information was kindly communicated to us by Carlos van Hasselt). This work was the sole Rembrandt in the sale catalogue and since its dimensions (measured, according to the catalogue, in Utrecht feet and from inside the frame) correspond almost exactly with the Rembrandt of De Roore (measured in Rhineland feet) it must be assumed that this was the Rembrandt painting which D'Ablaing had purchased at the De Roore auction. F. Lugt probably never consulted this sale catalogue. According to his notes, he, too, believed that the painting in the De Roore collection was identical with the Hague *Saul and David.*

14. Kindly communicated by L. Kuiper, chief restorer of paintings in the Rijksmuseum Amsterdam. It is assumed that the work did not differ considerably in dimensions from those quoted above.

15. This type of harp was played in the 15th and 16th centuries. See, for example, King David playing the harp in the altarpiece by Albert Dürer, *The Adoration of the Holy Trinity,* 1511 (Kunsthistorisches Museum, Vienna, Inv. No. 838) and a *Company Singing, accompanied by the Harp,* after Dirck Barendsz., (of c. 1550; Kurfürstliche Galerie, Munich). The same harp is to be seen in a drawing by Rembrandt, entitled *Nathan admonishing David,* c. 1652-53 (Benesch, V, Cat. No. 918, ill. 1129).
Both in David's dress and in the shape of the harp, Rembrandt has followed what was at the time an out-dated mode. Van de Waal has already pointed out that where religious pieces were concerned, it must surely have been taken that "the new fashion was worldly and sinful and was accordingly not in keeping with the sacred nature of the subject" (see H. van de Waal, *Drie eeuwen vaderlandse geschied-uitbeelding, 1500-1800. Een iconologische studie,* 1, The Hague, 1952, p. 62).

16. *Inter alia:* J. Veth, *Rembrandt's Leven en Kunst,* Amsterdam, 1906, p. 171; W. Weisbach, *Rembrandt,* Berlin, 1926, pp. 518-519; Cat. M. (1935), No. 621.

17. E. Michel, *Rembrandt. Sa vie, son œuvre et son temps,* Paris, 1893, p. 446; L. Réau, *Iconographie de l'Art Chrétien. Iconographie de la Bible,* 1, Paris, 1956, No. 263; G. Knuttel, *Rembrandt. De meester en zijn werk,* Amsterdam, 1956, p. 211.

18. *Biblia, dat is: de gantsche H. Schrifture, vervattende alle de Canonijcke Boecken des Ouden en des Nieuwen Testaments. Nu eerst, door last der ... Heeren Staten Generael ... uyt de oorspronckelijcke talen in onse Neder-landtsche tale getrouwelijck over-geset. Met nieuwe bij-gevoegde verklaringen ... ende nieuwe registers over beyde de Testamenten,* Leiden, 1637.

19. J. Rosenberg, *Rembrandt, Life & Work,* London, 1968³, p. 228.

20. The story of Saul and David is also to be found in *Flavii Josephi hooghberoemde Joodsche historien ende boecken,* Amsterdam, 1626, Fol. 56-57. J. Rosenberg, *Rembrandt, Life & Work,* London, 1968³, p. 182, assumed an influence had been exerted by the writings of Menno Simons; David's playing of the harp does not, however, occur in these writings. See *Opera Menno Symons, ofte Groot Sommarie...,* 1646, pp. 281-282.

21. Prof. M.H. Gans of Amsterdam has informed us that in the Hebrew text the word used (*oween*), derived from the substantive (*noun*) for eye, hardly ever occurs. In the Aramaic free translation it occurs as *kamien* and this is translated as spy upon, lurk, watch secretly.
J. Rosenberg, *Rembrandt. Life & Work,* London, 1968³, p. 228, note 61, saw some relation between the figure of Saul and one of the Doomed in Michelangelo's *The Last Judgment:* both are covering one eye.

22. C. Tümpel, "Studien zur Ikonograpie der Historien Rembrandt's", *Nederlands Kunsthistorisch Jaarboek,* 20, 1969, p. 138.

23. I. Smidt-Dörrenberg, *David en Saul. Variationen über ein Thema von Rembrandt,* Vienna, 1969, p. 23: "Rembrandt has not represented any particular scene at all. He has painted these two people, Saul and David in their special nature, fatefulness and their dialogue, which comprises their wide-ranging story and their whole tragedy".

24. Copy after Rembrandt/School of Rembrandt, 162 x 218 mm, auction at Amsterdam (F. Müller), 15/16 June 1926, No. 424; Rembrandt School, 339 x 250 mm, Warsaw, University Library; copy, after Rembrandt, 207 x 306 mm, Sir Robert Mond's collection, Cat. No. 430.

25. Benesch, VI, Cat. No. C 76, ill. 1630; see there for literature. H. Gerson is, however, of the opinion that the Hague painting was executed by a pupil or pupils of Rembrandt "after a drawing of the master in the manner of Benesch C 76 (which is itself a copy)".

26. B., No. 27; Hollstein, Vol. 10, p. 79. It is known that Rembrandt owned prints by Lucas van Leyden. See for example, R. Fuchs, *Rembrandt en Amsterdam,* Rotterdam, 1968, p. 76, No. 193 (Inventory of Rembrandt's possessions, 165).

27. The Books of Samuel formerly formed part of the Book of Kings; this is why we read: *1 Re 18.* Hollstein, Vol. 6, p. 251, No. 1, with ill.; C. van de Velde, *Frans Floris. Leven en werk,* Brussels, 1975, pp. 395-396, No. P 15, ill. 168.

28. Hollstein, Vol. 8, p. 247, Nos. 491-500[10]; *Toneel ofte Vertooch der Bybelsche Historien,* Amsterdam, 1659, ill. 79.

29. The two canvases were not originally meant for these organ wings but were attached to them at a later date, when they were altered to fit the required shape. They are to regain their original, rectangular shape after being restored. When the canvases were attached to the wings is not known but according to a description dating from 1665, the paintings had already been fitted by then (see P. Dirkse, "De Nieuwe Zijds Kapel en de inrichting in de 17de eeuw", *Spiegel Historiael* 12, 1977, pp. 12-13).

30. N. Knüpfer, Utrecht, Centraal Museum, Inv. No. 11148 (see J.I. Kuznetzow, "Nikolaus Knüpfer (1603?-1655)", *Oud Holland,* 88, 1974, p. 182, Cat. No. 7, ill. 2).

31. J.L.A.A.M. van Rijckevorsel, *Rembrandt en de traditie,* Rotterdam, 1932, p. 210. There seems to be no foundation for the suggestion that Spinoza was, as a young man, the model for the figure of David (A. Ch. Coppier, "Rembrandt et Spinoza", *Revue des deux Mondes,* 32, 1916, p. 160).

32. W. Valentiner, "Ein Altersentwurf Rembrandts", *Genius,* 2, 1920, pp. 44-56. Benesch, V, No. 947, ill. 1156.

33. L. Réau, *Iconographie de l'Art Chrétien. Iconographie de la Bible* 1, Paris, 1956, No. 263; G. Bandmann, *Melancholie und Musik. Iconographische Studien,* Cologne, 1960, p. 11; R. Klibansky, E. Panovsky and F. Saxl, *Saturn and Melancholy,* London, 1964, pp. 46, 81; E. Kirschbaum S.J. etc., *Lexikon der christlichen Ikonographie,* 4, Nachträge, Rome, 1972, p. 605.
The fact that we find the story of Saul and David more than once on the wings of organs demonstrates once again the theme's relation to the world of music.

34. Communicated by L. de Vries; see also A. Blankert, "Heraclitus en Democritus", *Nederlands Kunsthistorisch Jaarboek* 18, 1967, pp. 53-54.

35. Br.-G., No. 526. See also V. Bloch, *Rembrandt Today,* Amsterdam, 1970, p. 45; H. Gerson, "Rembrandt pro domo", *Gazette des Beaux Arts,* 78, 1971, pp. 193-200.

36. A.B. de Vries, "Nog eens Saul en David in het Mauritshuis", *Album Amicorum J.G. van Gelder,* The Hague, 1973, p. 347.

37. How rapidly and irresponsibly opinions are uttered (or repeated) is clear from the remarks of Nicholas Ward Jackson, associated in 1973 with the auctioneering firm of Sotheby-Parke Bernet in New York, who, in *The New York Times* of 19 January 1973, gave expression to his blunt and entirely negative opinion regarding Rembrandt's authorship, without backing it up with any argument based on personal observation. See also K. Roberts, "Review: 'Art in Seventeenth Century Holland' at the National Gallery", *Burlington Magazine,* 118, 1976, p. 784, regarding *The Man with the Golden Helmet* (Br.-G., No. 128) and the *Saul and David.*

38. For literature see Br.-G., No. 526.

39. A.B. de Vries, "Nog eens Saul en David in het Mauritshuis", *Album Amicorum J.G. van Gelder,* The Hague, 1973, p. 349.

40. H.E. van Gelder, *Rembrandt, Saul en David. Petrus verloochent Christus,* Leiden, 1948, p. 21: "On some occasion an attempt was made to make two paintings of it but later on the two canvases were joined together again; the seam is still visible. However, the section above David's head was apparently incomplete and was filled in by painting a woman's head there; this ugly addition was removed when the work was restored after the 1898 exhibition, being replaced by a simple and even background".
The *Saul and David* was restored in 1898 by W.A. Hopman (see the article by C. Flugi van Aspermont in the *Amsterdammer* of 27 November 1898). It is possible that after removing the old layers of varnish, Hopman described the subject on the piece inserted in the top righthand corner as the figure of a woman. H.E. van Gelder had presumably heard something to this effect. The radiograph refutes the thesis that Hopman substituted another piece of linen for the fragment in the top right-hand corner. Moreover, neither Décisy's etching after this paintnig (in *l'Art,* 48, 1890, opp. p. 152, given as in the collection of Ph. George) nor the photograph of this painting dating from c. 1895 (Fig. 135) show the figure of a woman in the top right-hand corner. Gerson appears to have misinterpreted H.E. van Gelder in this respect (Br.-G., No. 526).

41. On the reverse of the photo we read: *763 — Rembrandt — David and Saül — L 3332 — 1 M 30 x 1 M 65.* These dimensions correspond fairly closely with the actual dimensions. It is most regrettable that the records of the firm of Durand-Ruel in Paris should have been destroyed during the Commune of 1870 so that we have no information as to the provenance of the *Saul and David* before that date.

42. J. Bruyn, *Rembrandt's keuze van Bijbelse onderwerpen,* Utrecht, 1958; esp. pp. 18, 19.

43. Bremen, Kunsthalle, Inv. No. 55/669. Not mentioned in K. Lilienfeld, *Arent de Gelder. Sein Leben und seine Kunst,* The Hague, 1914.

44. G. Bandmann's thesis in *Melancholie und Musik. Ikonographische Studien,* Cologne, 1960, p. 15, to the effect that the work was commissioned by a society of musicians seems to us to be beyond proof.

45. H.d.G. *Urkunden,* pp. 260-262, No. 213. Concerns a story of David and Jonathan, also from the First Book of Samuel, *viz.,* I Samuel 18, verses 1-5 and I Samuel 20, verses 1-43.

46. In view of the theme (the Old Testament story of Saul and David), it is also conceivable that one of the Amsterdam "churchwardens" commissioned the work. Compare, for example, the organ panels painted by David Colijns (1582-1668), showing *David with Goliath's Head* and *Saul Threatening David with a Javelin as he Plays the Harp.* See also note 29; A. Blankert, *Kunst als regeringszaak in Amsterdam in de 17e eeuw. Rondom schilderijen van Ferdinand Bol,* Lochem, 1975, ill. 39: F. Bol, *The Offering of Gifts at the Construction of Solomon's Temple,* signed, canvas 157 x 171 cm., Amsterdam, Hervormde Gemeente (Reformed Dutch Church).

137. Homer.

XII

Homer

Plate XVI; Fig. 137

Canvas, 108.0 x 82.3 cm. Signed and dated ...*andt f. 1663.*

Cat. Br. (1895), No. 584; Valentiner, p. 466; H.d.G., no. 217; Cat. M. (1935), No. 584; Br., No. 483; Bauch, No. 244; G., No. 371; Br.-G., No. 483; Cat. H. (1977), No. 584.

TECHNICAL DATA

The original canvas has 13 warp and 12 weft threads per sq. cm; there are two relining canvases.

Examination using ultra-violet rays and infra-red photography did not yield any special information. The X-radiograph corresponds with the painting; there are no striking *pentimenti* (Fig. 138). The light parts of the head, painted *impasto*, and similar painted parts of the garment, show up clearly in detail. In the X-ray photograph there is no indication whatever of the left hand.

Parts of the detail in the right-hand bottom corner of the painting can also be traced in the X-radiograph. Those places where the painting has sustained fairly severe damage are recognizable from the dark patches, especially in the lowest areas and higher up too, in the cloak.

The *craquelure* varies from comparatively fine cracks to very wide grooves. In general, the paint of the background contains relatively coarse grains of pigment and there is a fine network of cracks. This paint does not, however, seem to be the original layer, most of it appearing to have come from old and some from more recent restoration. Here, that is to say, one can, in various places, see a layer of paint underneath the smooth top layer, one that differs in texture and has a coarser network of cracks, and this may be the original layer. It is true that the yellow to the left of the head looks more reliable, but there is retouching here too.

The cap, painted in grey, brown and black, has a network of wide cracks, the grooves of which, some very wide, have been filled up with a brown varnish. The thickly painted head shows normal *craquelure* in the lighter areas, while once again very broad cracks occur in the areas of shadow. The same applies to the beard.

The garments Homer is wearing also show a normal network of cracks in the lighter areas and very coarse cracking in the dark ones. On the right shoulder and sleeve, the yellow paint of the shawl, partly

138. X-ray photograph.

139. Macrophotograph. Detail of the lower part of the painting. The paint surface scorched (magnification x 2).

mixed with white, is very thick and has apparently been applied partly with a palette knife.

Many parts of the cloak have been restored, especially in its lower regions and to the left. In some places one also finds remnants of the old paint layer, which seems to have been scorched (Fig. 139) (see note 17). There is only a little *craquelure* on the right hand and there seems to have been old retouching. There is old *craquelure* in the remains of the paint below, to the right, on the inkwell and fingers.

The first layer of the ground is of a light shade of yellow and pink, composed of plenty of chalk and a little ochre. One or two other layers follow this one, preparatory layers, that is to say, in a rather darker tone of reddish brown, which in the main are composed of chalk, ochres and umber, mixed with a little white lead. On top of these reddish ground layers dark greyish-brown underpainting was detected in various places in the background, cloak, head and beard, into which umber and a great deal of coarse white lead have been worked. Below, to the right, under the topmost layer, a thin dark-brown layer made up of carbon black and umber was found. In the shadowy areas of the head, in the cap and on the beard, the greyish-brown underpainting mentioned above has been only partly covered by a lighter toplayer so that the tone of the dark areas is also determined by this underpainting.

The white in the painting is white lead, in which traces of copper, silver and tin were detected. The brown, red and yellow pigments which occur in the cap, face and beard consist of ochres, but the yellow ribbon across the forehead consists of lead-tin yellow, mixed with white lead. The yellow on the right shoulder and sleeve is also largely composed of lead-tin yellow and white lead, but yellow ochre is present too.

No red lake pigment was detected in this painting, neither in the flesh tones nor in the areas of shadow.

On the left of the painting, where it has been cut down (see below), the date *1663* and a remnant of

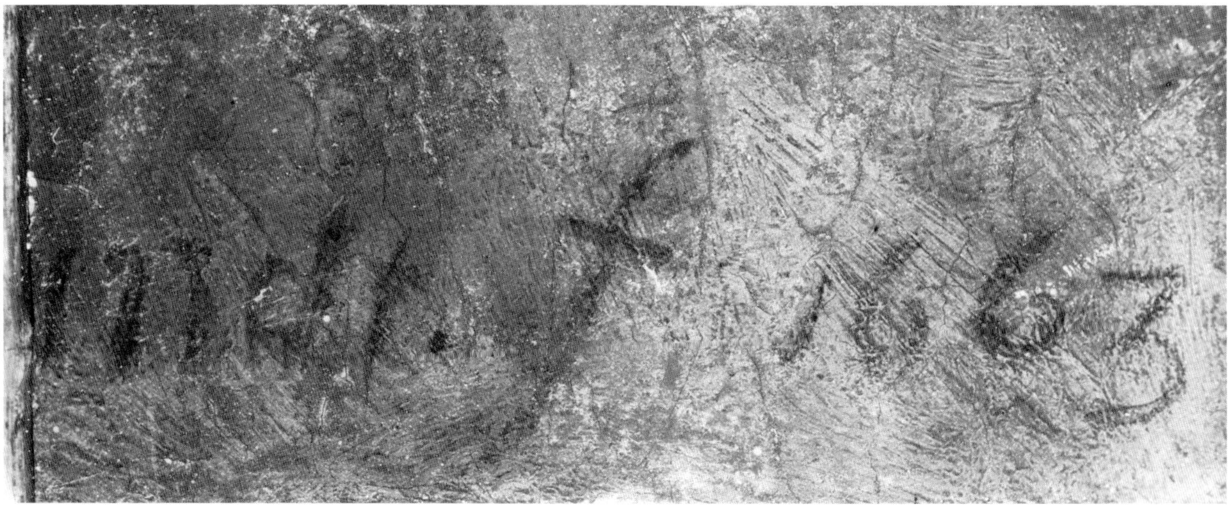

140. The truncated signature and date.

the truncated signature are still present (Fig. 140). Part of the cracks in the top layer continues through the signature. During later restoration parts of the old paint of the signature have been covered by thin retouching.

HISTORICAL DATA

In 1894, Bredius purchased a painting in London, representing a seated old man which was signed and dated... *andt f. 1663.* Nothing is known as regards its provenance except that about 1885 the work had been in the keeping of S.T. Smith Esq., of London [1]. Even at the time of purchase Bredius thought that this blind old man represented Homer. He had noticed that the head bore a strong resemblance to a painted portrait of a bust, which is to be seen in Rembrandt's *Aristotle* (Br.-G., No. 478). This painting was in England prior to 1894, changing hands in that year [2] (Fig. 141).

It was not until a study of the Ruffo Collection in Messina during the 17th century was published by the Marchese Vincenzo Ruffo in 1916 that it was possible to establish that both the *Homer* in the Mauritshuis and the *Aristotle* (dated 1653), then in a private American collection (Br.-G., No. 478), had been painted for Don Antonio Ruffo's collection [3]. The invoice, dated 30 July 1661, was published at the same time; it bore Rembrandt's instructions and also showed that the *Homer* had been shipped to Messina. This painting had not been commissioned by Don Antonio Ruffo, but Rembrandt put it in unfinished condition with the *Alexander,* which Ruffo had indeed commissioned and which was despatched with the same consignment [4]. On 12 November 1662, the

141. Rembrandt. Aristotle with the Bust of Homer, 1653. *New York, The Metropolitan Museum of Art.*

Homer was shipped back to Amsterdam so that it might be completed. From a highly detailed letter which has been preserved, we learn that the *Alexander* had not met with the commissioner's approval but that he was prepared to accept the *Homer,* although at a reduced price, partly as compensation for the *Alexander,* which was made up of four pieces of canvas (see *Appendix IV*).

Rembrandt, however, would not accept this. He brushed aside the complaints of his patron and stood by this original prices. He did, however, declare himself ready to complete the Homer, if he were to be informed of the dimensions required (see *Appendix IV*) [5].

After Rembrandt had received the painting back —the letter of complaint which, incidentally also contained three new commissions, had reached him in the meantime—he scribbled a short note to Ruffo saying: "If each piece is 6 palms (hands) broad and 8 high, the proportions will be good and the Gentleman will not think the price too high, your respectful servant Rembrandt van rhijn" [6] (Fig. 142). According to the date, Rembrandt completed the canvas in 1663, whereupon it was again shipped off to Messina. The date of arrival is given as 20 May 1664 [7].

In 1673 an inventory was drawn up of Ruffo's collection and in this we find descriptions of all three paintings mentioned, the *Aristotle, Alexander* and *Homer,* under Nos. 221, 222 and 223. On the occasion of the marriage of Don Antonio's eldest son, Placido, it was also laid down in that same year that a nucleus of 100 paintings was to be kept together and always handed down from eldest son to eldest son. The three paintings by Rembrandt fell within this stipulation [8].

It is as good as certain that the collection remained intact until the death of Don Caligoro Ruffo, who died of the plague in Messina in 1743. In 1750 the Ruffo family became divided into two branches, that of the "Principi della Scaletta" and that of the "Principi della Floresta" [9]

What became of the "hundred paintings" in the original Ruffo collection after 1750 cannot be established with any certainty. Vincenzo Ruffo himself pointed out that as far as this period was concerned he had had to have recourse to suppositions and further research. It is possible that the "hundred paintings" or at least a considerable portion of them did remain together in the collection until 1818. In Sicily that year the right of primogeniture was abolished. Vincenzo Ruffo also mentions the earthquake in Messina in 1783, during which the family palace had sustained damage [10]. Finally, information supplied by a member of the family told of a great fire which had raged in the Villa Ruffo di Gazzi outside Naples (?) in 1848, causing the loss of many paintings. The same source also stated that only one painting of minor importance belonging to the Dutch School had been saved from this fire, so that the *Homer* cannot have been meant [11].

Corrado Ricci, who took Vincenzo Ruffo's article as basis, but who had also obtained further notes from Vincenzo's brother, Barone Giaocchino Ruffo Calcagno dei Principi della Floresta, claimed that when the family had split up into two branches in 1750, the Principi della Scaletta had taken the "hundred paintings" off to Naples; that the three Rembrandts were definitely no longer present in Messina when the law of primogeniture was abrogated in 1818 (and indeed, the *Aristotle* was exhibited in London in 1815, as a portrait of the Dutch 17th century poet P.C. Hooft); and, finally, that it was quite possible that in 1848 the *Homer* had still been in the Villa di Gazzi and could have sustained damage there [12]. Neither did Hoogewerff consider this excluded [13].

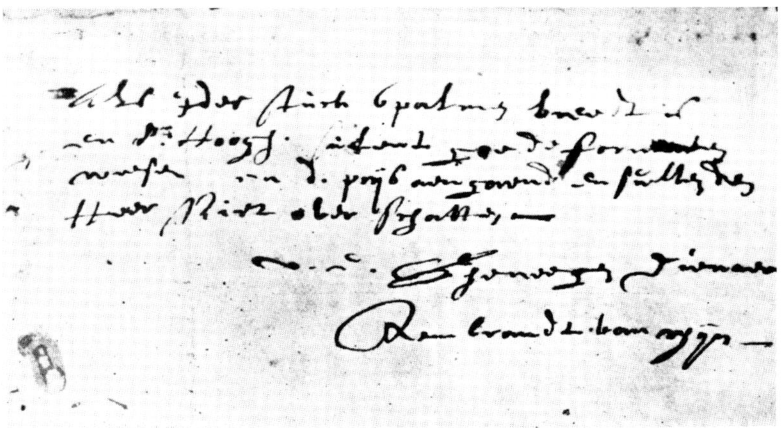

142. Rembrandt. Autograph note. 1661.
Archives of the Ruffo Family.

Here we can only repeat that further research may perhaps bring some clarification. What is sure is that the *Aristotle* was disposed of before 1815, and probably several years before then, since the real subject of the painting had already been lost sight of. As regards the *Alexander,* we are still obliged to assume that the painting has been lost. Attempts to identify this work with paintings of Rembrandt we still know have not proved convincing [14].

It is known that the Scottish painter Gavin Hamilton (1723-1798) brought two paintings by Salvator Rosa to England about 1770 and that both had once belonged to the "hundred paintings" in the Ruffo collection [15]. This indicates that after 1750 Don Ruffo's stipulations were being disregarded and Vincenzo Ruffo had, indeed, already made a passing reference to this [16].

We are therefore left in the dark as to what happened to the *Homer.* It seems probable that during the second half of the 18th century this painting, too, disappeared from the Ruffo collection, perhaps after the earthquake in Messina in 1783 (does the fire damage Bredius refers to indicate this?) [17], or perhaps from Naples. Since the subject matter of the work (*Homer*) had also been lost sight of, this painting, too, may have been in England for a considerable time before 1885, the year in which it re-appeared.

Bredius loaned the *Homer* to the Mauritshuis in 1894, and bequeathed it to the gallery in 1946.

Collections

Don Antonio Ruffo, Messina (Sicily), 1661, 1663

The Ruffo Family, certainly until 1750

S.T. Smith Esq., London, 1885

T. Humphry Ward and Son, London, 1894

Dr. A. Bredius, The Hague; on loan to the Mauritshuis, 1894-1946

Bredius Bequest, 1946

Dimensions quoted

1661	Upper corners rounded off
1663	8 x 6 palms = 206.4 x 154.8 cm
1894	108 x 82.4 cm
1977	108 x 82.3 cm

Prices

1663	500 florins
c. 1885	12 shillings
1894	800 pounds—offered by the art dealer Ward in London on 19 February for 2,400 pounds

ICONOGRAPHY AND STYLE

Blind Homer is seen seated, turned towards the right. His lips are parted and he is holding a staff in front of him, in his left hand. With his right hand he is making a didactic gesture. He is dressed in a dark-brown cloak with wide sleeves and has a golden yellow shawl over his cloak. He is wearing a poet's fillet on his brow; on his head he has a cap with a peak at the back [18]. Below, right, are visible two finger-tips, an inkpot and a sheet of paper (Fig. 137).

The technical investigation and historical data have revealed that this *Homer* was originally a larger work. Two young men were to be seen on the right, described as *discepoli* [19]. A small strip is missing on the left, on which the first five letters of the signature must once have been visible (the letters *...andt* and the date *f. 1663* have been preserved). Since, in its present form, the dimensions of the work are 108.0 x 82.3 cm, but these were formerly 8 x 6 *palmen* (hands) = 206.4 x 154.8 cm, 98.4 cm are missing in the height and 72.5 cm in the width [20].

The invoice dated 30 July 1661 (see note 4 and *Appendix IV*) shows that this *Homer* was originally rounded off at the top and that Rembrandt had done this so that the painting would match the *Aristotle,* when the *Alexander* was hung between the two [21].

Conceived by Rembrandt as a "triptych", the paintings were originally tall [22]. They can, it is true, never have been hung on Ruffo's walls as Rembrandt had meant them to be, since in the winter of 1660 Guercino had completed a painting commissioned from him by Antonio Ruffo, intended as a companion piece to Rembrandt's *Aristotle* [23].

Even today we are unable to give a satisfactory answer to the question whether Rembrandt himself conceived the idea of illustrating the historical link between Aristotle and Alexander the Great and the admiration both felt for Homer, or whether we ought perhaps to see a humanist friend or mentor of the artist as the "auctor intellectualis" of this idea. All three figures were already present *in nuce* in the *Aristotle* painting of 1653 [24].

The historical source which combines these three famous figures of classical antiquity is to be found in Plutarch's life of Alexander (Plutarch: c. 46-125 A.D.). In his work we read among other things of Aristotle's appointment as tutor to the youthful Alexander, who, when a young general, would always carry with him a copy of Homer's *Iliad,* edited by Aristotle, placing it under his pillow at night, next to his sword [25].

Besides this historical detail, nowadays looked upon as merely legendary, the Aristotelian conception

143. The Head of Homer.

of the threefold activity of man—in the poetic, the contemplative and the active life—may have formed the basis for this version of Homer, Aristotle and Alexander [26].

Although Homer is shown as a blind poet, especially in sculptures (he appears only rarely in paintings), he should be seen here in the first place as the instructor of the young, as is indicated by the two *discepoli* who were to be seen in the originally much larger work (see note 19).

This curious subject is based on the *Life of Homer* attributed in the 17th century to Herodotus [27]. After many vicissitudes, Homer is said to have arrived on the island of Chios, where Glaucus, a herdsman, took pity on him and brought him to his master. The latter appointed him as tutor to his children. This story of Homer's life was re-told more or less in detail in introductions to various editions of the *Iliad* and/or the *Odyssey,* for example, in the Dutch translations by Dirck Volckertsz. Coornhert (1561), by G. van Staveren (1651) and—very extensively—by Jan Hendrik Glazemaker (1658) [28].

The motif of Homer dictating his verses or teaching the young had so far been known to us only through a painting by Piero Francesco Mola (1612-1666), but it has been rightly emphasized that these two versions of this apparently rare theme lie worlds apart [29]. We do happen to have a painting of this subject by Aert de Gelder (Fig. 144), but in reverse, which is based on Rembrandt's composition. Here however, there are four, not two, pupils receiving instruction. When this work was auctioned in 1783, it was called *The Schoolmaster*—a figure, apparently, in no way suggesting Homer [30].

The head of Homer (Fig. 143) as Rembrandt has painted it here is without any doubt based on the Hellenistic bust (probably of plaster) which the artist owned, as he owned also a bust of Aristotle together with other antique busts [31]. Whereas the artist represented this bust of Homer as such in his painting of *Aristotle,* in his *Homer* he has transposed the sculpture into his own—the painter's—idiom. The blind old poet is seen leaning on his stick; he is wearing a cap to protect his head from the cold and about his body he has flung a broad cloak [32]. Although Homer has remained clearly recognizable here, it would be hard to point to another sculpture being "translated" into a work of painting in such a way that a static, idealized portrait has become a personality vibrating with feeling—a transformation accomplished, moreover, in so very personal and moving a manner [33]. This poet and teacher is so convincing in appearance that we scarcely notice the loss of the two subsidiary figures.

144. Aert de Gelder. Homer Teaching, 1682. *Boston, Museum of Fine Arts.*

Some years before he painted this *Home*r, Rembrandt had drawn *Homer reciting Verses,* surrounded by an audience of all ages, in an *Album Amicorum* for Jan Six (1652; Benesch, V, p. 267, Cat. No. 913) (Fig. 145) [34]. A drawing in Stockholm can be regarded as a preliminary sketch for the painting he sent Ruffo, and must have been executed circa 1660-1661, when the artist was working on both the *Alexander* and the *Homer* (see *Historical data;* Benesch, V, p. 305, Cat. No. 1066). The horizontal form is what we notice first; then that both upper corners are rounded off, which is also the case with the final work. The poet's posture corresponds in the main

145. Rembrandt. Homer reciting verses, 1652. Drawing.
Amsterdam, Six Collection.

146. Rembrandt. Homer teaching. Drawing.
Stockholm, Nationalmuseum.

with that in the painting, although there are many differences, for example the left background, the view on the right, the attitude of the hands, and so on (Fig. 146).

When Bredius acquired this painting in 1894, it must have been in very poor condition indeed. Hauser, the Berlin restorer, worked on it between 1894 and 1897 and in 1897 we find Six speaking of "kill or cure" [35].

We must conclude from the technical data that the background has been largely overpainted, while admitting that its "autumn colours" are not without their effect. Best preserved are the head and shawl of the cloak and here it is the light and the brushwork which explain the fascination this portrait of a poet, illumined with inner light, exercises. It is a fascination impossible to express adequately in words [36]. The golden-yellow of the shawl has been applied broadly with the palette knife [37]. It is not possible to find out exactly what Rembrandt did between November 1661 and approx. mid-1663 to complete the work (see *Historical data* and *Appendix IV*). The broad painting of the shawl can be compared with that in the *Self Portrait of Rembrandt as Zeuxis painting a Woman* (Cologne, Wallraf-Richartz Museum) (Br.-G., No. 61), which he probably painted about 1663 or a few years later [38]. It is possible, therefore, that the venturesome detail was included during the last stages of work on this painting. The hands, on the contrary, seem weakly modelled, if we compare them, for instance, with the hands in his *Matthew and the Angel* (1661; Br.-G., No. 614), It looks as though the painter has simply added a few quick changes, now visible as *pentimenti*.

NOTES

1. Purchased by Bredius from T. Humphry Ward, London, as *Portrait of an Old Man*; in 1885 the painting was with S.T. Smith Esq., who, according to his notepaper, was the curator of the Bridgewater Gallery, the Earl of Ellesmere's collection.

2. It appears from a letter from Bredius, dated 9 June 1894, addressed to the Minister of Home Affairs, that he called the painting a "portrait of an old man, presumably meant to be Homer".
Collections: Sir Abraham Hume, Bart., Ashridge Park; Earl Brownlow, Ashridge Park; Rodolphe Kann, Paris. See also Th. Rousseau, "Aristotle Contemplating the Bust of Homer", *The Metropolitan Museum of Art Bulletin*, 20, 1962, p. 155; Cat. Br. (1895), p. 338.

3. Ruffo, pp. 21-64, 95-128, 165-192, 237-256, 284-320, 369-388. See the *Appendix IV* for the texts regarding the relations existing between Ruffo and Rembrandt and the course of affairs with respect to the *Alexander* and *Homer* paintings. Hoogewerff, in 1917, was the first to identify the *Homer* and *Aristotle* mentioned in the Ruffo archives with the two works concerned. His identification of the *Alexander* has not been sustained (see note 14).

4. Ruffo, pp. 127-128; Ricci, p. 18, pp. 21-22.

5. Ruffo, pp. 165-166.

6. Ruffo, p. 166; Ricci, pp. 18-19.

7. Ricci, p. 30.

8. For a description of the paintings and for the stipulation, see Ruffo, p. 318.

9. Ruffo, pp. 377-378; Ricci, p. 43.

10. Ruffo, p. 379.

11. Ruffo, pp. 379-380.

12. Ricci, pp. 8, 43, 48.

13. Hoogewerff, 1917, p. 135.
We have received no response so far to our request for further information addressed to the Archives in Naples and to a descendant of the Ruffo family.

14. There is no agreement as to the identification of the *Alexander* from the Ruffo collection (Br.-G., Nos. 479-480). See Held (1969) pp. 8-11, note 31, and Br.-G., No. 480, they state the various hypotheses but offer no solution.

15. Ruffo, p. 318, Nos. 242, 243, representing "Pythagoras Emerging from the Underworld" and "Pythagoras and the Fishermen" (now respectively in the Kimbell Art Museum, Fort Worth, Texas, U.S.A., Cat. 1972, pp. 76-80, with ill., and in the Gemäldegalerie in Berlin-Dahlem respectively, (Cat. 1975, p. 365, Inv. No. 1/59, with ill.). The first work was presumably exhibited at "The British Institution" (1821, No. 28); see also: exh. cat. *Salvator Rosa*, London (Hayward Gallery), 1973, p. 33, No. 36, ill. 37.
Regarding Gavin Hamilton, see D. Irwin, "Gavin Hamilton: archeologist, painter and dealer", *The Art Bulletin*, 44, 1962, pp. 87-111; see also H. Honour, *Neo-Classicism*, Harmondsworth, 1968, pp. 45, 88 *inter alia*.

16. Ruffo, p. 379.

17. Hoogewerff, 1917, p. 135, note 1.

18. F. Schmidt Degener, "Rembrandt en Homerus", *Feestbundel Dr. Abraham Bredius aangeboden den achttienden April 1915*, Amsterdam, 1915, p. 24: "A sailor's cap, with a broad peak hanging down his neck, covers his grey hair, as if the storms of the Odyssey had blown over the head of the poet himself". The cap seen in this painting bears some resemblance to that in the preliminary drawing in Stockholm (Benesch, V, p. 305, Cat. No. 1066, ill. 1283), but even more to the headgear worn by Nathan in the two drawings *Nathan Admonishing David* (Benesch, V, p. 274, Cat.

Nos. 947 and 948, ills. 1156 and 1159). See also the paintings by Aert de Gelder: *Homer Teaching the Young,* Boston (Museum of Fine Arts), inv. No. 39.45, and *Esther and Mordecai,* Budapest (Museum of Fine Arts), Cat. 1967, p. 255, Inv. No. 1342, ill. 260.

19. Ruffo, p. 318: *Omero seduto che insegna a 2 discepoli, mezza figura al naturale, 8 x 6 palmi.*

20. In the province of Messina the "palm" (hand) measured 0.258 metres (see *Enciclopedia Italiana,* 26, Rome, 1935, p. 146). Hoogewerff, 1917, p. 135 calculated 8 x 6 palms as approx. 192 x 144 cm. How he, and all the authors who followed him, arrived at these measurements is not known to us.
Since in our country dimensions were given in "feet" and "inches" (*voeten* and *duimen*), Rembrandt received the information regarding required dimensions from Sicily.

21. Ruffo, pp. 127-128; Ricci, p. 22.

22. Compare, for example, Rembrandt's words: "If Each piece is 6 palms Broad and 8 High, the proportions will be good..." (see text against note 6 and note 6 itself) and the dimensions quoted in the inventory of 1673: 8 x 6 palms (see note 8).

23. Ruffo, pp. 100-102. See the drawing by Guercino, which may have served as a preliminary sketch for the painting, now no longer known to us, intended as a companion piece for the *Aristotle:* Held, 1969, p. 6, note 15, ill. 2; Jacob Rosenberg was the first to draw attention to this (J. Rosenberg, "Rembrandt and Guercino" *The Art Quarterly,* 7, 1944, pp. 129-134). It is no longer possible to ascertain how the three Rembrandt paintings were hung in Ruffo's collection, since the inventory was compiled in alphabetical order.

24. It does not appear from the papers V. Ruffo published in 1916 that Don Antonio Ruffo gave details in his first commission. Presumably he merely ordered "a philosopher". Did Rembrandt conceive the *Aristotle* completely independently? H.E. van Gelder's hypothesis, put forward in *Rembrandt en zijn tijd,* Amsterdam (no year), pp. 32-33, 38, that Jacobus Heyblock, headmaster in 1670 of the Latin School along the *Singel* in Amsterdam, was possibly the *auctor intellectualis,* should be given serious consideration. Rembrandt made a drawing illustrating *The Presentation in the Temple,* signed and dated *Rembrandt f. 1661* in his *Album Amicorum* (Benesch, V, No. 1057, ill. 1275). When the second commission arrived in 1660, that is, for the *Alexander,* would Rembrandt have sent off the *Homer* entirely on his own initiative, to allow his patron to see and eventually buy it, even though it was only half-finished? That Ruffo did not seem even then to have thought of the relation between Aristotle, Alexander and Homer, is suggested by the commission he gave to Giacinto Brandi after Rembrandt's death (*una mezza figura;* see Ruffo, p. 186).

25. Held, 1969, p. 19. *Plutarchus, een jongeling verovert de wereld (Alexander de Grote), vertaald en toegelicht door S.L. Radt,* Zeist, 1965, pp. 15-16, Ch. 7-8.

26. J.A. Emmens, *Rembrandt en de regels van de kunst,* Utrecht, 1968, p. 174 and note 305.

27. In the 17th century the biography was attributed to Herodotus but is nowadays attributed to the pseudo-Herodotus, Heraclitus Ponticus the Elder, c. 388-310 B.C. (?).

28. *Deerste twaelf boecken Odysseae, dat is de dolinghe van Ulysse, bescreven int Griecx, wten Latijne in rijm verduytscht* by Dierick Coornhert, Haerlem (J. van Zuren) 1561; *De dooling van Ulisses...* translated by G.V.S., Amsterdam (G. van Goedesberg and Kl. Fransz.) 1651; *Iliaden van Homerus, Prins der Grieksche Poëten...* New translation by J.H. Glazemaker..., Amsterdam 1658. In the Royal Library at The Hague there are 11 Dutch and 8 Latin editions of the *Iliad* and/or *Odyssey* dating from the 16th and 17th centuries (published in the Low Countries).
For the esteem in which Homer was held by men of letters in the Netherlands see: Held, 1969, pp. 19-20.
Homer was also on the curriculum of the Latin School (for that matter see E.J. Kuiper, *De Hollandse "Schoolordre" van 1625. Een studie van het onderwijs op de Latijnse scholen in Nederland in de 17e en 18e eeuw,* Groningen, 1958, pp. 20-21, 51, 130, 169, 217).

29. Von Einem, p. 199, ill. 175.

30. Lugt, I, No. 3615, No. 65; Lugt, I, No. 5767, No. 67; K. Lilienfeld, *Arent de Gelder, Sein Leben und seine Kunst,* The Hague, 1914, Nos. 147, 148; Boston, Museum of Fine Arts, Inv. No. 39.45: canvas, 101 x 127.5 cm. (This painting is identical with Lilienfeld Nos. 147 and 148).

31. As regards Rembrandt's collection of antique busts, see R.W. Scheller, "Rembrandt en de encyclopedische Kunstkamer", *Oud Holland,* 84, 1969, pp. 126-128. J. Six in "De Homerus van Rembrandt", *Oud Holland* 15, 1897, p. 6, leaves the question as to which bust of Homer Rembrandt used undecided. Held's proposal (Held, 1969, p. 18, ill. 14, notes 59 and 60) to accept the bust in the museum in Boston as the model should be given serious consideration.

32. Mention has been made more than once of the unusual dress and headgear Rembrandt's *Aristotle* is wearing. They appear to be based on the imagination (Held, 1969, pp. 15-16). Homer's dress and the remarkable cap he is wearing do not appear to have been based on classical models either. In his narrow-minded way, Abraham Breughel had already written in his letter to Ruffo of 24 January 1670 as follows: "Li pictori grandi studino a faijre vedere un bel corpo niudo, e dove si vede il sapere del disegnio, ma al contrario, un inniorante cherca di coprire di vestiti ouscuri goffi, et il contorno in cognito questi sorti di pictori..." (Ruffo, p. 186; Ricci, p. 32).
Held drew a hypothetical parallel between Homer's blindness and that of Rembrandt's father during the last years of his life, and then with the blindness of the father of Tobias (Held, 1969, p. 41; p. 124 and note 31). It is, indeed, remarkable that Rembrandt, the man who thought and acted via his eyes, should have been so intensely fascinated by blindness.
Finally, here is not the proper place to go into the question as to whether Rembrandt has "interpreted the ancient theme in Christian terms" (Von Einem, p. 200).

33. Von Einem, p. 200.

34. Does this drawing represent *Homer on Parnassus?*

35. J. Six, "De Homerus van Rembrandt", *Oud Holland,* 15, 1897, p. 9.

36. Von Einem, p. 200.

37. It seems hardly likely to us that this heavy shawl, painted with the palette knife, would be of *silk,* as Bredius and many authors after him wrote (Cat. Br. (1895), p. 337).

38. A. Blankert, "Rembrandt, Zeuxis and Ideal Beauty", *Album Amicorum J.G. van Gelder,* The Hague, 1973, pp. 32-39.

147. Self-Portrait in Later Life.

XIII

Self-Portrait in Later Life

Plate XVII; Fig. 147

Canvas, 63.5 x 57.8 cm. Signed and dated *Rembrandt f. 1669*

Valentiner, p. 479; H.d.G., No. 527; Br., No. 62; Bauch, No. 342; G., No. 420; Br.-G., No. 62; Cat. H. (1977), No. 840.

TECHNICAL DATA

The work has been painted on a canvas with 11 warp and 14 weft threads per sq. cm. There is no trace of relining. Here and there, on the reverse, the ground has come through small apertures in the linen fabric. Neither the canvas itself nor the X-ray photograph revealed any information which would point to the present canvas having been substituted for the original. We may accordingly assume that the original canvas is still serving its purpose today, and this must be said to be exceptional. The canvas has been attached to its stretcher with old, hand-forged nails and there are some centimetres of fold-over along the edges.

Examination using ultra-violet light and fluorescence photography yielded no special information, except that it revealed a little retouching here and there. The infra-red photograph shows that retouching has taken place near the eyes among other places (Fig. 150).

The X-radiograph indicates that the ground consists of a thin layer of primer containing white lead (Fig. 149). In those places where the ground is very thin indeed (scoured?) dark patches are visible in the X-ray photograph. The X-ray image of the headgear reveals fairly heavy painting in white lead, which does not match the headgear seen in the picture and in which a flattish cap or headcloth can be discerned. Since it is hardly plausible that a white lead underpainting of the present barret is involved here, one is justified in concluding that at first the artist painted a flat cap or headcloth and changed this later. For the rest, the X-radiograph corresponds with the surface view of the picture, a portrait painted directly, without white lead underpainting, so that the brush strokes in the lighter areas are visible on the X-radiograph (Fig. 148).

In the thickly painted, lighter areas of the forehead and of the barret the *craquelure* is rather coarse, with wide cracks. The *craquelure* on the face takes, on the whole, the form of a network of cracks of finer structure. In other places the cracks are less pro-

148. X-ray photograph. The Head.

149. X-ray photograph.

150. Infra-red photograph. The head with part of cap.

nounced, often consisting of small individual ones, in the background especially.

On the whole, the paint layer is thin; in various places, particularly in the background and the hair, the bare canvas shows through. Dark underpainting can be seen here and there in the white of the collar, of the forehead and also in the grey and brown of the barret. Here it has been applied on the thick white layer of white lead of the original cap or headcloth. A dark under-layer is also visible on the right side of the face, where it shows as a greyish tint in the white. All this may have resulted, in part, from a certain degree of wearing away of the surface of the original paint.

An overpainted layer of old paint containing a lot of red ochre was encountered in the uppermost areas of the coat.

A dark strip, about 2 cm broad, runs across the entire top edge of the picture, the paint of which, a blackish-brown, appears to be original, or at least old. Below this strip the dark paint has been partly over-painted with the greyish-green paint of the back-ground, which gives the impression of being of later date (restoration). In various places, above the barret, for instance, the dark paint has come through the grey-green and the same can be seen along the entire left edge of the painting. Along all four edges of the painting the canvas has been folded back a few centimetres over the stretcher and is covered with the same blackish-brown paint.

Examination of the pigments used showed that the dark, greyish-brown first layer of ground consists of coarse white lead, umber, bone black, red and yellow ochres. This ground has been covered with a second ground layer of blackish-brown made up of bone black, Cologne earth and a little ochre. In places, a third layer has been found composed as the lowest layer of ground and followed by another blackish-brown layer. It is on this dark layer that the portrait has been painted. The 2 cm broad dark strip along the top has been glazed with a red lake pigment. Here and there in the background, one can still find old paint with coarse pigment (umber, white lead, red ochres) next to and under later overpainting with finer pigments—above the head, for example, bordering on the dark band mentioned above. The yellow and brown in the head and barret is composed of ochres; red ochres and possibly vermilion, here and there, have been used as red pigments in the eyes, nose and mouth, and these have been generously covered with a red lake glaze in the darker areas. Red lake particles have likewise been blended with the white lead in the flesh tones, with ochres present too. Traces of silver and copper were found in the white lead.

The signature lies just above the right shoulder of the figure on the left of the painting (Fig. 151). There is little *craquelure* in the paint composing the background here, yet it appears to continue into the paint of the signature. This, however, tells us little about authenticity or age, especially as there are doubts as to the genuineness of the background too. There is also doubt as to the origin of an extra stroke of dark paint, next to the second *6* in the date.

151. Signature and date

HISTORICAL DATA

When, in 1835, G.F. Waagen, director of the former "Gemäldegalerie des Königlichen Museums" in Berlin (1794-1864), went on his first journey to England to study art, the Neeld collection was one of the items on his programme. It was not until his second visit, however, in 1850, that he had an opportunity to see the collection [1].

Joseph Neeld (1789-1856), who had built Grittleton House, owned a large collection of paintings, including two works by Rembrandt: *Joseph Accused by Potiphar's Wife,* now in the museum at Berlin-Dahlem (1655; Br.-G., No. 524), and the self-portrait discussed here. Concerning this portrait, Waagen wrote: "Portrait of Rembrandt himself in his later years: very warm and transparent in colouring, but over broad in treatment" [2].

At the winter exhibition of the Royal Academy in London in 1899 this self-portrait was exhibited for the first time and described in the catalogue under item No. 4 as follows: "Portrait of the painter. Bust to r., looking at the spectator; dark dress, coloured turban, long grey hair; dark background. Signed and dated. Rembrandt. 1660 (?). Canvas (oval), 23 1/2 x 20 in" [3] (Fig. 152). This was the first occasion upon which the signature and the date were mentioned. It is striking that doubts were already being expressed as early as 1899 as regards the dating: in the second, revised impression of the catalogue the signature and dating were given as "Rembrandt f 1669" [4].

The canvas went to Berlin via the London art market (Douglas; Knoedler) and entered the collection of Marcus Kappel, one of the many private collectors to be advised by Bode [5].

The work was shown at the Rijksmuseum in Amsterdam during the city's historical exhibition in 1925 and then left at the museum on long-term loan by M. Kappel's heirs [6]. On Kappel's death the painting came into the possession of his niece and nephew, Mrs. E. Ettlinger-Rathenau and Dr. Ernest G. Rathenau, in Berlin, who later lived in Oxford and New York. They had extended the loan but in the summer of 1940 the work was taken by the occupying power to Germany, where it was intended for the "Führermuseum" in Linz, Austria. This museum, fortunately, failed to materialize. After Germany's capitulation, the self-portrait was one of the works

152. Reproduction after the illustration in W. Bode and C. Hofstede de Groot, *Rembrandt. Beschreibendes Verzeichnis seiner Gemälde* 7, Paris 1902, No. 507.

of art found at Alt-Aussee in the Salzkammergut, in the former saltmine fortified and guarded during the war. This had been a large depot for works of art looted by the Nazis. Rembrandt's *Self-Portrait* was among the first twenty-six paintings removed from the Netherlands to be returned by the American military command in October 1945. Returned, that is to say, on condition that they should find their way to their rightful owners.

After consultation with Mr. Rathenau, who was also acting on his sister's behalf, the Mauritshuis was given the opportunity to acquire the work. Despite the shortage of foreign exchange pertaining shortly after the war, particularly the shortage of dollars, both the owners and the authorities (The Minister of Finance, the Minister of Education, Arts and Sciences and the President of the Netherlands Bank) gave their fullest co-operation in order that this late self-portrait of Rembrandt should be saved for the Dutch nation. The "Rembrandt Society", the Rijksmuseum (by means of a generous advance provided by the "Friends of the Rijksmuseum Society" and a number of private persons then made the purchase possible [7].

Collections

Joseph Neeld, London, before 1850

John Neeld, Grittleton House, near Chippenham, Wiltshire, England, c. 1885

A.W. Neeld, Grittleton House, near Chippenham, Wiltshire, England, 1899

R.L. Douglas, art dealer, London

Knoedler and Co., art dealers, London

M. Kappel, Berlin, c. 1912-c. 1930

E.G. Rathenau and Mrs. E. Ettlinger-Rathenau, Berlin, later in Oxford and New York

Amsterdam, Rijksmuseum, on loan, 1925-1940

"The Mauritshuis"—Royal Collection of Paintings, The Hague, 1947

Dimensions quoted

1885 all corners rounded off

1899 all corners rounded off, 23 1/2 x 20 in = approx. 59 x 51 cm

1914 rectangular, 67 x 52 cm

1977 63.5 x 57.8 cm

ICONOGRAPHY AND STYLE

Rembrandt has painted an almost half-length portrait of himself with the hands not showing. The body is turned to the right, but the head is turned less, and faces the spectator. He is dressed in a dark coat with a V-shaped shirt collar, and is wearing a barret-type cap. His grey hair falls in heavy curls onto his right shoulder (Fig. 147).

There has never been any doubt as to the identity of the sitter.

It goes without saying that the date, *1669,* gave rise to no problems for those who trusted in its accuracy. On the contrary, this so-called firm piece of information led, automatically, it seems, to all manner of interpretation of the expression and mood of an aging artist who felt his life coming to an end [8].

Even when the painting was first shown to the public in 1899, there already proved to be no consensus of opinion regarding its date. Was it *1660* or *1669*? (see *Historical data*). It is more than likely that Bode had his friend Hauser restore this self-portrait, described as dark and opaque, and that Hauser, even if he did not renew the signature and date altogether, at least made it more legible. We are therefore left with this question: *1660* or *1669* or even *1666*? Has something been added to the *0* or not? (see Fig. 151).

In 1966, when one of Rembrandt's late self-portraits (National Gallery, London; Br.-G., No. 55)

153. Rembrandt. Self-Portrait, 1669. *London, National Gallery.*

154. Rembrandt. Self-Portrait, 1660 (?). *Paris, Musée du Louvre.*

155. Rembrandt. Self-Portrait, c. 1665 (?). Detail. *London, Kenwood House, The Iveagh Bequest.*

156. Photograph taken during restoration, 1954.

(Fig. 153) was being cleaned and restored, the date of this work became clearly distinguishable as *1669*. Close examination made it more than probable that we should be justified in regarding both signature and date as authentic [9].

The simplest solution would be to retain the *9*, now clearly visible, as the last figure of the date on the painting in The Hague, and to leave the question open whether this or the London work must be taken as the very last self-portrait.

When we compare the self-portraits Rembrandt painted during the last decade of his life (Br.-G., No. 50, 1658; Br.-G., No. 51, 1659; Br.-G., No. 52; Br.-G., No. 53, 1660 (?); Br.-G., No. 54, 1660; Br.-G., No. 59, 1661; Br.-G., No. 60; Br.-G., No. 61), accepting these dates with some reservation, it is at least clear that Rembrandt was portraying himself in varying moods and with different expressions.

As soon as we begin to look closely at such details as the fulness or leanness of the cheeks, the length of the curls in the grey hair, the expression in, or the intensity of, the gaze, we find that they do not, after all, help us very much to date these portraits.

If, for example, we compare his self-portrait in New York (Br.- G., No. 54) which bears the presumably original date 1660 [10] with *Rembrandt at his Easel* in Paris (Br.-G., No. 53) (Fig. 154), which may possibly also have been painted in 1660, we do indeed see before us two figures which resemble each other, but their expression differs very much.

Moreover, Rembrandt's self-portraits during the last ten years of his life very often differ in the manner in which they have been painted. For instance, the barret in the Hague self-portrait, which has been painted on top of the white artist's cap the figure was originally wearing (see *Technical data*), has been added with broad strokes of the brush while the paler areas of the face have been firmly painted; touches round the nose, eyes and mouth have been added with very short brushstrokes, which amount almost to *pointillism* [11]. This we have not found in any other self-portrait. The X-ray photographs at our disposal (those of several late self-portraits from the 'sixties) also failed to provide any definitive solution to the problem of supplying this Hague canvas with an exact date.

The painting was put on exhibition in 1899 in an oval frame, while in Valentiner (1908) it is reproduced with the corners rounded off. Fold-marks were not found on the canvas, so that the frame must have been fitted over the old rectangular canvas and its stretcher. The painting was presumably cleaned when in Berlin, as already stated, by A. Hauser, a protégé of Bode. On this occasion, the canvas was presumably put into a rectangular frame once more, since a photograph taken at that time (Fig. 156) shows the work as rectangular. One notices, too, that the figure of Rembrandt seems, as it were, to be sagging downwards [12]. Does this explain Schmidt-Degener's supposition that the canvas must formerly have been of larger dimensions? [13].

In the Neeld collection the dimensions were quoted as 59 x 51 cm, while in the Kappel collection they were said to be 67 x 52 cm, thus indicating a difference in height of 8 cm. This has naturally influenced the positioning, the *mise en page,* of the figure in relation to the total surface of the canvas.

In 1954 the layers of badly-yellowed varnish were removed, with the result that a dark, blackish-brown strip, approximately 2 cm wide, became clearly visible along the top edge. This technical examination showed that the paint here seems to be of ancient origin. A similar strip is also visible, though rather less distinct, down the left side, while the folded-over edges fixed on to the stretcher are all covered with the same heavy, blackish-brown paint. Since there appears to have been a good deal of restoration in the grey background around the head, we may assume that Rembrandt had originally envisaged a much darker background. We may also assume, however, by analogy with other late self-portraits, that round the head he worked from light to dark, to suggest space (see *Technical data*).

The curious, practically straight border along the top permits the assumption that the painter saw this as the limit for his composition. Since the restoration of 1954, the dark strips along the edges have been hidden behind the widened inner rim (rabbet) of the frame. It seems to us that this improves the proportion between the figure (head and chest) and the total surface [14].

NOTES

1. G.F. Waagen, *Kunstwerke und Künstler in England* 2, Berlin, 1838, p. 211.

2. G.F. Waagen, *Treasures of Art in Great Britain* 2, London, 1854, p. 246.

3. Exh. cat. *Works by Rembrandt,* London (Royal Academy), 1899, No. 4.

4. The following authors mentioned no signature or date: Dutuit, p. 47; E. Michel, *Rembrandt, sa vie, son œuvre et son temps,* Paris, 1893, p. 483.
According to the notes these authors made regarding the 1899 exhibition, F. Lugt takes into account the possibility of a 1660 dating, while Hofstede de Groot was of the view that the painting was signed and dated *Rembrandt f. 1669.*
A. Bredius ("De Rembrandt-Tentoonstelling te Londen" in *De Amsterdammer, Weekblad voor Nederland,* 22 and 29 January and 5 and 12 February 1899) wrote: "The last portrait of the painter appears to be No. 4 belonging to Sir A.W. Neeld; at least, one can read the year on it: 1669. One could wish that this signature be very closely studied once more; in brilliant sunlight, for instance. It was formerly read as 1660...". According to Bredius the varnish on the painting was "untransparent", which was the reason for these differing readings of the date.

5. W. von Bode, *Die Gemäldesammlung Marcus Kappel in Berlin,* Berlin, 1914, No. 21, with ill.

6. Exh. cat. *Historische tentoonstelling,* Amsterdam (Rijksmuseum en Stedelijk Museum), 1925, p. 524.

7. *Jaarverslag* (Annual Report) *Mauritshuis over 1947,* The Hague, 1948, p. 48.

8. Schmidt-Degener in exh. cat. *Rembrandt,* Amsterdam (Rijksmuseum), 1935, No. 32: "This last self-portrait shows features which wear a contented smile yet which seem somewhat fatigued. Although his life closes with this portrait full of resignation and equipoise, one is struck by the fact that at 63 he makes the impression of being a prematurely aged and exhausted old man. The cheeks are unhealthily puffed, the hair white under the gaily coloured artist's cap."; W. Pinder, *Rembrandts Selbstbildnisse,* Leipzig, 1943, p. 108: "Now the might of the Universe—represented for the painter by light and space—has merged imperceptibly into the might of the I: Man as the image of the Universal".

9. G. Martin, "A Rembrandt Self-Portrait from his last year", *Burlington Magazine,* 109, 1967, p. 355, ills. 1, 2.

10. Communicated by word of mouth by Miss Margaretta Salinger, Metropolitan Museum, New York.

11. Prof. J. Bruyn drew our attention to a very similar handling of the paint in Rembrandt's portrait of the poet Jeremias de Decker (signed and dated 1666) in the Hermitage in Leningrad (Br.-G., No. 320).

12. Also illustrated as an oval in: W. von Bode and C. Hofstede de Groot, *Rembrandt. Beschreibendes Verzeichniss seiner Gemälde,* 7, Paris, 1902, p. 80, with ill. (see our Fig. 151). A rectangular framed picture is illustrated in: W. von Bode, *Die Gemäldesammlung Marcus Kappel in Berlin,* Berlin, 1914, No. 21; H.d.G., No. 527 (appeared in 1916; the text still refers to an oval painting).

13. Exh. cat. *Rembrandt,* Amsterdam (Rijksmuseum), 1935, No. 32.

14. See also: S.J. Gudlaugsson, *Vijfentwintig jaar aanwinsten Mauritshuis,* Den Haag, 1970, No. 29, with ill. in colour.

157. Old Copy after Rembrandt. Study of an Old Woman (Rembrandt's Mother).

1

Old copy after Rembrandt

Study of an Old Woman

(Rembrandt's Mother)

Fig. 157

Panel, 18.3 x 14.0 cm. Unsigned, undated; probably 17th century.

Cat. Br. (1895), No. 556; Valentiner, p. 35 (copy); H.d.G., No. 686 (authentic?); Cat. M. (1935), No. 556; Br., No. 67; Br.-G., No. 67 (copy); Cat. H. (1977), No. 556 ("may not be autograph").

TECHNICAL DATA

The old woman's portrait has been painted on a thick oak panel in which the grain of the wood runs horizontally, in contrast to most panels which are taller than they are wide. At the sides the edges have been bevelled in the normal manner [1].

Investigation using ultra-violet light and infra-red photography produced but little information, except that various retouchings became clearly visible in and around the eyes and elsewhere (Fig. 158).

Unlike that of the other paintings on panels which we examined, the X-ray photograph in this case shows little contrast (Fig. 159). The clear picture of the grain of the wood shows that on this panel the material used for the ground was not chalk only, as on the other panels, but a priming containing a large quantity of white lead. The presence of white lead in this ground and also the absence of thicker underpainting in white lead in the light areas explain why the face and collar painted thinly in white lead show up so badly in the X-radiograph. According to the radiograph, the hair and the dark coat have been deliberately left blank in the thin white lead underpainting of the background. Neither the X-radiograph nor the radiograph obtained by electron emission indicated any *pentimenti*.

In the light areas of the face and background the *craquelure* consists of a fine and fairly regular network of cracks. In some places on the face "spider's-web" cracking is to be seen, surrounding slight indentations in the surface of the paint, presumably caused by local impact.

The cracks are rather wider in the dark paint of the hair, yet *craquelure* is almost entirely absent from the dark coat, a great part of which has been overpainted during earlier restoration. It is only along the bottom edge that there are regular and fairly wide cracks in the black coat, along a strip a few centimetres high. There is no *craquelure* in the blackish-brown of the eyes, yet here, too, retouching is involved, as was said above. The paint layers are thin

158. Infra-red photograph.

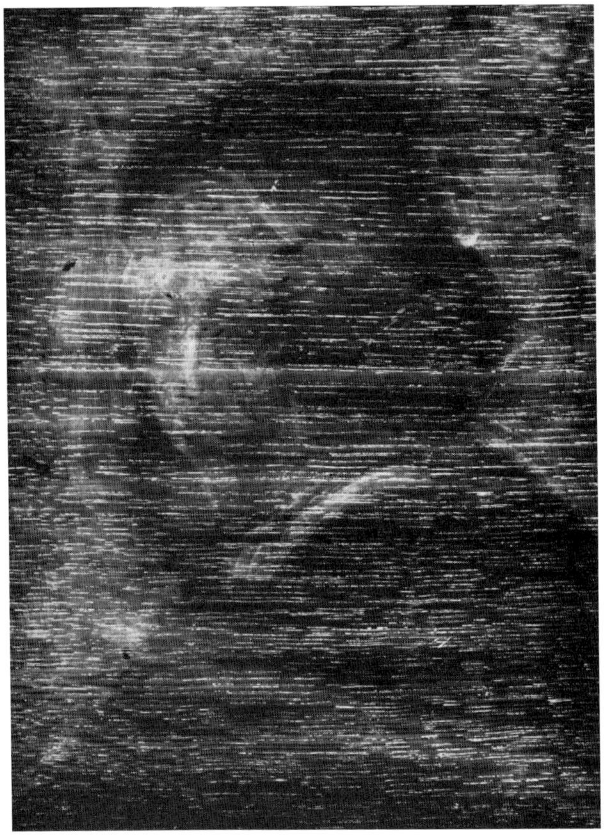

159. X-ray photograph.

in this work and the wood or its grain is visible in several places.

The ground consists of a mixture of white lead and chalk, over which, in the background areas, a second layer of thin white lead has been applied. The background has been painted in greyish tints, made up of white lead, carbon black and various ochres containing many coarse grains of pigment. Coarse-grained brown ochres and white lead were also discovered in the original areas of the coat in addition to carbon black. The face and the collar have been underpainted with a thin dark grey layer consisting of white lead and carbon black with some brown ochre.

In various places, the flesh tones, painted in white lead and ochres, have been thinly glazed with red lake pigment.

The white lead on the collar has the composition of old white lead with the trace elements silver, copper and manganese. The red-jewelled head ornament has been painted with a thick layer of a red lake pigment and a little red ochre. In the green jewel there is malachite, mixed with a fairly large quantity of blue azurite, the yellow in this place consisting of yellow ochre. A rather large amount of coarse white lead has been blended into the yellow as it has also in the grey of the head ornament.

Blue is present in very small quantities in the form of light touches in both eyelids, and looks like azurite.

The dark brown of the coat consists of Cologne earth mixed with black pigment and brown ochre.

There is no signature on the painting nor were any remnants of one detected.

HISTORICAL DATA

At the end of the 19th century this *Study of an Old Woman* formed part of the collection of Monseigneur C.J.H. Franssen, Honorary Chamberlain of His Holiness the Pope. This collection was auctioned in Rotterdam on 17 March 1890 [2]. Item No. 21 was listed as: "G. Dou (?). Head and shoulders Portrait of an Old Woman. Panel. H. 18. Br. 13 c.". In his copy of the sale catalogue A. Bredius noted: "Excellent model, finely yet broadly executed. Certainly RHL's mother; pale grey background; partly in impasto; early Dou. ƒ41" [3].

Bredius bought the painting, loaning it to the Mauritshuis in 1890 and bequeathing it to the gallery in 1946.

Collections

Mgr. C.J.H. Franssen, Grubbenvorst (Limburg, Holland), 1890

160. Rembrandt. The Artist's Mother, 1628. Etching. B. 354.

161. Rembrandt. The Artist's Mother, 1631. Etching, B. 349.

Dr. A. Bredius, The Hague, on loan to the Mauritshuis, 1890-1946

Bredius Bequest, 1946

Dimensions quoted

1890 18 x 13 cm
1895 17 x 13 cm
1977 18.3 x 14.0 cm

Price

1890 41 florins

ICONOGRAPHY AND STYLE

Study of the head of an old woman, looking to the left. She is wearing a fur cap, under which a decorative head-shawl can be seen, part of it falling down on to her left shoulder. It is sewn with stones and is gathered together on the forehead by one large gem (Fig. 157).

Tradition has it—and tradition is probably right—that this *Study of an Old Woman* represents Rembrandt's mother [4].

Rembrandt's mother, Neeltgen Willemsdr. van Zuytbrouck was born around the year 1570 and was the daughter of Willem Adriaensz. van Zuytbrouck and Lysbeth Cornelisdr. van Tetrode. Her father was a baker with a shop on the Warmoesgracht, now the Fish Market, in Leiden. She married a miller, Harmen Gerritsz. van Rijn in the Calvinist church of St. Peter's in Leiden on 8 October 1589 [5]. The couple had nine children, of whom Rembrandt was the last but one [6]. Neeltgen Willemsdr. was buried in St. Peter's Church in Leiden on 14 September 1640 [7].

In the inventory of Rembrandt's etching plates which were among the possessions of the art dealer and publisher Clement de Jonghe († 1677) and were auctioned in 1679, item No. 10 refers to an etching plate entitled *Rembrandt's Mother.* Since De Jonghe presumably acquired these plates around 1658, directly or indirectly from Rembrandt's auctioned belongings, one may be almost certain that the woman in this etching has rightly been identified as Rembrandt's mother. It is highly probable that this etching is identical with B. 349, which bears the monogram *RHL* and is dated *1631* [8] (Fig. 161).

The woman in the Hague painting looks very much like the woman referred to as "Rembrandt's mother" in the etching B. 349. Yet the resemblance between this painting and the etching B. 354 (Fig. 160), which also represents Rembrandt's mother and is monogrammed *RHL* and dated *1628,* is still more striking [9]. Münz, too, sees a direct link between this etching, B. 354, and the painting in The Hague [10].

Painted portraits, a single drawing (Benesch, I, No. 55), and a fairly large number of etchings were considered during the 18th and 19th centuries to be portraits of Rembrandt's mother. This means that there has, in any case, been a fairly long tradition of painted, drawn and etched portraits connected with the artist's mother [11]. It is noteworthy that the portrait of Rembrandt's mother in Windsor Castle (Br.-G., No. 70), which was probably acquired directly from Rembrandt about the year 1629 and offered as a gift to King Charles I in 1633, was listed in an inventory in 1640 as "an old woman with a greate scarfe uppon her heade with a peaked falling band" [12].

If we compare the etchings in which Rembrandt's mother has probably been portrayed [13] with the painted portraits Rembrandt made of her (Br.-G., Nos. 63, 64, 67, 68, 69, 70, 71) we notice that the head-dress the old woman is wearing in the etchings corresponds more often with the customary everyday wear of an older woman than the head-dress we see in some of the paintings [14].

From this we may conclude that Rembrandt painted his mother not only as a sitter for portraits but also in some biblical role, such as, for instance, the prophetess Anna [15].

Many versions of this *Study of an Old Woman*[16] are known. It would seem to us that only the panel in the Fogg Art Museum in Cambridge (Mass.) (Fig. 162) is roughly of the same quality as the work in The Hague. We may ask ourselves why so many versions of this small portrait were made. Was it the fact that the sitter was the mother of a famous painter which led to so many copies, or was it the fact that it was a character-study of an old woman which made the picture so popular? There can be no doubt that this small portrait is not Rembrandt's own work (see also the *Technical data*). The work lacks the firmness of form and daring touch which we find practically everywhere in Rembrandt's youthful production. Since there has been a fairly considerable amount of retouching (e.g. round the eyes and mouth) we cannot say much regarding the way the details have been painted. It must also be borne in mind that at the Franssen auction this small work was sold as a Dou, but that Bredius later, like Martin after him, always stood by the attribution of the work to Rembrandt. It was not until the abridged Mauritshuis catalogue of 1949 was published that the painting ceased to be regarded as a Rembrandt or a Dou [17].

162. Old Copy after Rembrandt. The Artist's Mother. *Cambridge (Mass.), The Fogg Art Museum.*

It is highly probable that the still undiscovered original (by Rembrandt or Dou) was oval in shape, since the majority of the copies known to us have been painted as ovals (see note 16).

This Hague *Study of an Old Woman* is probably a 17th century painting. The dendrochronological research carried out by J. Bauch particularly gives reason to suppose this (see note 1).

NOTES

1. J. Bauch has ascertained that the last heartwood growth ring on this panel must date from 1600.

2. Lugt, I, No. 48893. H.d.G., No. 686 states incorrectly that this painting is probably identical with the painting from the F.J.O. Boymans auction of 31 August 1811, item No. 79B (Lugt, I, No. 8060). But that painting's dimensions are 18 x 14 *pouces,* whereas those of The Hague work are 18.3 x 14 *cm.*

3. In the keeping of the Netherlands Institute for Art History, The Hague.

4. D. de Hoop Scheffer, "Nogmaals de inventarislijst van Clement de Jonghe", *De Kroniek van het Rembrandthuis,* 26, 1972, pp. 126-128.

5. H.d.G., *Urkunden,* 3, No. 4.

6. Münz, 1953, p. 142; J. Rosenberg, S. Slive, E.H. ter Kuile, *Dutch Art and Architecture. 1600-1800,* Harmondsworth, 1972, p. 77.

7. H.d.G., *Urkunden,* p. 86, No. 80.

8. D. de Hoop Scheffer and K.G. Boon, "De inventarislijst van Clement de Jonghe en Rembrandts etsplaten", *De Kroniek van het Rembrandthuis,* 25, 1971, pp. 1-18; D. de Hoop Scheffer, "Nogmaals de inventarislijst van Clement de Jonghe", *De Kroniek van het Rembrandthuis,* 26, 1972, pp. 126-128. B. 349 = Münz, No. 302 = Hollstein, Vol. 18, p. 155, Vol. 19, p. 266.

9. B. 354 = Münz, No. 82 = Hollstein, Vol. 18, p. 157, Vol. 19, p. 267.

10. Münz, No. 82.

11. Münz, 1953, p. 143; see also note 8.

12. O. Millar, "Abraham van der Doort's catalogue of the collections of Charles I", *The Walpole Society,* 37, 1958-60 (pub. 1960), p. 60, No. 101; J.G. van Gelder, "Rembrandt and his Circle, *Burlington Magazine,* 95, 1953, p. 37 and note 4.

13.

Bartsch No.	= Münz No.	= Hollstein vol. 18, p.	vol. 19, p.
343	85	152	264
348	86	154	265
349	302*	155	266
351	87	156	267
352	83	156	267
354	82	157	267

* as amended by Van Vliet.

14. For that matter the facial features of the women differ in the paintings mentioned, although there is undoubtedly a marked resemblance in the overall characterization. In Gerson's revised edition of Bredius (Br.-G.), all the paintings referred to as "Rembrandt's Mother" have this title placed between inverted commas, indicating that Gerson himself is not quite sure of the sitter's identity.

15. C. Tümpel, "Studien zur Ikonographie der Historien Rembrandts", *Nederlands Kunsthistorisch Jaarboek,* 20, 1969, pp. 178-179.

16. 1) Salm-Salm collection, Bocholt; 24.2 x 19.3 cm; oval, originally rectangular; H.d.G., No. 686.1; 2) Herzog Anton-Ulrich Museum, Brunswick; panel, 23 x 18 cm, already in the Salzdahlmner Galerie in 1776; H.d.G., No. 686.2; 3) W.C. Alexander collection, London; panel, 21.8 x 16.8 cm; H.d.G., No. 686.3; 4) L. Janssens collection, Brussels; auctioned at Sedelmeyer's, Paris, 25 May 1907, item No. 159; panel, 29 x 22.5 cm; formerly oval; H.d.G., No. 686.5; 5) Lord Rossmore collection at Rossmore, U.K.; 37 x 29 cm; formerly oval; H.d.G., No. 686.4; 6) Auction in London, 12 June 1912, No. 30; panel, 21.7 x 17.5 cm; oval; H.d.G., No. 686.6; 7) Fogg Art Museum, donated by J.P. Warburg; panel, 24.8 x 19.7 cm; oval; 8) Musée d'Art et d'Histoire, Geneva (provenance: King of Saxony's collection (?), panel, 23.7 x 19 cm; 9) Warsaw, Nationalmuseum (Gerrit Dou); panel, 23.8 x 19 cm; formerly oval (provenance: collections, Potocki, Ossolinski, Tarnovski, acquired 1942); 10) A. Delmotte-Neyrinck collection, Antwerp, 1969 (provenance: F. de Hoffmann collection; Brussels, 1936; G. Marseau, art dealer, Brussels, 1936); formerly oval; 11) P. Jurschewitz collection, Paris, 1927; Art market, Munich (Steinmeyer), 1965; panel, 28 x 22 cm; formerly oval; 12) O. Bondy collection, Vienna (provenance: A.S. Drey, art dealer, Munich); auctioned in New York, 3 March 1949, item No. 77, with ill.; panel, 25 x 20 cm; oval; 13) R. Chasles etc. auction, Brussels, 16 December 1929, item No. 29 (attributed to G. Dou); formerly oval; 14) Düsseldorf auction (Pongs), 17 October 1953, item No. 19, with ill. (as by G. Dou); panel, 23 x 19 cm; formerly oval; 15) Phönix Aktiengesellschaft für Zahnbedarf, Essen, 1961; 16) W.F.J. Laan auction, Geneva (Moos), 9 June 1934, item No. 13, with ill.; (provenance: Auction, Christie's, London) 31 May 1920, item No. 83; Art Collection Association); panel, 23.3 x 19 cm; formerly oval; 17) A.L. Nicholson collection, Wimbledon, England.

17. Abridged Cat. Mauritshuis, 1949, p. 67, under Rembrandt, No. 556, annotated: "Probably not the artist's own work either".

It is quite possible that some of the seventeen versions are mentioned twice, as we do not know exactly what has happened to the paintings since Hofstede de Groot's list was published (1916, English edition). There are certainly great differences of quality between the many versions, which were painted at various dates too.

163. Circle of Rembrandt. Minerva.

2

Circle of Rembrandt

Minerva

Fig. 163

Panel, 60.1 x 51.8 cm. Unsigned, undated.

H.d.G., p. 467 (not as Rembrandt); Cat. M. (1935), No. 626; Bauch, p. 219 (as G. Dou?); Cat. H. (1977), No. 626 ("possibly painted by Hendrick Pot").

TECHNICAL DATA

The thin oak panel, fitted with a cradle, is not the original support. This is apparent from the presence of a fairly thick, smooth white priming or layer of plaster on the panel, on to which the paint-film has been glued and from which it easily comes off. The layer of plaster has no *craquelure,* as has an original layer of old priming which forms a whole with the paint layer. When the painting was transferred from the old support to the new panel, it must have been planed off on the reverse side until the paint-film was reached, for no remnants of an earlier support or of priming were found. Drastic restoration of this kind was being performed as early as the 18th century and occurred fairly frequently in the 19th century as well.

Examination under ultra-violet radiation and by means of infra-red photography, did not yield any special information. In so far as it has not suffered interference from the battens of the cradle, the X-ray photograph gives a good picture, full of contrast, in which no *pentimenti* were detected (Fig. 164).

In the light areas of the figure, and elsewhere, there is a *craquelure* which ranges from a fine network of cracks to irregular, discontinuous wider cracks. In the more thickly painted layers, these wide cracks reveal brownish-black underpainting, which is probably the cause of this form of premature cracking. The dark areas in the painting have been largely overpainted and have little or no *craquelure,* the same being true of the foreground.

Despite the presence in places of thicker layers, the surface of the paint makes a smooth flattened impression almost everywhere. This may probably have come about as the result of strong pressure on the paint-film when it was transferred to the new panel [1].

The thick, uniform white layer of plaster (ground) consists of chalk mixed with a little white lead. The paint can be easily separated from the plaster and between the two lies a thin, greyish-yellow layer of glue. The white in the painting is white lead with the usual contaminations of copper, silver and tin. The

164. X-ray photograph.

yellow of the globe and the jewels and that found in other places consists of yellow ochre. The blue of the collar is azurite; owing to the layer of yellow varnish this blue makes a greenish impression. The red in the jewels consists of red ochre and vermilion, glazed with a fairly thick layer of red lake pigment.

There is no signature on the painting nor were the remnants of one found.

HISTORICAL DATA

Nothing is known of this painting's provenance. It was loaned to the Mauritshuis by A. Bredius in 1899 and bequeathed to the gallery by him in 1946 [2].

Collections

Dr. A. Bredius, The Hague, on loan to the Mauritshuis, 1899-1946

Bredius Bequest, 1946

Dimensions quoted

1899 61.7 x 53.5 cm

1977 60.1 x 51.8 cm

ICONOGRAPHY AND STYLE

Minerva is seated in the left upper half of the painting, in an armchair, on a dais over which a green cloth has been thrown. Behind her, to the right, rises a massive pillar. She is reading in a book which has been propped open against a pile of smaller volumes lying on a table covered with a green cloth. Her head is supported by her left hand, with her left elbow resting on the table. She is clasping the girdle round her waist with her right hand. Her head is adorned with a string of pearls and a laurel wreath, her fair hair falling down over her shoulders. Over her purple robe with its green girdle she is wearing a red cloak trimmed with gold brocade and held together by a clasp. A white under-garment is visible round her neck and on her left arm. To the right, on the wall, hangs a shield bearing the head of Medusa and a game-bag; between them a lance has been painted. In the foreground, in front of the table, a number of objects are seen lying against the body of a fallen over lute with two plaster heads to the left, and to the right a few books. Behind them we see the shell of a great tortoise. Further to the right there is a globe and behind it a small armchair upholstered in gold leather, with a number of colourful pieces of material lying on the seat (Fig. 163).

The female figure should be interpreted in the first place as Minerva in view of her attributes, the Medusa shield and the lance. In his early years Rembrandt painted this Goddess of War and Wisdom on more than one occasion and often with the Medusa shield, a lance, books and a globe as her attributes (see Br.-G., No. 466 (c. 1631) and No. 469 (dated 1635)).

165. Rembrandt. Minerva.
Berlin-Dahlem, Gemäldegalerie.

The *Minerva* in the Berlin Museum (Br.-G., No. 466) (Fig. 165) bears the closest resemblance to the Hague *Minerva.* The Berlin painting is in all probability the painting which was described in the inventory of the possessions of Stadhouder Frederick Henry in 1632 under item No. 89: "Een stuck schilderij de Melancolij, sijnde een vrouw sittende op eenen stoel aen een taeffel daerop liggende boecken, een luyt ende andere instrumenten, door Jan Lievensz. [3]. We cannot attach much credence to this attribution to Jan Lievens, since the compiler of this inventory shows that he was unable to distinguish between Rembrandt and Lievens (see No. V, *Simeon's Song of Praise,* p. 77).

In 1953, basing his opinion on a certain resemblance with the Berlin painting and on the 17th cen-

166. Detail of the undecipherable title of the book on the foreground.

tury description, J.G. van Gelder also referred to the Hague painting as representing *Melancholy* [4]. He indicated a number of objects which would be appropriate in any such allegory, also mentioning an etching by Castiglione in this connection [5]. It does not seem very likely to us that Minerva, the Goddess of Wisdom, would be identified with Melancholy. It is striking, all the same, that the Hague Minerva—in contrast to the Berlin painting—is resting her head on her hand, a characteristic gesture in illustrations of Melancholy [6].

We are of the opinion that in both these paintings Minerva is portrayed as the patroness of the sciences. The book [7] (Fig. 166), lute, plaster casts and globe seen on the floor in the foreground in the Hague painting are all objects which bear some relation to the Arts and Sciences. Similar objects are to be found in portraits of painters, studio interiors and still-lifes of the 16th, 17th and 18th centuries.

The shell of the tortoise is also open to such interpretation. It is quite conceivable that the painter had seen such a curiosity in Leiden and added it to the items in the foreground as a scientific object [8].

When Bredius lent this painting to the Mauritshuis in 1899, he described it as follows: "*Minerva.* Dutch School about 1628, not marked. This painting could possibly be a very early work of Rembrandt's (± 1627-28). The style of painting is highly reminiscent of that in a work in the possession of a Mr. Weber in Hamburg *(The Presentation in the Temple),* while the same accessories are seen in two similar works by Rembrandt, one in the Museum in Berlin and the other in the possession of Mons. P. Charbonneaux in Rheims." [9].

Since then the painting has been attributed to such artists as G. Dou, W. de Poorter and H. Pot, with appropriate—well justified—reservations [10].

In our view, the association of the still-life in the foreground with Rembrandt's circle in Leiden is quite acceptable. The lighting has undoubtedly certain "Rembrandtesque" features, though not the strong contrasts we may expect from him during his Leiden period. The colours have a certain attractiveness and diversity, but the draughtsmanship is not strong, while it is difficult to place the composition—surprising as it may be with the figure of Minerva placed in the upper left corner—in Rembrandt's immediate vicinity. We are left with the question of whether we are concerned here with some as yet unidentified painter of Rembrandt's circle or whether there is reason to doubt the 17th century origin of the work. Technical investigation has not been able to provide any clue.

This new loan to the Mauritshuis was mentioned in a newspaper article dated 16 June 1899. We read: "A painting belonging to Dr. Bredius has been placed on temporary exhibition in the Mauritshuis which the owner has not been able to identify with any certainty". When the work was restored by A. Hauser in Berlin "a twig appeared on Minerva's head, which is also to be found in the painting (mentioned above) in Berlin, and on the same occasion a right hand was revealed over which the cloak had been painted. In the top lefthand corner even an entire window with the branches of a vine, through which the light fell, disappeared, yielding place to a wall" [11].

To conclude we do not accept the proposed attributions to G. Dou, W. de Poorter and H. Pot. We are, however, reluctant to suggest a more convincing name for the author of this picture, painted, as we believe, in the 17th, if not the 18th, century.

NOTES

1. For the highly flattening effect of a transfer of this kind on the paint layer see also R.H. Marijnissen, *Dégradation, Conservation et Restauration de l'œuvre d'art,* Brussels, 1967, pp. 187, 314.

2. A. Bredius, "Jaarverslag Mauritshuis over 1899", *Verslagen omtrent 's Rijks verzamelingen van geschiedenis en kunst,* 22, The Hague, 1900, p. 56; Cat. M. (1935), No. 626.

3. Drossaers-Scheurleer, I, p. 185, No. 89; Drossaers-Scheurleer, I, p. 523, No. 39; Cat. Berlin Staatliche Museen), 1975, No. 828C.

4. J.G. van Gelder, "Rembrandt's vroegste ontwikkeling", *Mededelingen der Koninklijke Nederlandse Akademie van Wetenschappen, afd. Letterkunde,* N.S., Vol. 16, No. 5, 1953, pp. 293-296.

5. R. Klibansky, E. Panovsky and F. Saxl, *Saturn and Melancholy,* Edinburgh, 1958, p. 390, ill. 135.

6. See, for example, A. Blankert, "Heraclitus en Democritus", *Nederlands Kunsthistorisch Jaarboek,* 18, 1967, pp. 53-54.

7. See exh. cat. *Tot Lering en Vermaak,* Amsterdam (Rijksmuseum), 1976, Cat. No. 74. Even with the help of photographic enlargements it was not possible to read the title of the book in the foreground.

8. Exh. cat. *Leidse universiteit 400,* Amsterdam, 1975 (Rijksmuseum), Cat. Nos. D 22, D 25, D 26, with ill. It is apparent from this that in the Botanical Garden at Leiden the shells of tortoises were to be seen amid all kinds of *naturalia.*

9. A. Bredius, "Jaarverslag Mauritshuis over 1899", *Verslagen omtrent 's Rijksverzamelingen van geschiedenis en kunst,* 22, The Hague, 1900, p. 56; the works mentioned are Br.-G., Nos. 535 and 465 (now: Denver (U.S.A.), Art Museum).

10. Bauch, p. 219, Fig. 180: "G. Dou (?)"; J.G. van Gelder, "Rembrandt's vroegste ontwikkeling", *Mededelingen der Koninklijke Nederlandse Akademie van Wetenschappen, afd. Letterkunde,* N.S., Vol. 16, No. 5, p. 293, note 55: "W. de Poorter?"; Cat. Mauritshuis, 1977, No. 626: "H. Pot?".

11. *Nieuwe Rotterdamsche Courant,* 16 June 1899.

167. Pastiche in the manner of Rembrandt. Travellers Resting.

3

Pastiche in the manner of Rembrandt

Travellers Resting

Fig. 167

Paper on panel, 38.0 x 43.0 cm. Signed *Rembrandt f.*

Cat. Br. (1895), No. 579; H.d.G., No. 89; Cat. M. (1935), No. 579; Br., No. 556; Bauch, No. 50 (copy after Rembrandt); Br.-G., No. 556 (not Rembrandt); Cat. H. (1977), No. 579 ("possibly by an 18th century follower of Rembrandt").

TECHNICAL DATA

Painted on paper, the texture of which is visible in places, where the paint layers have worn thin. The paper is fairly thick (0.2 - 0.3 mm) and consists of fibres of flax.

This painted sheet of paper has been affixed to an oak panel, with a thick layer of grey paint between paper and wood. On either side of the panel strips of wood 2.6 cm wide have been attached with glue (mitred), with the result that the painting has been widened by 1.4 cm on either side. There is no paper on these two side strips; the joins have been covered with white plaster and the painting continues on them. The paper runs to the edges at the top and bottom of the panel. All four sides of the panel are bevelled.

The examination using ultra-violet light and infra-red photography yielded no special information. The X-ray investigation revealed that the underlying layers contain so much white lead that only fragments of the picture can be discerned on the radiograph (Fig. 168). The additional investigation by means of electron emission radiography did not, however, reveal any alterations or, more particularly, *pentimenti*.

There is comparatively little *craquelure* in the surface of the paint. In the group of figures, painted fairly thickly, and in the other bright areas of the work too, (roofs, sky, rocks) there is a certain amount of irregular cracking, especially in the white, yet less than one generally finds in old paintings done on canvas or panels. However, in this respect it should be noted that we have no data on the formation of *craquelure* in old paintings done on paper or on paper stuck on panel.

The yellowish-green and brown central area has been painted thinly and smoothly and displays little cracking. There are no coarse grains of pigment in the paint. Scratching in the wet paint (with the wooden tip of the brush) has, however, been done in more than one place, so that the outlines of the roofs, for example, have acquired their colour from the whitish-yellow layer of ground and from the paper.

168. X-ray photograph.

On the right, too, in the dark mass of rocks, certain pictorial effects have been achieved in the same manner. The uppermost layer of paint has been badly worn away in the dark areas at the top, to the right, and also lower down in the painting, so that the whitish-yellow of the ground and of the paper has become visible in many places.

The very thin whitish-yellow preparatory layer on the paper consists of white lead. The thick layer between paper and panel is made up of a large quantity of white lead, umber and a little brown and yellow ochre. Here the silver and copper, usually found as trace elements in the white lead on old paintings, seem to be present in obviously lower concentrations than in the other paintings examined. The yellow consists of yellow ochre and the greenish-yellowish-brown tints of the roofs and background are composed of yellow ochre, brown ochre and umbers.

169. Signature.

New pigments dating from the 19th century or later were not detected.

The signature in the foreground cannot be judged by the *craquelure,* since the thin and worn paint in the same area does not display any cracks (Fig. 169). The signature has been applied in black paint. It lies on the original paint layer and has partly worn off with this layer—which suggests a certain age. There are also places where the signature appears to have been retouched.

HISTORICAL DATA

This painting is probably identical with that which was auctioned as item No. 65 at the sale of the De la Roque collection in Paris in April 1745, together with a painting by Rembrandt entitled *Artist in his Studio* (Br.-G., No. 419). It is noticeable that even at that date the work was not attributed to Rembrandt. We read: "Le second, qui est de l'Ecole de ce Maître, représente une espèce d'Etable placée au bas d'une Tour au pied de la quelle il y a des Figures éclairées par une lumière vive qui se trouve cachée" [1]. According to a note in the copy of the sale catalogue kept in the Netherlands Institute for Art History in The Hague, both paintings were sold to a certain Nelson for 96 livres (pounds?) the pair.

This small painting was later to be found in the collection of the Dowager Countess of Morton, who died in the Old Hall near East Bergholt, Suffolk, on 23 April 1849. The collection was auctioned on 27 April 1850 at Christie and Manson's in London [2]. This work, item No. 13, is described as follows in the sale catalogue: "Rembrandt. The reposo, in a cavern—*effect of fire light*" [3]. According to a note in the copy of the sale catalogue kept at the Netherlands Institute for Art History, The Hague, the price it fetched was [£] 16 [s] 5 [d] 6.

In April 1894 in Leeds, Bredius bought the painting for the Mauritshuis from a Mr. W. Howgate for 620 florins, Mr. W. Nijhoff acting as intermediary [4].

Collections

De la Roque collection, Paris, 1745

The Dowager Countess of Morton, Old Hall, Suffolk, England, 1850

W. Howgate, Leeds

"The Mauritshuis"—Royal Collection of Paintings. The Hague, 1894

Dimensions quoted

1745 39.1 x 33.7 cm
1895 38.3 x 35.0 cm
1977 38.0 x 34.0 cm

Prices

1745 96 livres (pounds?)
1850 £6.5.6d
1894 620 florins

ICONOGRAPHY AND STYLE

A man is seen from behind, seated under an arch with a staff at his side. He stands out as a silhouette against an evenly-lighted wall. In the middle distance, a mother is sitting with her child and a cradle, casting a dark shadow on the wall of a dilapidated building. A third figure (a man or woman?) is talking to the young mother, while behind them a man is lying down and appears to be sleeping in a shed, next to his horse or mule. The scene is illumined by a camp fire and by moonlight (Fig. 167).

From 1850 onwards this work, painted on paper, was considered to be by Rembrandt and to represent *The Rest on the Flight into Egypt.* In 1949, however, doubt was cast on its attribution to Rembrandt [5]. Since then Bauch, Rosenberg and Gerson have declared themselves to be against such an attribution [6]. As early as 1935, Martin had already altered the title into *Travellers Resting* (*Rustende reizigers),* because neither the number of persons involved nor the horse fitted in with the Bible story [7].

The subject still evades exact interpretation, unless we are to assume that the artist's intention was to paint a family scene in a romantic manner.

The technical research has already given some good reason to doubt that this is Rembrandt's own work, while art-historical analysis rejects the attribution to him without hesitation. As for the style, it is surprising that so many renowned experts should have accepted the attribution to Rembrandt for so long. Since it is painted on paper, it was associated with the sketch on paper (and pasted to wood) entitled *The Entombment of Christ* (Br.-G., No. 554), yet every comparison of style between the two works breaks down.

There is, in our view, every reason to suppose that we are confronted here with an 18th century Rembrandt pastiche. It does sometimes happen that pastiches are based on etchings which were once attributed to Rembrandt or were Rembrandtesque in style. Inquiries made in Germany elicited no information, although there is reason to believe that this small picture may have been painted in Southern Germany in the first half of the 18th century [8]. The cracked wall of the dilapidated house, the rather clumsily painted horse or mule and the absence of any main theme forcefully presented, rule out the attribution to Rembrandt.

NOTES

1. Lugt, I, No. 619 (no date known). We are indebted to the chairman of the Amsterdam Rembrandt Research Team for this information regarding provenance. De la Roque (1672-1744) was editor of the "Mercure". The sale catalogue was compiled by Edm. Fr. Gersaint.

2. Lugt, II, No. 19829; George (Douglas), Count of Morton, since 1791 Baron Douglas of Lochleven, County Kinross, married Susan Elizabeth Buller-Yarde-Buller in 1814. The Count of Morton died in 1827 at Dalmahoy, near Edinburgh, and in 1831 the Countess married Edward Godfrey († 1842).

3. A copy is kept at the Netherlands Institute for Art History in The Hague.

4. This is apparent from a document, dated 6 April 1894.

5. Abridged Cat. Mauritshuis, 1949, p. 68, No. 579: "Doubt has probably rightly been cast on the attribution".

6. K. Bauch, in *Der frühe Rembrandt und seine Zeit,* Berlin, 1960, p. 133, Fig. 98, takes it to be a copy after Rembrandt. Bauch, p. 4, No. 50; J. Rosenberg, *Rembrandt. Life and Work,* London, 1968[3], p. 371; Br.-G., No. 556.

7. Cat. M. (1935), p. 283, No. 579.

8. Written communication, dated 2 August 1973, from Dr. A. Mayer-Meintschell of Dresden, who, at least as regards the period of origin, agrees with the supplementary information we were able to obtain concerning provenance (see note 1).

EKTACHROMES:

De Schutter, Antwerp

PHOTOGRAPHS

A.C.L., Brussels: 34
J.P. Anders, Berlin: 111
Art Promotion, Amsterdam: 78
Ashmolean Museum, Oxford: 22
British Museum, London: 6
A. Dingjan, The Hague: 17, 43, 77, 156
Foto-Commissie Rijksmuseum, Amsterdam: 5, 11, 12, 23, 46, 57c, 59, 60, 61, 81, 82, 83, 88, 97, 98, 160, 161
Gemeente Archief Amsterdam: 58
Germanisches Nationalmuseum, Nuremberg: 3, 4
Greater London Council, London: 155
R. Kleinhempel, Hamburg: 45
Lichtbeelden-Instituut, Amsterdam: 145
Mauritshuis, The Hague: 1, 2, 8-9, 18-21, 25-32, 37-41, 47, 49-55, 57 a, b, d, 63-73, 79, 84-87, 89-95, 101, 103-108, 113-116, 119, 137-140, 143, 147-151, 157-159, 163 164 16669
National Gallery London: 53
Nationalmuseum, Stockholm: 14, 146
Photograph Services, The Metropolitan Museum of Art, New York: 134, 141
Prentenkabinet, Leiden: 75
Réunion des Musées Nationaux, Paris: 44, 128, 154
Staatliche Kunstsammlungen, Dresden: 48
Stedelijk Museum, Amsterdam: 61
W. Steinkopf, Berlin: 165

Appendices

I. THE METHODS APPLIED IN THE TECHNICAL INVESTIGATION

The aim of the technical examination performed within the framework of this project was to supply data concerning the material structure of the paintings, concerning alterations to their composition, concerning restoration and retouching and, wherever possible, concerning the signatures and dates [1, 2, 3].

1. *PHYSICAL METHODS*

a. *Examination and photography using ultra-violet light, infra-red light and X-rays*

In addition to conventional photography and microphotography in visible light, photography using ultraviolet, infra-red and X-rays was employed.

Ultra-violet light (quartz lamp, 366 mm) was used to detect overpainting or local retouching, including that in signatures and dates. In addition to the fluorescence image, the reflected ultra-violet image was photographed, after the visible fluorescent rays had been filtered out, in order to obtain supplementary information concerning possible anomalies in the paint surface. The results obtained by both methods were, however, rather disappointing. This was mainly because the fluorescence engendered by the varnish and impurities on the surface of the painting caused so much interference that it was often impossible to obtain the information desired.

Examination using infra-red light took place visually, employing an infra-red image converter, and also photographically, employing polaroid infra-red film, the source of radiation being a 250 Watt excess-voltage lamp with filter. The infra-red image converter proved to retain its sensitivity to radiation up to 1300 nm. For some paintings infra-red reflectography was also used [4].

The infra-red examination served to detect any alterations which might have been made in the original composition and also to make the signatures, monograms and dates on the paintings stand out more clearly, or to trace alterations to these. It is also possible by this means to reveal earlier damage to the support and paint layers and restoration work too.

In the X-ray photography the total picture was photographed in all cases, using Structurix-D.7 (Gevaert) film of 30 x 40 cm. X-ray equipment was used in which the voltage and current could vary between 5 and 200 kV and between 5 and 10 mA respectively [5]. Practically all the radiographs illustrated were taken with 55 kV and 10 mA. The principal aim of the X-ray examination is to obtain more knowledge concerning the structure of the paintings. In interpreting the radiographs certain results yielded by the microscopic and chemical investigation have been used, in particular, data concerning the structure, relative thickness and especially the chemical composition of the layers of ground and paint in various places on the painting.

Another important feature of the X-ray examination is to trace alterations in the composition. These may show up clearly or less clearly on the X-radiograph, depending on their size and the pigments used, white lead playing a very dominant rôle in this respect.

The weave of the old original linen is usually clearly visible on the X-ray photographs, with plenty of contrast, despite the presence of one or even two sheets of relining. In order to ascertain the number of warp and weft threads per sq. cm—the thread-count—the number of threads in an area 5 cm square was counted in various places, chosen at random on the X-radiograph; in six different places on larger canvases and in four on smaller ones. The counts were repeated several times, the average results divided by five and rounded up or down in the usual manner. Furthermore, the X-radiographs usually yield a good picture of any damage and repair the painting may have undergone in the past, both in the support and in the paint layers.

In the case of the painting which had been done on copper, electron emission radiography was employed, since X-ray photography could not be applied [6]. When this technique is used, the painting is radiated with hard X-rays (in this case of 200 kV). This induces electron emission in the layers of paint, which is registered on a photographic film. Owing to their greater emission of electrons, the areas painted in white lead, lead-tin yellow and vermilion show up darker on the photographic film than do the other pigments. As a result, the electron emission radiograph obtained is the opposite of the X-ray photograph, as regards the gradations of black and white, and if we are to compare it with such a photograph, it has to be converted into a positive.

This technique was also employed in respect of a few of the other paintings in order to acquire more information about possible alterations, especially in those cases where no clear X-ray picture could be obtained owing to the presence of a large quantity of white lead in the underlying layers.

It can be said that, in general, this method proved to yield far less information than the normal X-ray examination, because the electrons emitted come chiefly from the uppermost layer of paint. For this reason, *pentimenti,* for instance, often failed to be recorded.

b. *Microscopic examination of the surface*

The microscopic examination of the front and reverse of the paintings was performed with a Zeiss stereomicroscope (10-40 x magnification) on an operation stand with built-in illumination (operation microscope). This examination gives a good idea of the way the work was painted (thin, with glazing or with impasto), of the texture of the paint surface and of the degree of coarseness of the pigments used (size of grain). In this way, it is far easier than when using the naked eye or a magnifying glass to see where underlying paint layers have come to the surface and made themselves manifest in the colouring, or how certain pictorial effects have been achieved, e.g. by using the palette knife or by scratching in the wet paint with a hard, pointed object.

With the stereo-microscope it is also possible to investigate signs of aging in the surface of the paint, such as *craquelure* patterns, abrasion and other damage dating from the past; the same applies to restoration work. It is possible by this means to study the edges of wide cracks and of small paint losses and thereby to examine the layer structure of the painting.

Finally, this is one of the few methods besides examination using ultra-violet and infra-red light by which it is possible to study signatures and dates more closely. A difficulty encountered now and again was the obstacle presented by dirty and cracked layers of varnish.

A fairly large amount of information can be obtained using the methods enumerated above. The great advantage they offer is that no damage of any kind is done to the object studied. For the purpose of this research project, it was, however, desirable to collect more information concerning the paint-layer structure and the nature and composition of the materials used than these methods could provide. For this reason, it was necessary to apply physical and chemical techniques proper to analytical chemistry.

2. *PHYSICAL AND CHEMICAL ANALYSIS OF MATERIALS*

a. *Collecting the samples*

One of the important consequences of analytical investigation is that it necessitates the removal of small samples of material from the painting. In recent decennia, however, methods of analysis have been evolved whereby from a tenth to a few thousandths of a milligram of matter is sufficient to determine its composition.

With the aid of the Zeiss stereo-microscope samples are usually taken from the edges of the paintings which are normally covered by the frames. In these places, however, the old layers of paint have often been damaged or restored and overpainted and it may be difficult to trace the proper original areas. Consultation of the X-ray, infra-red and fluorescence photographs proved most helpful in this work, and even essential, while the X-ray photographs also provided information regarding the representativeness of the area under examination. In those cases in which it was judged necessary to take a small sample of paint from areas within the frame, this was only done after the director of the gallery had been consulted, and then only from places which were not regarded as essential parts of the painting concerned. Moreover, the operation was performed in such a way that it remained unvisible to the naked eye—the sample usually taken from the edge of an already existing small paint loss or crack.

b. *Microscopic examination*

To begin with, the samples of paint, wood, linen or paper were examined microscopically in reflected and transmitted light, using magnifications from 10x to 400x. The better to study the layer structure and the structure of individual layers, paint cross-sections were prepared of some samples suitable for this purpose. Apart from a few, the samples were, however, far too small to enable good paint cross-sections in plastic to be made from them, suitable for illustration in colour. Moreover they were usually incomplete as regards the layer structure. Where good paint cross-sections have been illustrated in the literature on this subject, these have almost always been prepared from larger samples, taken from paintings in course of treatment in the restorer's studio. This was not, however, the case with any of the paintings we examined.

The microscopic slide mounts of the paint samples were made with Canada balsam diluted with xylene or toluene. The microscopic examination covered the colour, size of grain, shape and structure and also the birefringence of separate particles of pigment. By comparison with specimens of authentic old pigments, chiefly originating from the Hafkenscheid collection, it was possible to recognize some pigments and their admixtures under the microscope with a great degree of probability [8]. These include the various ochres, ivory or bone black, charcoal black, chalk, Cassel or Cologne earth, smalt, azurite and vermilion.

c. *Microchemical examination*

In the process of the microscopic identification of pigments, important supplementary information can be obtained by observing the transformations small particles of paint undergo when heated and set aglow on a platinum plate. This applies in particular to yellow and red ochres, azurite, smalt, bone black, Cologne earth and chalk.

d. *X-ray diffraction analysis according to Debije-Scherrer*

This technique was applied to practically every paint sample, since it makes it possible to identify most pigments directly and with certainty. The apparatus used was a Philips PW 1009 Generator, 1 kW diffraction tube (40 kV-25 mA), monochromatic Cu K_α-radiation and large Debije-Scherrer powder cameras. The amount of paint required for a diffractogram lies between 0.1 and 0.01 mg; sometimes even less is sufficient, depending on the pigment.

In the case of mixed pigments it is often difficult to identify all the constituents in the complicated diffraction pattern. Then, too, should the mixture contain a great deal of white lead—which is often the case—other constituents, composed of lighter elements, do not usually produce reflections to a recognizable degree and thus can not be identified. However, this method is non-destructive and leaves the sample unaffected, thus making it possible to perform microscopic, microchemical or spectrographical examination on the paint particles, after the X-ray diffraction photographs have been taken, this being done especially to be able to identify small quantities of additional pigments or to track down typical trace elements.

e. *Emission spectrography*

The spectrograph used was a Hilger Medium Quartz Spectrograph E 498 with RVS generator and adjuster (8 Ampères). The cathode-layer technique was employed with image on the slit. The paint samples, which vary in weight between 1 mg and 0.02 mg, were cleansed as far as possible of varnish and other foreign matter, then inserted into the hole in the Ringsdorff-electrode and covered with a layer of powdered graphite. The excitation in a direct-current arc was carried out in air or in a mixture of equal parts of argon and oxygen in a Schöntag cuvette.

The spectra thus obtained afford a good picture of the characteristic elements present in the pigments of the paint sample. Since this method is very sensitive, elements of secondary components and also of characteristic or non-characteristic impurities can be traced (trace elements).

The limits of detectability of a few elements were determined by experiment. In respect of typical trace elements in old white lead, such as silver and copper, they amount to less than one millionth part of one milligramme.

Spectrographic analysis made it possible to identify the pigments in those cases where X-ray diffraction analysis and the microscopic examination had failed to give sufficient information regarding their composition —especially that of mixtures of pigments. This method is destructive and is accordingly applied in the final stage of the analytical investigation.

f. *Dendrochronological examination*

In connection with this research, the panels of seven paintings were submitted to a dendrochronological examination by J. Bauch [9]. The aim of this examination was to ascertain the year the tree from which the panel had been taken was felled, this being done by studying the annual growth rings in the wood. Accordingly, the results only provide information of the *terminus post quem* situation—the date *after* which the work must have been painted.

No examination was made of the binding media in the various paint layers, since this, with the research it would have entailed, would have taken too much time [10]. Effective micro-techniques for analyzing and identifying oils, resins and mixtures of them in small paint samples have yet to be developed, while one is also confronted with the difficult problem of the original composition of these binding media. In old paintings their composition must have undergone drastic change as a result of chemical and physical processes, and especially under the influence of the surroundings and the way they have been handled during the course of the centuries (restoration, re-lining etc.) [11].

Red lake pigments found on many paintings have also not been more precisely identified. When found on the surface—directly underneath the varnish and partly merged into it—these lake pigments may very well come from (old) restoration, since as paintings age and when they are cleaned, the original red lake pigment is often wholly or partly lost [12]. Moreover, these red lakes had often been applied very thinly in parts of the painting of great pictorial importance, so that no samples could be taken.

NOTES

1. Highly valued assistance was given in this research work by Mr. L. Kuiper, at the time restorer at the Mauritshuis (surface-examination, sampling, photography, ultra-violet, infra-red and X-ray examination), Ir. R. Breek and Ing. J.W. van Wilsem (X-ray diffraction), Dr. E.R. Groeneveld (spectrography) and W. Verschuren (photography, ultra-violet, infra-red and X-ray photography), attached to the Forensic Science Laboratory in Rijswijk. This laboratory is specialized in analyzing small paint samples using modern instrumental methods. It has also performed investigations over the years into many dubious or faked paintings and signatures, including the Vermeer forgeries by Han van Meegeren and several supposed Rembrandts; see W. Froentjes in *Aspects of Art Forgery,* The Hague 1962, pp. 39-53. The research performed for this present work, however, provided the laboratory with a unique opportunity to gain experience with original paint samples from paintings by Rembrandt and a few of his contemporaries.

2. See "Kunst en Chemie", supplement to the *Chemisch Weekblad,* 67, 1971, pp. K 1-35, including J. Bruyn, "Hoe werken kunstgeschiedenis en natuurwetenschappen samen?", pp. 7-8 and W. Froentjes, "Natuurwetenschappelijk onderzoek van Rembrandts in het Mauritshuis", pp. 21-22.

3. A useful survey of publications on technical and scientific research into paintings by Rembrandt up to 1972 is to be found in H. von Sonnenburg, "Technical aspects: Scientific Examination" in *Rembrandt after three hundred years: a Symposium - Rembrandt and his Followers,* Chicago (The Art Institute of Chicago) 1973, pp. 83-101. Also H. von Sonnenburg, "Maltechnische Gesichtspunkte zur Rembrandtforschung", *Maltechnik-Restauro,* 82, 1976, pp. 9-24.

4. The investigation was carried out by Dr. J.R.J. van Asperen de Boer, former assistant-director of the Central Research Laboratory for Objects of Art and Science in Amsterdam, to whom we extend our thanks.
For a closer description of the technique employed see J.R.J. van Asperen de Boer, *Infrared Reflectography,* Amsterdam 1970. Dissertation, University of Amsterdam.

5. A special X-ray apparatus was kindly lent for a period by the firm of Philips-Nederland, for which loan we would like to express our thanks. At a later stage, the X-ray equip-

ment of the Forensic Science Laboratory was used, *viz.*, the Baltospot and the Baltograph.

6. C.F. Bridgman, S. Keck and H.F. Sherwood, "The Radiography of Panel Paintings by Electron Emission", *Studies in Conservation*, 3, 1958, pp. 175-182.

7. *a.* The observation involved here concerns the determination of whether the paint of the signature and date forms a whole with the paint of the work itself. This can provide the first important indication that painting and signature are contemporaneous. Here, of course, there must first be a reasonable degree of certainty that the surface paint in the area concerned is original. Experience teaches that if this microscopic observation has to take place through the layer of varnish, there may easily be a question of optical illusion. Particularly if the varnish is thick, old and contaminated, or if it has small internal cracks, it can prove exceedingly difficult, if not impossible, to make out whether or not there is another, underlying and thin layer of varnish between the paint of the signature and date and that of the painting itself. The same applies to ascertaining whether a congruent and continuous pattern of cracking is present. In such cases it will be necessary first to remove the varnish at the place concerned, if reliable results are to be obtained and there are often objections to doing this. It was not possible in our research either to remove the varnish for this purpose.
It often happens that signatures and dates have to an extent been repainted or painted over, at times on top of an old layer of varnish. It is often far from easy to detect such retouching or overpainting, especially through the varnish. Either may be so old that the structure and the pattern of cracks in the overpainted parts can no longer be distinguished from those of the original paint, whether of signature and date or of the painting itself.
Partly in view of the nature of the paint employed, it could hardly be expected to obtain relevant information as to the age of the signatures from chemical analysis, quite apart from the technical difficulties involved.

b. (See Introduction) The multi-disciplinary character of any study of signatures and dates proceeds from the nature of the criteria to be investigated. On the one hand, it is a matter of age characteristics (contemporaneity) which have to be determined by scientific methods (see 7a above) and for which more research is required. On the other hand, it concerns the authenticity of the "writing" in the signature, for which one has to apply methods employed in the comparative study of handwriting (*not* graphology). Finally, the material important for research will have to be selected by the art historian with great care.
In performing this research into handwriting, it is necessary to analyse a sufficiently large number (scores) of authentic signatures and dates (or those still to be regarded as authentic, despite retouching) from various periods. The aim of this analysis is to enquire into whether a sufficiently large number of characteristics (variables) are repeated often enough to characterize Rembrandt's "handwriting" in his painted signatures and dates. Use could possibly be made here of modern statistical methods which are also being applied in the Netherlands in court cases, when often only one disputed signature is involved. See W. Froentjes, "Schriftonderzoek en statistiek", *Nederlands Juristenblad*, 1969, pp. 821-829. All manner of questions arise here, of course. For instance, the extent to which specific motorial features characteristic of an ordinary written signature are changed when this signature (and/or date) is painted in with a brush; also whether perhaps certain characteristic ways of handling the brush manifest themselves.
It will be necessary, too, to include in this research Rembrandt's presumably authentic signatures and handwriting in the few letters of his which are known to us, and on his drawings and also the signatures on etchings, even though written in reverse. In order to be able to evaluate these characteristics properly, the researcher will, as has already been said, need to possess a knowledge and understanding of the special features of 17th century handwriting.

8. The Hafkenscheid collection of old pigments and dyestuffs dates from the beginning of the 19th century and is in the possession of the Laboratory of General and Inorganic Chemistry, Dyestuffs Department, of the Technological University at Delft. We are grateful to Professor P.M. Heertjes and Professor G.A.M. Diepen for placing samples from their collection at our disposal.

9. We thank Dr. J. Bauch for his interesting contribution to our research. J. Bauch, D. Eckstein and M. Meier-Siem, "Dating of Wood of Panels by a Dendrochronological Analysis of the Tree Rings", *Nederlands Kunsthistorisch Jaarboek*, 23, 1972, pp. 485-496. See also J. Bauch and D. Eckstein, "Dendrochronological Dating of Oak Panels of Dutch Seventeenth Century Paintings", *Studies in Conservation*, 15, 1970, pp. 45-50, and the literature it quotes.

10. When examining the composition of the ground on a large number of paintings by Rembrandt, Kühn also performed some summary research into the binding media used. H. Kühn, "Untersuchungen zu den Malgründen Rembrandts", *Jahrbuch der Staatlichen Kunstsammlungen in Baden-Württemberg*, 2, 1965, pp. 189-210. H. Kühn, "Untersuchungen zu den Pigmenten und Malgründen Rembrandts, durchgeführt an den Gemälden der Staatlichen Kunstsammlungen Kassel", *Maltechnik-Restauro*, 82, 1976, pp. 25-33.

11. See R.H. Marijnissen, *Dégradation, conservation et restauration de l'œuvre d'art*, Brussels 1967, Chapter I. On this see J.R.J. van Asperen de Boer in the *Nederlands Kunsthistorisch Jaarboek*, 26, 1975, pp. 24 and 25.

12. R.H. Marijnissen, *Dégradation, conservation et restauration de l'œuvre d'art*, Brussels 1967, Chapter I, p. 65 et seq.

II. THE RESULTS OF THE TECHNICAL INVESTIGATION

Summary and observations

The main findings of the technical and scientific examination of the paintings are shown in a table at the end of this appendix. The following comments should facilitate their evaluation and interpretation. Relevant data yielded by the research performed by a few other authors have been incorporated in these comments, which also include some results obtained in our own investigations but not mentioned elsewhere in this work or in the table. The present writer hopes to treat a number of the technical and scientific aspects of methods and results which could not be given adequate attention in the present work in a separate publication.

When considering the findings of the examination of the stratigraphic structure and composition of the layers of paint, it should be borne in mind that various data mentioned in the chapters on each individual painting and also in the table are based on the examination of a single—or at most two or three—minute samples of paint taken from certain small areas of the paintings. We were also limited in our choice of these places, which were confined mainly to the edges of the paintings and to spots where the paint-film had already sustained some damage [1]. In the case of the larger paintings on canvas, which, owing to their more complicated structure and problems, called for more extensive examination and consequently the taking of samples from several places, the conditions for choosing samples were, on the whole, more favourable than in the case of the panels. The simpler structure and smaller dimensions of the latter meant one could make do with fewer samples to achieve comparable results. The data obtained through the examination of these samples have, as described elsewhere, been supplemented by a study of the paintings using the operation microscope and other physical methods.

When evaluating the results, one is, of course, confronted with the question as to how far the findings based on examination limited to a few places in the painting also apply to those large areas from which one has not been able to take samples for scrutiny. The uncertainty arising here becomes all the greater, if we know only little about the technique and the materials the artist was wont to employ or should these display great variety. Both conditions apply to Rembrandt's work.

All the same, certain general conclusions in the table should be taken to be correct. This applies to the composition of the ground, for one thing, there being very good reasons for assuming that this is practically uniform over the entire surface of the panel or canvas.

On the other hand, one should bear in mind that in places the structure and the composition of certain layers may differ to a greater or lesser degree from the pattern resulting from the limited areas investigated. The X-ray photograph too can supply only limited information in this respect, dependent upon the use of white lead in the various layers.

As a consequence of the inevitable limitations imposed on the investigation, existing—but undetected—layers may be missing in the table, while others may not have been assimilated into it with perfect accuracy. There is also a real chance that some of the data obtained refers to old restoration not recognized as such.

1. The first column shows the titles of the thirteen Rembrandt paintings examined, arranged in chronological order. The three works not considered as being by Rembrandt have been added at the end.

2. In column 2 the year in which the oak tree which supplied the panel was felled is shown in respect of five of the paintings done on panels [2]. In two cases (Nos. VII and VIII) this date could not be determined, while in two other cases (Nos. 2 and 3) it was not relevant. In the case of six paintings on canvas the two figures after the word "linen" indicate the number of warp and weft threads per square centimetre in the original canvas [3]. As a result of irregularities in the weave, the figures quoted are only accurate within a margin of 1 thread per cm. The oldest canvas examined, that of *Dr. Nicolaas Tulp's Anatomy Lesson,* No. VI, had the finest weave of all the canvases examined. The later the painting, the coarser the weave proved to be. This finding corresponds with the results of the examination of a large number of 17th century paintings in the Central Museum at Utrecht [4].

3. In the third column the pigments are listed which were detected in the (first) layer of ground, or first preparatory layer, applied to the support.

With one exception, only chalk was found on the panels. Here the colour of the ground is yellowish-white. Usually the layer is very thin and present principally in the irregularities of the wood.

This thin ground of chalk (and glue) was the customary way of preparing panels during the 17th century and we also found it, for instance, on a panel by Jan Lievens (*Study of an Old Man*) and on one by Carel Fabritius (*Head of a Polish Jew*), both in the Mauritshuis (Inv. Nos. 85 and 828 respectively) [5].

Regarding the three Mauritshuis paintings on panel (Nos. III, VII, VIII) Kühn examined during his research into the composition of the grounds in paintings by Rembrandt, he reports an exceptional dark brown ground in the *Bathsheba* (No. VIII—referred to as *Suzanna at the Bath*), composed of umber, chalk and smalt [6]. This finding does not correspond with our own: on the original panel we detected the usual yellowish-white ground of chalk only. A dark brown layer of ground is, however, present on the strip added later, and this contains chalk, white lead, umber and black. Consequently, Kühn will not have examined the original ground but will probably have taken his sample from the added strip or possibly from along the top edge, where dark layers had originally been painted.

The panel on which the *Study of an Old Woman* (No. I) has been painted, has been prepared with a ground of chalk mixed with white lead, a combination Kühn detected on four panels by Rembrandt (Br.-G., Nos. 2, 38, 178 and 572) [6].

In the painting done on copper, *Study of a Man Laughing* (No. II), which corresponds in its dimensions and structure with the *Self-Portrait* on copper in Stockholm (Br.-G., No. 11), the composition of the ground was found to be the same as in the Stockholm painting [7].

A wide variety in the composition of the ground was found in the six paintings done on canvas. The colour of the lower layer ranges from pale red (*Homer,* No. XII) to dark brown (*Self-Portrait in Later Life,* No. XIII), depending on the nature and the relative quantities of the constituent pigments. There is also quite a degree of variety in the coarseness of the pigments, their homogeneity and the thickness of the layers. Thus the *Dr. Nicolaas Tulp's Anatomy Lesson* (No. VI) has a comparatively thick (± 0.2 mm) and fairly homogeneous first ground layer, composed of well-mixed, fine pigments, whereas the first ground of the paintings from later periods we examined is generally more heterogeneous with coarser pigments and in places, for example in the *Two Negroes* (No. X), much thinner (0.1 mm).

The materials detected in the grounds correspond entirely with what one would expect from the literature, and in particular with Kühn's investigations [5]. In four of the five Mauritshuis paintings on canvas he examined (Nos. IX, X, XI, XII, XIII) he found practically the same components in the ground layers as we did [6]. Only in the case of the *Portrait of a Man with Grey Curly Hair* (No. IX) does he mentions an unusual white ground of chalk and white lead, while we found a thin red layer composed predominantly of red ochre. It is probable that in this case Kühn examined a spot along the edge, which had been restored. We did not encounter any ground containing quartz as an essential component, apart from traces which may occur as natural contamination in earth-colours (Nos. IX and X).

A greyish ground was found in three paintings on canvas in the Mauritshuis by Aert de Gelder, *viz., Judah and Tamar, The Temple Entrance* and the *Portrait of Herman Boerhave* (Inv. Nos. 40, 737 and 757). This consisted of coarse white lead and a very small amount of ochre—a combination we did not find in the paintings by Rembrandt we examined. Kühn, too, detected a similar ground on two canvases by Aert de Gelder.

4. The fourth column contains information regarding the layers between the (first) ground and the actual painting, with the exception of local underpainting in the figures. These are layers, which, although observed only in places, extend, it is assumed, either over the entire painting, or at least over large areas of the work.

The discovery of gold leaf between the ground and the paint layers in the *Study of a Man Laughing* (No. II), painted on copper, may be seen as a notable and unexpected result obtained in this part of the technical examination. This is all the more so, because this same, unusual technique also proved to have been employed for the *Self-Portrait* on copper in Stockholm (Br.-G., No. 11) and *Rembrandt's Mother* in Salzburg (Br.-G., No. 63)—likewise painted on copper [7].

In the case of five panels, small amounts of white lead were detected on the ground of chalk, and in the X-ray photographs too, pale stripes caused by a thin layer of white lead (or containing white lead) showed up. It did not become equally clear everywhere, however, whether we are concerned here with a second, very thin, preparatory layer of white lead only or whether this white lead forms part of a thin pale brown priming layer (*imprimitura*) applied onto the chalk ground (*Andromeda,* No. IV; *Bathsheba,* No. VIII), or even part of the paint layer. Here we must also bear in mind that it had proved possible to show the presence of very small quantities of white lead, when using the micro analysis techniques.

The brown intermediate layer detected on some of the panels and rendered rather transparent, probably by the Cologne earth, is not present all over the paintings and may be lacking underneath the figures. In the dark areas of foreground and background and in the areas of shadow, this layer often comes to the surface, thus becoming part of the top paint layer.

Especially in view of the publications of Van de Wetering's (preliminary) findings concerning Rembrandts technique of painting during his Leiden period, this brown transparent layer should be seen as a "dootverf", i.e. as the paint of the dead-coloured preparatory stage of the painting [8].

Whereas a certain degree of uniformity of structure and composition was found on the panels, this was not the case with the canvases we examined. Generally speaking, in most paintings on canvas the second layer, sometimes being of nearly the same colour, composition and thickness as the first (ground) layer, extends, it is assumed, over the entire surface and should be taken for a second layer of ground ("double priming"). Other intermediate layers were, on the other hand not found everywhere, especially not underneath the figures. The variety encountered here is confirmed by the literature on the subject. Joyce Plesters [9] and Hendy and Lucas [10] have described the build-up and composition of four late Rembrandts painted on canvas. In his investigations into the grounds, Kühn also made brief mention of the intermediate layers applied to a number of paintings after the ground, and, in his latest publication, he also analysed parts of the surface paint [6].

Apart from the variations mentioned, there is a certain correspondence between our findings and those of the investigators referred to, in particular as regards the colour and components of the layers of ground [11].

5. Column 5 shows that in both panels and canvases, dark brown, dark grey or black layers were found as

underpainting in the light areas of the figures, especially in the heads and collars. In the dark areas where these layers sometimes have come to the surface, they contribute to the dark colouring.

6. In column 6 the pigments are listed which were identified in the final layer of paint, using the methods described. They give us a fairly complete picture of the artist's palette.

White lead was detected in the white areas in the form of a fine-grained pigment. The coarse, almost round grains of white lead in coloured underlying layers consist of agglomerations of the finer particles. In many cases X-ray diffraction examination of the samples of white lead revealed the presence of *normal lead carbonate,* varying between approximately 20 % to 40 %. There were some paintings, however (among them, the *Self-Portrait in a Plumed Hat,* No. VII), in which no lead carbonate was to be found in the white lead (less than 10 %).

Among the samples of old pigments (of the 18th and 19th centuries) in our possession there were also five samples of white lead. In the collection from which they came, they were referred to as "Schulpen wit" (also known in English as "flake white"), "Duitsland schulpen", "Cremnitzer" wit, "Inlands wit" and "Hollands lootwit". These ancient samples proved on examination to contain large quantities of normal lead carbonate, ranging between 40 % to 60 %. Kühn also found similarly—and surprisingly—large quantities of normal lead carbonate—a white pigment inferior in quality to white lead—in the paintings of Jan Vermeer [12].

An analysis of the five samples mentioned using X-ray diffraction and energy dispersive X-ray fluorescence spectrometry showed 27 % *calcium carbonate* or *chalk* to be present in the "Hollands lootwit", whereas the other four samples contained no chalk.

The examination of the old samples of white lead provided convincing proof of Van de Graaf's view, based on 17th and 18th century literature, that two kinds of white lead were on the market in those days [12]. There was pure white lead, known as "Schulpwit" (flake white), which took the form, as in our samples, of small, shell-shaped particles, and, in addition, there was a specifically cheaper Dutch product known as "lootwit", which was a mixture of white lead and chalk and consequently equivalent to our sample of "Hollands lootwit".

Where we found white lead together with chalk in the underlying layers of the paintings we examined, it may be presumed that the cheaper "Hollands lootwit", obtained via the trade, was used. On the *Nightwatch* Van de Wetering and his collaborators detected an underlying layer of "lootwit" with about 25 % of chalk [11].

Chalk, which is normally used only in layers of priming, was detected by us in one painting, the *Andromeda* (No. IV), used as colouring matter, i.e. in the white of the flowers. However, it is quite possible that this chalk was a substratum for a possibly yellow organic pigment which has faded with the passage of time.

The yellow pigments were principally *yellow ochres* in a wide range of shades, from light to dark yellow.

The old pigment *lead-tin yellow* was identified in five paintings. When examined using X-ray diffraction, this pigment proved to contain free tin dioxide in quantities which varied from painting to painting. This pigment, which investigators before 1940 often took to be massicot (lead monoxide), was rediscovered around that year by Jacobi on a number of 15th and 16th century German paintings [13].

Since then other research workers, among them Coremans and especially Kühn have detected this same pigment on numbers of other paintings (more than 200), dating from 1300 to 1750 [14]. It no longer occurs on paintings done after 1750, or, at least, it has not so far been encountered, although many paintings dating from after 1750 have been examined for this. It was accordingly concluded that this highly durable yellow colouring matter was no longer being prepared after the middle of the 18th century and that the recipe for making it had apparently been lost. This would make it possible to fix a *terminus ante* on statistical grounds for paintings in which lead-tin yellow occurs. In a Lexicon of Colours (Farben-Lexicon) of 1782 we did, however, find a simple recipe for the preparation of lead-tin yellow, which at that time was being used, among other things, in enamelling [15]. The yellow pigment we obtained on the basis of this recipe proved identical with the lead-tin yellow found on the paintings, the fractions of a lighter shade of yellow proving to contain varying amounts of free tin dioxide as in the paintings, too. Moreover, the existence of this recipe in 1782 means, that the preparation and use of this pigment must still have been popular after 1750.

Red ochre has been used in a variety of shades as red colouring matter in all the paintings. In addition, *vermilion* was identified in six paintings, but only as light touches in the flesh tones, near eyes, ears and in jewellery. In most places this vermilion had been covered with a red lake pigment [16].

Red lake pigments are present on the majority of paintings and applied as a thin glaze, but also in thicker layers.

Azurite has been used in six of the paintings as a blue pigment. In general only sparing use has been made of this pigment (scattered blue) [17]. On two of the paintings a little *smalt* was found, in addition to azurite. *Ultramarine (lapis lazuli)* was not found on one of the paintings [18].

The green pigment detected on two paintings was identified as *malachite. Green earth* was found nowhere in large and easily identifiable quantities but only (probably) as a subsidiary blend of other (yellow) ochres and umber.

The brown pigments usually consisted of *(red) brown ochres* and *umber;* in addition, *Cassel* or *Cologne earth* was found on a number of paintings, but mostly as a constituent of brown transparent intermediate layers.

Black pigment was almost always *bone or ivory black,* identified by the presence of calcium phosphate. Now and again the shape of the particles suggested the use of *charcoal black*.

Old literature (mainly 17th century) on the subject enables one to deduce that in Rembrandt's day about twenty different pigments were in use. Van de Graaf also arrives at this number for pigments [19]. Some of these are less suitable for use, however, when painting in oil, while others are not very durable. One of the few large-scale research projects concerning the pigments used in 16th and 17th century Dutch and Flemish paintings has been carried out by De Wild [20]. In a total of approximately fifty paintings he was able to identify fourteen different pigments.

The fourteen kinds of colours we detected in the paint layers are among the most frequently used. They were: white lead, chalk, yellow ochre, lead-tin yellow, red ochre, vermilion, red lake pigments, azurite, smalt, malachite, brown ochre, umber, Cologne earth, bone black or charcoal black. Of these fourteen pigments we found twelve on *Simeon's Song of Praise* (No. V) and only six on the *Self-Portrait in Later Life* (No. XIII) and the *Homer* (No. XII), which is a clear pointer to the more sober palette Rembrandt adopted in his later years and a confirmation of Maroger's words that he "could not have had more than five or six colours on his palette" [21].

7. The traces of silver, copper and tin mentioned in column 7, found by spectrographic analysis in various samples of white lead, confirm that the samples had come from old layers of paint. Since, however, these elements can occur in white lead up to about the mid-19th century, these findings provide no answer to the question as to whether the samples investigated came from original paint layers or from old restoration work. They are unable to tell us the approximate age of the paintings either, although they do supply us with a *terminus ante*. This was one of the reasons why no quantitative analysis was performed in addition to this limited qualitative examination—for instance, employing neutron activation analysis or atomic absorption spectrometry.

8. The results of the X-ray examination of the paintings are given in column 8. In the case of four panels electron emission radiography was applied in addition to the normal X-ray procedure. The former is indicated by "+ e.e.r.".

This technique did not throw up more information about any painting as regards changes which had come about in it, while in the case of the *Andromeda* (No. IV), for instance, nothing was revealed of the *pentimenti* present—which demonstrates the limited possibilities the method has to offer [22]. Although the X-ray examination provided a number of interesting data, it was unable to supply an answer to the question whether in some cases the alterations may have been made by the artist himself or whether they were made by others. Alterations were found, however, which, with the help of X-ray examination, it was possible to identify as restoration work done to (old) damage.

9. Finally, in column 9, technical details are shown for which there was no room in the other columns. They refer, among other things, to the use of a pointed object —the pointed end of the brush—for drawing or scratching in the paint before it had dried, the underlying layer(s) or the support becoming in this way integrated into the painting itself.

NOTES

1. See *Appendix I,* under 2a.
2. See *Appendix I,* under 2f.
3. See *Appendix I,* under 1a.
4. M.E. Houtzager, M. Meier-Siem and others, *Röntgenonderzoek van de oude schilderijen in het Centraal Museum te Utrecht,* Utrecht 1967.
5. Van de Graaf, p. 27.
6. H. Kühn, "Untersuchungen zu den Malgründen Rembrandts", *Jahrbuch der Staatlichen Kunstsammlungen in Baden-Württemberg,* 2, 1965, pp. 189-210. H. Kühn, "Untersuchungen zu den Pigmenten und Malgründen Rembrandts durchgeführt an den Gemälden der Staatlichen Kunstsammlungen Kassel", *Maltechnik-Restauro,* 82, 1976, pp. 25-33.
7. W. Froentjes, "Schilderde Rembrandt op goud", *Oud Holland,* 84, 1969, pp. 233-237.
Professor Carl Nordenfalk, former director of the National museum at Stockholm, lent his full co-operation on the examination of the ground and gold leaf of Rembrandt's *Self-portrait.*
8. E. van de Wetering in exh. cat. *Geschildert tot Leyden anno 1626,* Leiden (the Lakenhal), 1976-1977, pp. 23, 24. Also: E. van de Wetering, C.M. Groen and J.A. Mosk, "Beknopt verslag van de resultaten van het technisch onderzoek van Rembrandts Nachtwacht", *Bulletin van het Rijksmuseum,* 24, 1976, pp. 73-85.
Regarding "dead colouring" (*doodverven*) see also Lydia de Pauw-de Veen, *De begrippen 'schilder', 'schilderij' en 'schilderen' in de zeventiende eeuw,* Brussels 1969, p. 251. Also: John Hell, "Beobachtungen über Rembrandts Malweise und Probleme der Konservierung", *Kunstchronik,* 10, 1957, p. 139, and Van de Graaf, pp. 102-104. It was only after the present manuscript had been completed and translated that we were able to take cognizance of the extensive publications by Van de Wetering and Groen concerning their study of Rembrandt's technique during his Leiden period. Their interesting findings and conclusions have not therefore been discussed here. E. van de Wetering, "De jonge Rembrandt aan het werk", *Oud Holland,* 91, 1977, pp. 27-65. Karin Groen, "Schildertechnische aspecten van Rembrandts vroegste schilderijen", *Oud Holland,* 91, 1977, pp. 66-74.
9. Joyce Plesters, "Cross-sections and chemical analysis of Paint Samples", *Studies in Conservation,* 2, 1956, pp. 110-157.

SUMMARY OF THE RESULTS OF THE TECHNICAL INVESTIGATION

Title of Painting	Stratigraphic structure and composition of the layers			
	Support	First ground layer	Intermediate layers	Underpainting in the figures
1	2	3	4	5
I Self-portrait as a Young Man	oak panel (1595)	chalk; yellowish-white	white lead, in places	white lead
II Study of a Man Laughing	red copper ± 1 mm; cradle	white lead, chalk; greenish-white	gold leaf	—
III Head of an Old Man	oak panel (1569)	chalk; yellowish-white	brown layer (umber, brown ochre, white lead) *(imprimatura)*	dark greyish-brown layer beneath light areas of head and collar (white lead, umber and carbon black)
IV Andromeda	oak panel (1603)	chalk; yellowish-white	pale brown layer (umber) *(imprimatura);* white lead, in places	dark brown layer beneath light areas of figure; white lead
V Simeon's Song of Praise	oak panel (1589); upper edge heightened in form of an arc	chalk; yellowish-white	white lead, in places; brown transparent layer (umber, Cologne earth), in places	white lead; purplish-red and yellowish brown layer under Simeon's cloak (red lake, yellow, red and brown ochre); brown transparent layer beneath minor figures and in areas of shadow (see: column 4)
VI Dr. Nicolaas Tulp's Anatomy Lesson	linen 18-15; two relinings	white lead, chalk, red and yellow ochres; brownish-red	grey second ground layer (white lead, yellow ochre, umber, bone black); brownish-black layer (Cologne earth, bone black), in places	brownish-black layer beneath light areas of the figures (Cologne earth, carbon black) (see: column 4); white lead
VII Self-portrait in a Plumed Hat	oak panel	chalk; yellowish-white	white lead, in places	dark-brown layer beneath ligth areas of head and collar (brown ochre, Cologne earth, bone black); white lead
VIII Bathsheba	oak panel; 4 cm wide oak strip added along right hand side	original panel: chalk; yellowish white; added strip: umber, carbon black, white lead, chalk; dark greyish-brown	original panel: pale brown layer *(imprimatura);* white lead; added strip: black layer (bone black, red lake)	white lead; dark reddish-brown layer in areas of shadow of figure

	Further technical data		
Pigments in the final paint layer 6	Trace elements in the white lead 7	X-ray examination 8	Special features 9
white lead, yellow ochre, red ochre, red lake, azurite, brown ochre, umber, Cologne earth, bone black	silver, copper, tin	no pentimenti (+ e.e.r.)	an old grey paint layer on reverse of the panel (white lead, chalk, ochre, umber, carbon black)
white lead, yellow ochre, red ochre, vermilion, red lake, azurite, brown ochre, umber, (Cologne earth), bone black	no analysis	no pentimenti (+ e.e.r.)	scratching with a point in wet paint (moustache and beard); gold leaf visible here
white lead, yellow ochre, red ochre, vermilion, red lake, azurite, (green earth), umber, bone black	silver, copper	the original head-dress—small cap—has been overpainted with a black cap; small alterations in coat and collar	—
white lead, chalk, yellow ochre, red ochre, azurite, malachite, umber, bone black	silver, copper, tin	originally uncovered left leg and feet overpainted with garment and rock; garment widened across hips (+ e.e.r.)	outlines of the vegetation on the rocks drawn with a point in the wet paint
white lead, lead-tin yellow, yellow ochre, red ochre, red lake, vermilion, azurite, smalt, brown ochre, umber, Cologne earth, bone black	no analysis	no pentimenti	pattern of Simeon's cloak scratched with a point in the wet paint
white lead, yellow ochre, red ochre, red lake, vermilion, brown ochre, bone black	silver, copper, tin	hat of figure 8 has been overpainted; figure 3 originally more to the left; corpse's left arm originally higher; alterations to Dr. Tulp's hat and collar	small holes in paint layer indicate exposure to higher temperatures in earlier times; scratching with a point in the wet paint of corpse's beard and book
white lead, lead-tin yellow, yellow ochre, red ochre, red lake, brown ochre, Cologne earth, bone black	silver, copper, tin	no pentimenti	—
white lead, lead-tin yellow, yellow ochre, red ochre, vermilion, red lake, umber, bone black	silver, copper, tin	small changes in initial design of figure and garment	infra-red photograph shows earlier arc-shaped painting on top edge; a dark grey layer (carbon black and white lead) is present here beneath upper layer

SUMMARY OF THE RESULTS OF THE TECHNICAL INVESTIGATION

Title of Painting	Stratigraphic structure and composition of the layers			
	Support	First ground layer	Intermediate layers	Underpainting in the figures
1	2	3	4	5
IX Portrait of a Man with Grey Curly Hair	linen 11-13; one re-lining	red ochre, yellow ochre, chalk; pale red	dark brownish-grey second ground layer (chalk, white lead, red ochre, umber, carbon black)	dark layer beneath head, as described in column 4; black layer beneath white of collar
X Two Negroes	linen 14-12; one re-lining	chalk, white lead, yellow ochre, red ochre; pale red	greyish-brown layer (chalk, white lead, red ochre, umber, carbon black)	—
XI Saul and David	linen 14-14; two canvases sewn together; one re-lining	chalk, white lead, yellow ochre, umber, bone black; greyish-brown	greyish-brown second ground layer (see: column 3); black layer (bone black) in most places	dark grey layer beneath head and turban of Saul and head of David; partially under Saul's tunic and cloak (umber, carbon black, white lead); black layer beneath David's collar
XII Homer	linen 13-12; two re-linings	chalk, yellow ochre, red ochre; pink	reddish-brown ground layer(s) (white lead, chalk, yellow and red ochres, umber); greyish-brown layer (umber, white lead), in places; dark brown layer (umber, carbon black), in places	greyish-brown layer beneath figure (white lead, umber) (see: column 4)
XIII Self-portrait in Later Life	linen 11-14; no re-lining	white lead, yellow ochre, red ochre, umber, bone black; dark greyish-brown	blackish-brown second ground layer (red ochre, Cologne earth, carbon black); dark greyish-brown layer (see: column 3), in places; blackish-brown layer	blackish-brown layer beneath head and barret; white layer in places beneath hair
1 Study of an Old Woman	oak panel (1600)	chalk, white lead; yellowish-white	white lead, in places	dark grey layer beneath head and collar (white lead, brown ochre, carbon black); brownish red layer beneath coat (brown and red ochres)
2 Minerva	original panel removed; painting transferred onto new oak panel; cradle	white layer of plaster; chalk, white lead	layer of glue between plaster and paint layer; brownish-black layer, in places	white lead
3 Travellers Resting	paper (flax-fibre) on oak panel; between paper and panel a greyish-brown layer (white lead, ochres); panel enlarged on both sides	white lead	—	—

	Further technical data		
Pigments in the final paint layer 6	Trace elements in the white lead 7	X-ray examination 8	Special features 9
white lead, yellow ochre, red ochre, vermilion, red lake, brown ochre, bone black	silver, copper, tin	no pentimenti	—
white lead, yellow ochre, red ochre, brown ochre, Cologne-earth, carbon black	silver, copper, tin	foremost negro's shoulder-cloth originally hung across his chest	—
white lead, lead-tin yellow, yellow ochre, red ochre, red lake, azurite, smalt, brown ochre, bone black	silver, copper, tin	no pentimenti	painting cut in two pieces, later re-assembled; fragment of other old painting inserted; scratching with a point in wet paint of Saul's beard
white lead, lead-tin yellow, yellow ochre, red ochre, brown ochre, bone black	silver, copper, tin	no pentimenti	texture of surface of paint indicates localized exposure to heat; yellow paint on right sleeve applied with palette knife
white lead, yellow ochre, red ochre, red lake, brown ochre, bone black	silver, copper	cap originally lower, over-painted with a barret	original canvas still in use
white lead, yellow ochre, red lake, azurite, malachite, brown ochre, Cologne earth, carbon black	silver, copper	no pentimenti (+ e.e.r.)	—
white lead, yellow ochre, red lake, vermilion, azurite, umber	silver, copper, tin	no pentimenti	paint layer flattened by transfer
white lead, yellow ochre, brown ochre, umber, carbon black	silver, copper	no pentimenti (+ e.e.r.)	outlines of roofs among others scratched with a point in wet paint

10. Philip Hendy and A.S. Lucas, "The ground in pictures", *Museum,* 21, 1968, pp. 245-276.

11. Ben B. Johnson found a rather exceptional structure and composition of the layers on a panel when examining *The Raising of Lazarus* (Br.-G., no. 538). Ben B. Johnson, "Examination and Treatment of Rembrandt's Raising of Lazarus", *Los Angeles County Museum of Art Bulletin,* 20, 1974, pp. 18-35. See also H. von Sonnenburg, "Technical Aspects: Scientific Examination" in *Rembrandt after three hundred years: a Symposium - Rembrandt and his Followers,* Chicago (The Art Institute of Chicago), 1973, pp. 93, 94. Also E. van de Wetering, C.M. Groen and J.A. Mosk, "Beknopt verslag van de resultaten van het technisch onderzoek van Rembrandts Nachtwacht", *Bulletin van het Rijksmuseum,* 24, 1976, pp. 68-98.

12. H. Kühn, "A study of the pigments and the grounds used by Jan Vermeer", in *Report and studies in the History of Art* (National Gallery of Art, Washington D.C.), 1968, p. 157.

Van de Graaf, pp. 33-35. Also J.A. van de Graaf, "Betekenis en toepassing van "lootwit" en "schelpwit" in de XVIIde-eeuwse nederlandse schilderkunst", *Bulletin Institut Royal du Patrimoine Artistique,* 4, 1961, pp. 198-201.

Also Rutherford J. Gettens, Hermann Kühn and W.T. Chase, "Lead White", *Studies in Conservation,* 12, 1967, pp. 125-139.

13. R. Jacobi, "Ueber den in der Malerei verwendeten gelben Farbstoff der alten Meister", *Zeitschrift für angewandte Chemie,* 54, 1941, p. 28.

14. H. Kühn, "Lead-tin yellow", *Studies in Conservation,* 13, 1968, pp. 7-33.

15. C.F. Prangers, *Farbenlexicon,* Halle 1782, p. 266.

The recipe for preparing lead-tin yellow is as follows: lead must be melted in a stone crucible, to which tin is added in small doses at high temperature. The lead-tin yellow (Pb_2SnO_4) then forms on the surface of the molten metal. In addition, fractions of a lighter shade of yellow are formed which X-ray diffraction shows to contain varying quantities of free tin dioxide (SnO_2). The fact that besides pure lead-tin yellow, varying amounts of free tin dioxide were also detected in this pigment on the paintings too, may mean that the simple recipe we found, dating from 1782, was the 17th century method of preparation.

On the Rembrandt paintings we examined, we did not encounter the silicon containing lead-tin yellow II, which Kühn also described.

16. See Van de Graaf, p. 54.

17. Van de Graaf, p. 40, also mentions that, as in the case of ultramarine (lapis lazuli), the azurite was "strewn" over the white lead when it was not yet quite dry, so as to, as far as possible, avoid blending it with oil, the aim being to prevent losing their tint and becoming grey.

18. When investigating the pigments on thirty paintings by Jan Vermeer, Kühn discovered ultramarine (lapis lazuli) in the majority of cases (23) used as the blue pigment. Azurite was detected on six paintings only, and then always mixed with ultramarine or other pigments; see note 12.

It should be added that blue occupies a predominant place in Vermeer's palette, in contrast to Rembrandt's. This perhaps explains why Vermeer preferred lapis lazuli ("The diamond of all colours", according to Mayerne) to azurite, the former being more highly prized in his day.

19. Van de Graaf, p. 33.

20. M. de Wild, *Scientific Examination of Pictures,* London 1929.

21. J. Maroger, *The secret formulas and techniques of the Masters,* London 1948.

22. See also *Appendix I,* under 1a.

III. TO DR. NICOLAAS TULP'S ANATOMY LESSON

a) Decree made by the municipality of Amsterdam on behalf of the surgeons of this town, laying down the regulations for anatomy lessons.

Ordonnantie voor den Chirurgijns op 't stuk van de Anatomie.

I. Ordinarisse Lessen zullen gedaen worden alle Dijnsdagen en de Vrijdagen, ten een uure nae den middaghe, alwaer alle Chirurgijns, gehouden zullen wezen te comparere, op peene van dry stuyv. telkess te verbeuren.

II. De knegt van 't gildt sal op de Bestemde daghen een quartier uurs, voor de dagelijkxse lesse en een halv uur, voor d'anatomie, de plaetse daertoe bescheiden opdoen, en zal voorts daer blijven acht nemende dat geene kinders, of te andere die daer niets te doen hebben innekome.

III. Niemand zal onder de Lessen Anatomiae, oft andere onderlinge redene, de Lesse of 't anatomie aangaende niet lopen spreken, lachen of 't andersins luyde te zijn, de toehoorders of degeene, die de lesse doen zal eenigzins storen of te verlette.

IV. Als men Anatomiae doet, sal een iegelik tot d'oncoste betalen van elk lichaam zès stuyvers.

V. De toezienders zulle plaetse moge neme, soo sij inkomen, doch dat de Binnenste Banken voor d'Overigeyt, doctores, Mr. Chirurgijns gelaten werden, mede ygelyck, in syn genome plaetse moete blijve sitten, zonder op te mogen staen of te eenigsins d'andre te verletten.

VI. Wanneer het lichaam ter vertoninge bereydt wordt sal niemand dan de Chirurgijn die het gild bewilligt zal hebben, om de handt in 't snijden te leenen, de geene die verclaringe zal doen, ende den knegt om wat van noode is aen te dragen tegenwoordig mogen sijn.

VII. Niemand sal van het lichaem iet mogen wegdragen op de verbeurte van ses gulden, van welcke zes stuyvers en de ses guldens d'overluyde gehouden zullen wese reckeninge te doen, als d'Anatomiae gedae zal weze, in hande van de de Heeren Burgemeesters ofte derzelver Heeren gecommiteerden.

VIII. Oft Imand' van de zaken, in de tegenwoordige oft eenige der voorgaende Lessen, oft d'anatomie verhandelt, eenige vragen hadde voor te stellen, zal 't zelve mogen doen, waer op de geene die de Lessen en verclaringen over d'Anatomie doen sal ten eynde van de naest volgende bijeencomste zijn bedencke zal verclaren.

IX. In het vragen, antwoorden en allen onderlinge redene zal alle smadelijckheyt en de belagheid vermijdt, daer tegen alle beleeftheyt en soeticheyt onderlinge bewezen worden.

Op den 17 January 1606 zijn deze articelen bij mijne Heeren van de Gerechte Gearresteert, presentibus alle de Heeren Burgemeesters dempto Reijnier Pauw., en de alle de schepenen, Demptis Jan Thomasz. Ds Jan ten Grootenhuys, onderschout in kennisse van mij als secretaris onderteekent.

G. ROOSENBOOM.

b) Act drawn up by notary in Leiden on 8 March 1628, giving evidence of Hendrick van Uylenburgh's stay and his family relations in Leiden.

Gemeentelijke Archiefdienst van Leiden.
Notariële archieven, inv. nr. 331, akte nr. 15.
Akte van Notaris L. Vergeyl; 8 maart 1628.

Op huyden den VIIIen marty 1628 compareerde voor mij Laurens Vergeyl, notaris publyc, ende voor de naegemelde getugen: d'eersame Henrick van Ulenburch, coopman tot Amsterdam, als oom ende bloetvoocht van de nagelaten weeskinderen van za. Rombaut van Ulenburch, in sijn leven schilder tot Dansick, ende vervangende Ibel Haye Fries, weduwe, boedelhoutster ende medevoochdesse over haere kinderen gevonen ((= gewonnen)) bij de vern. Rombout van Ulenborch, haeren overleden man, ende verclaerde geconstitueert, machtich gemaect ende in sijne stede gestelt te hebben, gelijc hij doet bij desen, Robbrecht van der Burch, procur((eur)) voor den Hove van Hollandt, mitsgaders Johan van Kuyck, procu((reur)) voor de vierschare der stadt Leyden, ofte een van beyden, omme hen te opposeren tegens d'executie ende vercopinge bij Agniesgen Willemsdr van der Vorst, door Jan van Geesdorp, deurwaerder 's Hooffs van Hollant begost, ofte bij allen anderen te beginnen, op de schilderijen het eene genaempt het Oordeel (b), het derde Johannes onthoofddinge (a), het twede daer Moysis 't water uyt de steen slaet, het vierde ende vijffde een Poolsche ende Letousche wiltmarct, het seste een groenmarct, ende het sevende een blompoth met 2 naecte kinderkens, alle toebehorende de verss. weduwe ende kinderen van Rombout van Ulenburch ende berustende ten huyse van Sybrandt Fries geexedec... Dat dien eynde alle termijnen van rechten te observeren, sententie te solliciteren, deselve te horen pronunchieren, t' acquiesceren, off daer van te mogen provoceren, bij appèl, refermatie off anderssins; sulcx de gelegentheyt den saccke vereyschen ende haeren goeden raet gedraegen sal, Ende wijders in alle t' gunt verss. is ende daer aen cleeft alles te doen ende verrichten wat hij constituant allomme selffs present ende jegenwoordich zijnde soude cunnen ende vermogen te doen.

Belovende, ratificerende, ende approberende mede alle 't gunt in den verss. saecke uytten naem van de verss. weeskinderen alrede verrich es, onder gelijc verbant alsvoren, ende consenterende ende aldus gedaen binnen Leyden ten comptoire van vern. Jan van Kuyck, staende op de Lange Brugge; ter presentie van d' E. Nicolaus Dedel, professor in de universiteyt alhier, ende Cornelis Willemsz van Bilderbeec, clerc, als getu((gen)) hier toe beneffens mij notario gerequireert.

w.g. Nicolaus Dedel   w.g. Hendrick van Ulenborch
w.g. L. Vergeyl, Nots.   w.g. W. van Bilderbeec

1628

c) Notes compiled from various sources on restorationwork done to Dr. Tulp's Anatomy Lesson, before the painting came to hang in the Mauritshuis (1828).

29 januari 1700
"aen Milli voor Mons:r: Pool voor schoonmaecken van alle de schilderijen op het collegie - - - *f* 25" (the painter Jurriaan Pool (1666-1745) was married to the paintress Rachel Ruysch, daughter of Professor Fred. Ruysch, who was appointed in 1666 prelector of the Surgeons' Guild at Amsterdam).

29 juli 1709
"aen pictor blaupot (Pieter Blaupot, born 1655) voor 12 schilderijen schoon te maaken. Volgens quitanty - - - *f* 14."

9 mei 1732
"item voor alle de schilderijen te doen ophelderen of schoonmaken en te repareren de mantel van de prof. N. Tulpius, afgeschilferd zijnde versengt doordien een vuurige rook langen tijd tegen dat schone stuk van Rembrandts heeft geklommen en om zulks verder te verhoeden, is het kassien dat in de hoek bij het torentie heeft gestaan gezet naast de schoorsteen."

20 september 1732
"item in het stuk van Rembrants de mantel van de Heer professor nicolaas Tulp, oock gebrand zijnde voor bladders, en op enige plaatsen te verwen ten enemaal van het doek gebarsten, zo hebben de overlieden ook goed gevonden dien professor hoog loffelijker gedagtenisse, met een nuwen mantel te voorzien" (by Jan Maurits Quinkhard 1688-1772).

16 october 1747
"d'gilde knegt van der Waart geeft aan overlieden te kennen dat het schilderij Tulp door lekkatie mogt beschadigt worde hebben overlieden aan d'gilde knegt gesegt, dat door de timmerman te laten ondersoeken nevens d'schilder J:M Quinckhard"

6 juni 1752
"Alzoo overlieden van Haar Weledele Grootagtbaaren Heeren Burgemeesteren permissie hebben gekregen om het schilderij van d:Ed:Heer professor tulp te laaten verstellen en schoon te maaken door de schilder: Jan van dijk"

31 juli 1780
"Gesien hebbende dat de schilderijen der gildekamer nodig hebben van schoongemaakt te worden, is bij het volle collegie geresolveert, om J.Eeckels, J.Buijs en Quinkhard op aanstaande vrijdagnamiddag sijnde den 4 Aug:[s] boven te ontbieden, om te hooren totwelke prijsen sij Lieden het schoonmaken der schilderijen aannamen.
Waar op de Eerste te weeten Eeckels het bepaalde op *f* 250,, ,, .
Waar op de Tweede te weeten Quinkhard het bepaalde op *f* 150,, ,, .
Waar op de derde te weeten J.Buijs het bepaalde op *f* 84,, ,, .
dit bij het collegie in overweeging genomen hebbende, wierd goed gevonden, ten minste koste vande generaale kas, het aan J.Buijs over te geeven en de selve teegens aanstaande vrijdag namiddag sijnde den 11 Aug[s] boven te ontbieden, welke J. Buijs compareerde, en sijde, dat soo wanneer hij geweeten had, dat er reets voor het collegie iemand anders over gesprooken was, hij het om die prijs van *f* 84 ,, ,, . door een ander niet soude hebben laten aanneemen, te meer wijl hij sig seer geaffronteerd toonde van voor een schilderij-schoonmaker bij het collegie aangemerkt te worden, 't welk hij wel door andere onder zijn opsigt liet doen, maar dat hij een konstschilder is, welk caracter van konstschilder hij maintineerde en daarom het collegie voor het schoonmaken van de schilderijen bedankte. Waar op nagedaane omvraag collegialiter goedgevonden is den fijnschilder Quinkhard (Julius Henricus Quinkhard 1734-1795) teegens aanstaande maandag zijnde den 21 Aug[s] voor het collegie te ontbieden en hem te vraagen ofte hij voor die aangenoome Prijs van *f* 150 ,, ,, . niet alleenig de schilderijen beneevens de wapens voor de schoorsteen wel soude schoonmaken, opvernissen, de gaten die er in sijn te stoppen, maar ook dat geen dat er bij geschildert moeste worden, wel bij te schilderen en verder in soo een goede order te brengen, dat het de roem van andere meriteerde, het wel voorz: Quinkhard aangenomen heeft en op aanstaande woensdag sijnde den 23 deeser daar meede een begin soude maaken".

29 november 1808
"compareert Monsieur Spaan (Jan Spaan) als schoonmaker van schilderijen ten einde aan het schilderstuk op

de gildekamer van Rembrand de nodige reparatien te doen en hebben des wegens Administrateuren voor zo lange genoemde schilderstuk onder des zelfs berusting zal moeten verblijven, van den zelve ter hunner waarborg een hand gevordert en bekoomen."

2 juni 1817
"De Heeren Administrateuren van het Chirurgijns W[d] Fonds.
debet: aan J:Hulswit Amsterdam 1817

Voor een schilderij van Rembrandt verdoekt, schoongemaakt en geheel in order gebragt	*f* 440:—
Verschot aan linnen end raem ...	*f* 12:2
Transpoort heen weeder ...	*f* 1:11
	f 453:13"

d) Some notes on the restoration of the same painting since 1828:

1841
J.A. Hopman cleaned and varnished the painting.

1845
J.A. Hopman cleaned and varnished the painting.

1860
Etienne Leroy, Brussels: Relining; restoration indicated on a lithograph reproduced on page 106 (Fig. 83): "Le doigt du No. 4 est refait".

1877
W.A. Hopman relined and restored the painting. A report by the restorer is kept in the archives of the Mauritshuis (see Figs. 81 and 82).

1885
W.A. Hopman regenerated the varnish.

1891
W.A. Hopman regenerated the varnish.

1908
C.F.L. de Wild relined the painting with two canvases Some yellowed varnish was removed.

1925
D. de Wild removed some darkened overpainting and did some retouching. The varnish was repaired. (This probaly means that some old varnish was removed to allow of retouching, and that a fresh layer of varnish was applied.)

1951
J.C. Traas cleaned the painting removing several old layers of varnish. Much former overpainting was also removed or retouched. For the signature and date, see p. 90 and Figs. 57 a-d.

IV. REMBRANDT AND ANTONIO RUFFO

The financial transactions concerning the first painting Rembrandt did for Ruffo, the *Aristotle* (Br.-G., No. 478), were handled for the artist by Cornelis Gijsberts van Goor (1600-1675), of Amsterdam, shipowner and wealthy merchant in the Levant, while Giacomo di Battista, perhaps a relative of Giovanni Battista van den Broek, acted in Messina for Don Antonio. The painting was despatched on 13 June 1654 and arrived in Messina on 19 August of that year. The Dutch consul in the port, the painter and etcher Abraham Casenbroot, ten of whose paintings Don Antonio owned, was also concerned with the vessel's cargo. After his death, in 1658, Giovanni Baptista van den Broek succeeded him and it was he who was to act as intermediary when Don Antonio commissioned and purchased the *Alexandre the Great* and the *Homer*.

About the year 1660, after his mother's death and the apportionment of her estate, Don Antonio conceived the idea of expanding the family's collection of paintings by adding to it a few half-length figures. Rembrandt was commissioned to contribute a second half-length figure, while others were commissioned from a number of Italian painters. The paintings were to form a collection of historical personalities, particularly of philosophers.

This time Isac Just, a cousin or uncle of the wife-to-be of Gerrit van Ulenburch (Elisabeth Just, from Koningsbergen), acted on Rembrandt's behalf, while Carlo Bacchini and the Dutch consul, Giovanni Battista Vandambro (i.e. van den Broek), represented Don Antonio in Messina.

Rembrandt's painting was shipped to Messina via the island of Texel on 30 July 1661. The invoice, accompanied by a letter, with instructions from Rembrandt, has been preserved:

"Amsterdam 30 July 1661 Invoice for a painting entitled Alexander the Great, made by the hand of Painter Rembrant Van Ryn for the account of ...... of Messina for which painting I have paid in accordance with the agreement with said

Painter	F.	500—
And moreover for the canvas of Alexander and Homer ...	f.	18—
And moreover for their casing ...	f.	10—
and moreover for the frame ...	f.	7.10
and moreover for Customs duties ...	f.	9.09
and moreover for packing and casing ...	f.	10—
and moreover for conveyance to Texel on board ship ... and for convoy duty ... fees	F.	15.10
	f	70
for insurance from here to Messina à 10 p. 100 ...	f.	50.14
for arranging the insurance and calculation of course to Venice for Messires Moens. In duplicate ...d... f. 268 for 93.8 to be paid to Your Honour ...	f.	1.59
Sum (of)	F.	623. 2

Note that this painting has been despatched in the vessel Groot Croenenburigh, K. Captain Paul Custensen under attached Seal.
The Painter Rembrandt has informed as that Homer has still to be painted, the which he will do for F 500— To this end he is making an arch at the top of the canvas, by which it should match the other, so as to place Alexander in the centre, should such be ordered, let me be warned."

The invoice, in duplicate, is present in the Ruffo family archives.

The Homer had to be returned to Amsterdam for the painting to be finished, but the opportunity did not arise until a year later, when the Dutch consul traveled back to the Netherlands. On this occasion he took with him to Amsterdam a long memorandum from Don Antonio Ruffo to Rembrandt. The canvas with the as yet uncompleted Homer was, however, despatched by the vessel *Arion* on 16 November 1662, at the cost of three florins and was to be delivered to "Sig^{r}. Isach Justen" in Amsterdam.

The contents of the letter, full of complaints yet at the same time including new commissions, reads as follows:

"1662 1 November at Messina—Memorandum for the Consul, Mr. Giovanni Battista Vallembrot, for when he shall arrive in Amsterdam. He will make it clear to Mr. Isach Just how little satisfaction the friend in Messina derives from the painting of Alexander, which was done to his commission. The Aristotle has already been paid for, for which the order was given years ago by Mr. Giacomo di Battista for the account of the same person to Mr. Cornelio Vangaor. The said painting of Alexander, has been painted on four pieces of canvas sewn together, which makes four seams, so frightful, it is difficult to believe. Moreover, time will cause them to burst apart so that the painting will then be lost altogether. And among the 200 painted works which the said person owns by the best artists of Europe there is not one with a piece added to it as in this Alexander. Since this was originally a head only, on "sound" canvas, and Mr Painter Rembrandt then wanted to make a half-length figure of it, he decided, in order to save himself trouble or because he was so busy, to add pieces to the canvas, first of all vertically and then, since the painting then proved to be too narrow, he added pieces at the sides as well. To put matters right, together with the painting of Alexander, he sent another work—half-finished—of Homer on good and new linen, which will be the canvas for which he received 18 florins. The abovementioned painting of Homer, half-finished and packed in oilcloth and a crate, executed to the dimensions of the others, is now being returned in order to be completed, with the aim of making good the defect of the other, for which only a head may be charged for, thereby one might note that one could charge the half of the 500 florins which he has received for the two other works despatched earlier (paintings, the "Aristotle" and the"Alexander"). That would make 250 florins, a price four times as high as that charged in Italy by the most celebrated of painters. The latters have fixed a price of 25 scudi for a Head and 50 scudi for a half-length portrait. Besides, whereas the painting of Homer which (?) he is sending, is half-finished and will involve only half the trouble of painting an entire work. For the sewn-on pieces of canvas are so unsightly that it is neccesary to remove them. And should he not wish to show us this courtesy, which is reasonable and obligatory, the Alexander will be returned as well, in order to retrieve the price paid for it, for one is not obliged to keep in one's house a painting which is so expensive and, nevertheless, so faulty. This only befits the reputation and (the interests of) the friend of your Honour to do no less than what Mr. Vangaor did. And (befitting the interests) of the Painter Rembrandt to satisfy the eager desire of the customer, who, being thus satisfied, will not fail to have others done, or at least it lies within his intention to acquire half a dozen of them. If the Painter would send the sketches for these the same can be done on sheets of paper, in pencil, black or red, as he may choose. So that from these (sketches), which can be sent in a letter or by sea in a small box, the customer may see which are the most to his taste. And on his safe return from Amsterdam he can bring in the same crate and the oilcloth the completed painting of Homer with him."

When the consul arrived in Amsterdam this letter was handed to Rembrandt. The latter hastened to reply to his distant patron, having his defence translated into Italian and rejecting the complaints about the "Alexander": "I am grealy surprised by the manner in which they write of the Alexander, which has been executed so well. I think there must be few experts in Messina and since Your Honour complaints of the price as well as the canvas—but as Your Honour orders it to be sent back at your expense at your own risk, as with the sketch of the Homer too, I will make another Alexander—as regards the canvas, I found I had too little while painting, so that it was necessary to add to its length, but if the painting is hung in the proper light one will not notice this at all. Should your Honour be satisfied with the Alexander in this way, it is in order. Should Your Honour not wish to keep the Alexander—the lowest price is the 600 florins. And the Homer 500 florins and the cost of the canvas. The expenses are of course for Your Honour's account. Should you wish it to be executed, would you be so kind as to send me the exact measurements, which dimensions you desire?

I await your reply to this in order to have directions. Rembrandt Van Ryn."

The consul apparently arrived in Amsterdam before the ship *Arion* with Captain van Hol. At least in his reply to Ruffo's remarks and criticisms, Rembrandt asked expressly for the dimensions of the *Homer*, which had still to be finished.

The present work is set in Times, printed in June 1978 by Snoeck-Ducaju & Zoon, Ghent, with lithos supplied by Photogravure Tallon, Brussels, and bound by Splichal n.v., Turnhout, in 1250 numbered copies.

This copy is number 508